CHURCHILL'S
MOAT

CHURCHILL'S MOAT

The Channel War 1939 – 1945

ROBERT JACKSON

Airlife
England

Copyright © 1995 by Robert Jackson

First published in the UK in 1995
by Airlife Publishing Ltd

British Library Cataloguing in Publication Data
A catalogue record for this book
is available from the British Library

ISBN 1 85310 459 0

Typset by Litho Link Ltd, Welshpool, Powys, Wales
Printed by Butler and Tanner Ltd, Frome and London

Airlife Publishing Ltd
101 Longden Road, Shrewsbury SY3 9EB

Contents

Acknowledgements

In writing this book, I have been indebted to the following people who unstintingly delved into their personal memories and archives to provide me with experiences, photographs and other material. This story is theirs. L.E. 'Mick' Aldridge; H.G. Brown; A.E. Carver; D.J.T. Channell; Arthur Coleman; K. Colyer; Doreen M. Czarnota; Ken Davies; Paul Deacon; Richard and Yvonne Derwent; R.L. Fletcher; A.G. Frampton; Miss M.M.L. Gavan Duffy; Mrs Eileen Haynes; J.L. Hogg; David Horton; Eric Johnson; H.G.F. Male; R.A. Marsdale; Mrs Barbara Morgan; T.C. Parker; H.H. Richards; W.J. Rosser, DFC; Francis Thompson, DSC; R. Thorndike; Norman Wilkinson; Fred Winter.

The quotations in the chapter on the Dunkirk evacuation, by Commander Thomas Kerr, Lieutenant Stewart Gould, F.G. Hutchinson, W.T. Elmslie, Edward Faulkes, DCM, MM, Lieutenant-Commander Archie Buchanan, Tom Collins, W.E. Williamson, Reg Rushmere, Mrs B. Bowden, Troop CSM C.S. Best and Charlie White, were gleaned from correspondence gathered in the compilation of an earlier work of mine: *Dunkirk, the British Evacuation, 1940* (Arthur Barker Ltd, London, 1976).

CHAPTER ONE

First Encounters:
September 1939 – May 1940

They called it the Phoney War, and in many respects the term seemed justified. On the continent, from Belgium to the Swiss border, as late summer gave way to autumn and then a freezing winter, an army of men in baggy khaki uniforms that were the hallmark of the French Army faced another army of men in somewhat smarter field grey uniforms, and apart from one small and inconclusive Allied offensive in the Saar region there was little activity.

But on the high seas, as September gave way to October in that year of 1939, the war was already taking its toll. On 3 September, the day Britain declared war on the German *Reich*, the submarine U-30 torpedoed and sank the passenger liner *Athenia* off Ireland with the loss of 128 lives, the U-Boat's commander, *Kapitänleutnant* Lemp, having mistaken the vessel for a troopship; and on 14 September the aircraft carrier *Ark Royal* had a narrow escape when the U-39 fired a salvo of torpedoes at her west of the Hebrides. Luckily for the carrier, the torpedoes detonated prematurely and the submarine was sunk by the escorting destroyers *Faulknor*, *Foxhound* and *Firedrake*, which took the German crew prisoner.

Three days later, the Royal Navy's luck ran out. The U-29, commanded by *Kapitänleutnant* Schuhardt, was lying in wait in shipping lanes west of the English Channel when a large vessel was sighted. Schuhardt shadowed her, identified her as an aircraft carrier, and put three torpedoes into her. She was the 22,500-ton fleet carrier *Courageous*, and she went down with the loss of 515 of her crew.

By 13 October the Royal Navy's destroyers had evened the score to some extent, the *Fortuna* and *Forester* sinking the U-27 off the west coast of Scotland while the *Imogen* and *Ilex* sank the U-42 off the south-west coast of Ireland. On 14 October, the *Inglefield*, *Ivanhoe*, *Intrepid* and *Icarus* combined their efforts to destroy the U-45, but this success came only hours after the Germans had demonstrated the formidable destructive power of a U-boat in the hands of a skilled commander. On the night of 13/14 October, the U-47 under *Kapitänleutnant* Gunther Prien penetrated the defences of Scapa Flow naval base in the Orkneys and sank the battleship *Royal Oak* with the loss of 833 lives, a disaster that caused a ripple of shock and dismay to spread throughout Britain.

The loss of the *Courageous* and the *Royal Oak* was a serious double blow to the Home Fleet, whose resources, under Admiral Sir Charles Forbes, were already thinly stretched. The main base of the Home Fleet was Scapa Flow, but considerable naval strength was also deployed in the English Channel area at the outbreak of war, amounting to two battleships, two aircraft carriers (one of which was the *Courageous*), three cruisers and 37 destroyers.[1] Of these, 11 were at Portland, acting as a screening force for the battleships and aircraft carriers, while three more were at Portsmouth, seven at Dover and 16 at Plymouth, all tasked primarily with convoy escort duty.[2] In addition, minesweepers were deployed at all important points around the British coastline.

The first responsibility of the Royal Navy's southern commands was to transport and escort the British Expeditionary Force to France soon after the outbreak of war. In preparation for this, British and French naval forces laid the Dover Barrage, a network of minefields extending across the narrowest point of the English Channel. Some 3,600 mines had been sown by the beginning of October 1939, making it virtually impossible for U-boats to use the narrows as a means of egress to the western Atlantic. Three who attempted it in October were all sunk.[3] Until the capture of the French Atlantic ports, the Germans were forced to send their submarines into the Atlantic by the lengthy passage round the north of Scotland.

Mines, in fact, were potentially the most valuable and effective weapons deployed by either side in the early months of the war, and for a time the Germans enjoyed a definite advantage through the use of the magnetic mine, which was detonated by the magnetic field of a vessel passing over it. Such mines accounted for 59,027 tons of British coastal shipping in September and October 1939, and to compound the problem the entire British minesweeping service was equipped to deal only with moored contact mines that detonated on impact.

The Germans laid their mines by surface vessel, submarine (although it was not until later in the war that they developed a specialized minelaying U-boat, the Type XB) and aircraft. Foremost among the latter, in 1939, were the *Küstenflieger-gruppen* of the German Navy, operating Heinkel He 115 floatplanes. The first minelaying mission was flown on the night of 20/21 November 1939, when aircraft dropped mines without loss off Harwich and the mouth of the Thames, repeating the mission on the following night. Mines were free-dropped (i.e. without parachutes) from an altitude of 3,280 feet (1,000 m), their magnetic or acoustic fuses being armed by water pressure.

These pioneering minelaying sorties were flown by the He 115s of 3/*Kü.Fl.Gr.* 906, which on the night of 22/23 November was joined by aircraft of 3/*Kü.Fl.Gr.* 106. One of these aircraft dropped a magnetic mine on mud flats near Shoeburyness; the drop was observed from the shore and the authorities alerted. It was obvious that whatever the object was, there was a good chance of recovering it when the tide went out.

The Heinkel He 115 was widely used by the Germans for minelaying. This extremely rare photograph shows an ex-Norwegian example used for clandestine operations by the British. Note the absence of any markings.

The mine was dropped between 21.00 and 22.00 hours. Before midnight, two highly-skilled naval officers, Lieutenant-Commanders Ouvry and Lewis from HMS *Vernon*, the establishment responsible for developing underwater weapons, were called to the Admiralty, where they were interviewed by the First Sea Lord and the First Lord of the Admiralty, at that time Winston Churchill. By 01.30 hours they were on their way to Southend to set about the task of recovery, and before dawn, in pitch darkness and aided only by a lamp, they found the mine lying about 500 yards below high water mark, but as the tide was coming in they could make only a preliminary inspection before retiring to make their preparations for tackling it after the next high water.

The delicate and highly dangerous operation began early in the afternoon of 23 November, by which time a second mine had been found on the mud not far from the first. Ouvry, assisted by Chief Petty Officer Baldwin, went in first to tackle the mine, with their colleagues Lewis and Able

Degaussing gear fitted to a Wellington. The gun turrets have been removed and extra ballast fitted in the tail.

Seaman Vearncombe standing by at a safe distance in case the device exploded. After each pre-arranged step, Ouvry signalled his findings to the back-up team, so that if an accident did happen they could use the knowledge in tackling the second mine. In the event, the efforts of all four men were needed to defuse the weapon, which was made safe and transported to Portsmouth for detailed examination.

Once the magnetic mine's secrets were unlocked, the Admiralty initiated all technical measures to combat it. Before long, a research team under Rear-Admiral Wake-Walker had devised effective countermeasures in the form of a so-called degaussing girdle, an electric cable fitted to the hulls of ships to de-magnetize them.

As an alternative to this passive method, an offensive method was developed to deal with the mines; this involved triggering their detonator by creating a magnetic field. Vickers-Armstrongs Ltd were approached to modify a number of Wellington bombers to carry equipment consisting of generators with which to create an electromagnetic field generated by an aluminium coil encased in a circular 51-foot diameter balsa wood structure outside the aircraft. After a series of trials to establish the effectiveness of the idea

and such factors as optimum height and airspeed, the first aerial success was registered on 13 January 1940, and the subsequent operational task fell to the Wellingtons of No 1 General Reconnaissance Unit, RAF Coastal Command. Aircraft so modified were known as DWI (Directional Wireless Installation) Wellingtons. No 1 GRU was based at RAF Manston and its main area of operations was the Thames Estuary, the unarmed Wellingtons – their guns having been removed to save weight – usually being escorted by the Blenheims of No. 600 (Fighter) Squadron.[4]

These developments came just in time. In November 1939, enemy minelaying became so intensive that only a single channel into the Thames remained open, and in that month mines accounted for 27 ships totalling 120,958 tons. As the official naval historian Captain S.W. Roskill later wrote:

> While awaiting the arrival of the new sweep many extemporised measures were adopted, and together they just succeeded in keeping the east coast traffic moving. Though losses continued on a considerable scale in the New Year, and in the first seven months of the war no less than 128 ships totalling 429,899 tons fell victims to mines, we never again had to face as serious a crisis as that of the first autumn.[5]

Death of a merchant ship. Minelaying accounted for the majority of the ships sunk in the Channel area during the early months of the war.

While the Royal Navy followed its ancient tradition of engaging the enemy wherever and whenever possible, the Royal Air Force looked to its defences in readiness for an anticipated onslaught by Hitler's bombers. Until the mid-1930s, most of the RAF's offensive and defensive strength had been concentrated in a Fighting Area running from the Thames Estuary to the Bristol Channel and extending 35 miles inland. Throughout the 1920s France had been viewed as the principal threat to Britain's security, but the rise of Nazi-dominated Germany had changed the picture substantially. In 1936 the Air Defence of Great Britain, the single air command that had

Raising a barrage balloon. Balloons had a deterrent effect in that they forced attackers to fly higher, but brought down very few aircraft.

existed for eleven years, was broken up and replaced by four new commands: Bomber, Fighter, Coastal and Training, to which Balloon Command was added in 1938.

With the change of the command structure came the formation of new groups subordinate to Fighter Command. The first of these were No. 11 (Fighter) Group, with its headquarters at Uxbridge, and No. 12 (Fighter) Group with its HQ at Watnall in Nottinghamshire. The responsibility of No. 11 Group was the defence of southern and south-eastern England, while No. 12 Group's area of responsibility was the Midlands. Two more groups, Nos. 10 and 13, were formed later for the defence of the south-west and the north respectively.

In parallel with the reorganization of the fighter defences, Bomber Command gradually moved its assets to airfields in East Anglia and Yorkshire, from where its bombers would be better placed to strike at Germany. The majority of the bomber and fighter bases lay within a new defensive zone that was 26 miles wide, extending continuously from Portsmouth around the coast to the Tees. The first six miles of this, the coastal strip, was designated the Outer Artillery Zone, but this was abolished in 1937 and the fighter squadrons given a free hand to operate beyond the coastline within a new Aircraft Fighting Zone.

As well as the fighter squadrons, Fighter Command Headquarters at Stanmore in Middlesex also exercised operational control over Anti-Aircraft Command, Balloon Command and the Observer Corps, all of which also had their HQs at Stanmore. The re-equipment of AA Command was slow, but by mid-1940 its commander, Lieutenant-General Sir Frederick Pile, had deployed some 1,700 heavy guns – most of them modern 3.7- and 4.5-inch weapons – out of a recommended total, laid down in 1938, of 2,200. Light AA guns, mainly 40mm weapons, were harder to come by; in this case the recommended establishment was 1,900 for the defence of airfields and special targets such as aircraft factories, but in July 1940 only about 600 had been deployed. Pile did, however, have some

A battery of 3.7-inch anti-aircraft guns at a site on the south coast. Anti-Aircraft Command had deployed some 1,700 heavy AA guns by mid-1940.

4,000 searchlights at his disposal, and this was much closer to the approved total.

Of the airfields within the area of No. 11 Group, which extended from Suffolk to a point just west of Portland, seven were either on the coast or close to it. The most northerly was Martlesham Heath in Suffolk, a very secret place that was the home of the Aeroplane and Armament Experimental Establishment, responsible for the evaluation of new combat aircraft. With war imminent, the A&AEE moved to a safer location at Boscombe Down in Wiltshire on 1 September 1939. Martlesham's location near the east coast made it an ideal base from which to intercept raiders coming down over the North Sea, and in the first weeks of the war it was used by detachments of No. 17 Squadron (Hurricanes) No. 504 Squadron (Hurricanes) and No. 29 Squadron (Blenheims), all from Debden. On 7 December 1930 the Defiants of No. 264 Squadron

moved in from Sutton Bridge as a resident fighter unit.

Further south, at Rochford near Southend, the Spitfires of Nos. 54 and 74 Squadrons maintained regular detachments together with the Blenheim fighters of No. 600 Squadron, all deploying there from Hornchurch in Essex. Eastchurch, across the Thames Estuary, was non-operational, having been temporarily reduced to care and maintenance; in December 1939 the first contingents of Polish airmen arrived there, bewildered and demoralized by the disaster that had overwhelmed their homeland, and began re-training to carry on the fight in the Royal Air Force. Within just a few months, as the German *Blitzkrieg* smashed across Europe, Eastchurch was to become one of the busiest airfields in south-east England.

Manston, two miles west of Ramsgate in Kent, was a training establishment prior to the outbreak of war, the home of the School of Air Navigation and a School of Technical Training. When hostilities began these units moved out and operational squadrons moved in, first Nos 816 and 818 Squadrons of the Fleet Air Arm with Swordfish, then Nos 235 and 253 Squadrons of the RAF, which began to form there with Blenheims and Hurricanes respectively in October 1939. Both units trained on Fairey Battles for a time before receiving their operational equipment and moving on early in 1940, the former to North Coates within Coastal Command and the latter to Northolt.

In the meantime, Manston had officially transferred to Fighter Command on 15 November 1939, its first resident fighter unit being No. 79 Squadron, with Hurricanes. Number 600 Squadron also sent detachments there, its Blenheims patrolling the Thames Estuary after dark in the hope of catching Heinkel 115 minelayers.

Hawkinge, near Folkstone, was an Army Co-operation airfield at the outbreak of war, but quickly found use as a satellite airfield for squadrons of Fighter Command based further to the rear. Lympne, a few miles away to the west of Hythe, started the war as a Fleet Air Arm station; later, during the Battle of France, it was used by Army Co-operation Command, after which it also became a forward satellite airfield under the control of No. 11 Group for the fighter squadrons based closer to London.

All these airfields were to play a vital part in the air battles over the Channel and south-east England in the summer of 1940; but in September 1939 there was only one permanent fighter station in the Channel coastal area. This was Tangmere, near Chichester in Sussex, which had been a fighter airfield since it was re-activated in 1926. When war was declared it was the home of Nos 1 and 43 Squadrons, both with Hawker Hurricanes.

These, then, were the forward airfields, with only the Channel between them and any threat developing from the east. To their rear, in the protective screen around London, lay the principal fighter bases of No. 11 Group: Croydon, Biggin Hill, Kenley, West Malling, Hornchurch, Northolt and North Weald.

Far more obvious than fighters in the coastal area during the early days of the war were the

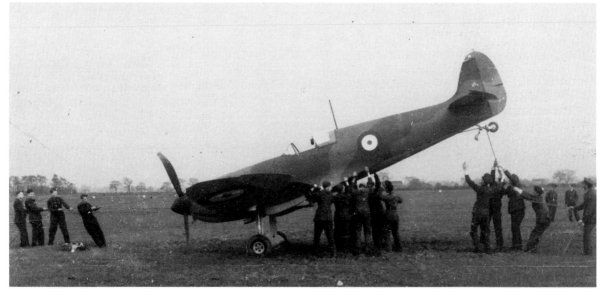

The new Spitfire was not the easiest of aircraft to handle on the ground, and taxying accidents were frequent. This Mk I has nosed over.

An Observer Corps post on the Channel coast. The Observers were of great value in the Battle of Britain.

radar masts. By September 1939 the planned chain of twenty radar stations at home – the Chain Home (CH) stations – had been completed, stretching from Southampton to Newcastle-upon-Tyne. Each had twin masts, the taller – 350 feet – for transmitting, and the shorter, 240 feet, for receiving. The CH stations, known for security reasons as Air Ministry Experimental Stations (AMES) could detect aircraft up to 100 miles away, and could give the bearing and an approximate indication of the height and number of an approaching formation. The main stations were being supplemented by another series, Chain Home Low (CHL) which were designed to detect aircraft flying below 3,000 feet.

These electronic eyes of Britain's defences were backed up by the human ones of the Observer Corps. While the radar stations were responsible for tracking enemy aircraft before they reached the English coast, the volunteers of the Observer Corps were responsible for tracking and reporting on them once they had crossed it. By

mid-1940 there were 31 Observer Corps groups in Britain, each incorporating between 30 and 50 posts that were manned around the clock.

Information from these reporting agencies, and later from signals intelligence gathered by the RAF's 'Y' Service, was passed by landline to HQ Fighter Command at Bentley Priory, where it was rapidly filtered and processed for re-transmission to the sector airfield operations rooms at key locations such as Biggin Hill and Hornchurch, which in turn passed it on to the fighter squadrons at readiness on their forward airfields.

It was a system that generally worked very well, especially after constant practice under actual operational conditions had smoothed away the rough edges, but at the beginning there were bound to be problems. During the first week of the war there were several false alarms generated by 'intruders' that turned out to be civil aircraft coming in from the continent, but just after dawn on 6 September a searchlight battery on Mersea island in the Thames Estuary alerted

No. 11 Group HQ to the presence of some incoming aircraft that were thought to be hostile. Various fighter squadrons were scrambled and became tangled with one another over the Thames Estuary; in the confusion two Hurricanes of No. 151 Squadron were shot down by Spitfires of No. 74 Squadron, one of the pilots being killed. On the ground, anti-aircraft batteries, their crews seeing what appeared to be a dogfight in progress overhead, also started firing. The chaos might have been much worse if the CO of No. 151 Squadron, Squadron Leader E.M. Donaldson, had not realized what was happening and shouted a warning over the R/T. This unfortunate incident, which went down in history as the Battle of Barking Creek, was later said to have been sparked off by a malfunction at the radar station at Canewdon, in the Thames Estuary, but a much more likely cause was an excess of zeal mingled with high tension.

As the winter approached, enemy minelaying activities remained the principal threat to sea traffic in the Channel area, with German destroyers playing an important role in these operations. Between 13 November 1939 and 19 January 1940, mines accounted for the loss of seven British warships in the Channel, including three destroyers, the *Blanche*, *Gypsy* and *Grenville*. (The other craft were two trawlers, a tug and a drifter,

Troops of the British Expeditionary Force marching through a south coast town prior to embarking for France, September 1940.

all in RN service). Apart from minesweeping, the Royal Navy's activities in the Channel during this period were fairly routine, the fast destroyers periodically ferrying VIPs – including HM King George VI – to French ports on inspection tours of the British Expeditionary Force.

Then, on the night of 1/2 March 1940, there came a new development. The 8,411-ton passenger ship *Domala* was bombed and set on fire off the Isle of Wight by German bombers, reportedly Heinkel He 111s of *Kampfgeschwader* 26. From now on, enemy bombers operated over the Channel at regular intervals, and on 20 March they sank the 5,439-ton freighter *Barn Hill* three miles south-south-west of Beachy Head. The focus of air operations, however, was in the North Sea area, and it was soon apparent why. On 9 April 1940, the Germans invaded Denmark and Norway. Less than a month later the *Luftwaffe* began mining the approaches to Dutch and Belgian seaports, and on 10 May the Germans lanched their *Blitzkrieg* into the Low Countries, simultaneously swinging a left hook through northern France. Within ten days, while the British Expeditionary Force embarked on a fighting retreat through Flanders, the armoured spearheads of the 2nd *Panzer* Division were within sight of the Channel coast at Boulogne.

By 23 May Boulogne had been encircled to landward and its garrison was engaged in fierce fighting. The British troops, drawn mainly from the 20th Guards Brigade (the 2nd Battalion Irish Guards and the 2nd Battalion Welsh Guards, supported by Royal Marines and some anti-tank artillery, together with the remnants of other units that had filtered into the town during the preceding days) soon found their position untenable, and at 15.00 hours orders were received to evacuate them. By this time the German artillery was in command of the heights around Boulogne, from which position it directed a steady stream of shellfire at the harbour and the destroyers that were arriving there, two by two, to carry out the evacuation. These craft – the destroyers *Vimy*, *Keith*, *Whitshed*, *Vimiera*, *Wild Swan*, *Venomous*, *Venetia* and *Windsor*, with a

French destroyer flotilla consisting of the *Cyclone*, *Orage* and *Frondeur* under *Capitaine* de Portzamparc lending their support – returned the enemy fire spiritedly, and it was heartening for the troops to see the naval 4.7s registering hits on the enemy.

Nevertheless, it seemed that the chances of carrying out a successful evacuation were slim, particularly when – just as the embarkation was getting under way at 18.30 hours – *Stukas* appeared overhead and subjected the ships to a vicious dive-bombing attack, setting on fire the *Orage*, which later had to be scuttled, putting the *Frondeur* out of action and near-missing the *Whitshed*. The last-named got away with her load of troops, mainly wounded, and as she steamed by the German-occupied Fort de la Crèche she fired a couple of salvoes, causing a big explosion. Other bombs exploded on the quays close to where the *Vimy* and *Keith* were berthed, flying splinters causing many casualties and killing the captains of both warships.[6]

The Germans were now close enough to use mortars and heavy machine-guns, which added their fire to the holocaust. All the while the naval gunners returned the fire as fast as they could, grimy with cordite, soaked through and caked with the mud that erupted from bomb bursts in the harbour, some of them wounded by the flying metal. They were far too occupied to notice that, overhead, small numbers of RAF Hurricanes were diving through the maze of friendly anti-aircraft bursts in an attempt to break up the enemy air attacks.

The destroyers *Keith* and *Vimy* backed out of the embattled harbour, their armament still hammering away, and were replaced by *Vimiera* and *Whitshed*, the latter still having room for more souls. These two ships quickly embarked some 500 men of the Welsh Guards and departed for Dover, their places being taken by *Wild Swan* and *Venomous*. A third destroyer, *Venetia*, also began her approach to the harbour, but as she reached the entrance she was badly hit and set on fire by a salvo from an enemy battery in the hills. Despite severe damage she backed off and regained the open sea, heavily ablaze and listing, but still firing with all guns that could be brought to bear. She later regained Dover with twenty ratings killed and eleven of all ranks wounded.

Wild Swan and *Venomous* now proceeded rapidly with the embarkation of the Irish Guards, completing the task shortly after 21.00. During the operation almost every German gun in the area was brought to bear on the two destroyers, which fortunately were hull down because of the low tide and their superstructures protected to some extent by installations on the quay. German tanks and infantry moved on to a parallel dock and also began to fire on the destroyers, which turned their 4.7s on this new threat. The effect was devastating; shrapnel scythed through the enemy troops and one tank, receiving a direct hit, was blasted into the air and turned a complete somersault. A minute later the gunners spotted a machine-gun firing from the upper storey of an hotel, and blasted away the building's entire top floor.

On the bullet-swept quay the Guardsmen never wavered. 'It says a great deal for the discipline of the troops,' wrote their commanding officer later, 'that no move was made towards the destroyers until I gave the order, and then the move was carried out slowly and efficiently.' This comment was substantiated by a naval officer: 'The courage and the bearing of the Guardsmen were magnificent, even under a tornado of fire with casualties occurring every second. They were as steady as though on parade and stood like rocks, without giving a damn for anything.'[7]

Both *Wild Swan* and *Venomous* were clear of the harbour by 21.30. An hour later the destroyer *Windsor* had lifted off some 600 troops, including a small number of wounded. The last warship to arrive was the *Vimiera*, which departed shortly before daybreak on 24 May with no fewer than 1,400 soldiers and civilians on board. Many of the civilians were Jews and Poles, who because of the special risks they would run under German occupation were permitted to embark once the destroyer had taken on her quota of troops. Nevertheless, about 300 Welsh Guards had to be left behind, and these fought on with other isolated groups well into the morning. In the Ville Haute, the remnants of the French 21st Infantry Division under General Lanquetot successfully resisted all attempts to dislodge them until, at 10.00, the Germans delivered an ultimatum: if the French did not surrender immediately the town would be systematically destroyed. Lanquetot felt compelled to accede to the enemy's demand in order to save civilian lives, and raised the white flag.

As the Germans entered the harbour area they encountered still more resistance from the ruined Gare Maritime railway station, where about 500 troops – what was left of a Welsh Guards company, 300 men of the Pioneer Corps and 100 or so Frenchmen – had dug in under the command of the Welsh Guards officer, Major Windsor Lewis. Despite heavy shelling from enemy tanks and mortars Lewis's force held out until 13.00 on 25 May, and only surrendered when stocks of food and ammunition were exhausted. With that, Boulogne passed completely into enemy hands.

Meanwhile, the Royal Navy had been hard at work reinforcing the Allied garrison at Calais, threatened by the 10th *Panzer* Division. The Germans were conscious of the fact that the ancient port would prove a tougher nut to crack than Boulogne; the terrain around Calais favoured the defenders, the town being surrounded by marshy land with a network of dykes running across it, and the nearest high ground was two miles away to the west. The town itself was stoutly protected by strong ramparts and ditches covering an eight-mile perimeter, on which there were eleven strongpoints at strategic intervals. In fact the port of Calais could be divided into two distinct areas, the new town and the old; the latter was surrounded by a sweeping moat of water that broadened out into the docks at its eastern extremity.

The man on whose shoulders fell the responsibility of organizing the Calais defence was Colonel R.T. Holland, the assistant adjutant general, who had been sent to the port to make

A train laden with cruiser tanks *en route* for the south coast and France. These armoured fighting vehicles were to prove no match against the German *Panzers*.

arrangements for evacuation. The British forces at his disposal initially comprised a single platoon of infantry from the 6th Argyll and Sutherland Highlanders, together with searchlight and anti-aircraft detachments which had set up their positions at two forts outside the main perimeter. There was also a French garrison manning the Citadel, the fortress that guarded the west flank of the old town, and a few coastal gun batteries manned by French sailors.

Beginning on 22 May, the 30th Brigade under Brigadier Claude Nicholson, comprising the 2nd Battalion the King's Royal Rifle Corps (60th

Rifles), the 1st Battalion the Rifle Brigade and the 1st Battalion Queen Victoria's Rifles, supported by 27 cruiser tanks of the 3rd Royal Tank Regiment, crossed to Calais on the transports *Kohistan* and *Benlawers*, carrying the armour and vehicles, and the troopships *Archangel* and *Royal Daffodil*, carrying the infantry. Escort was provided by the destroyers *Vimiera*, *Windsor* and *Venetia*.

The transports carrying the main body of the brigade did not reach Calais until the early afternoon of Thursday 23 May, the troops having embarked at Southampton after moving down from East Anglia. The convoy had then moved around the south coast to Dover, where Brigadier Nicholson had gone ashore briefly to confer with Vice-Admiral Sir Bertram Ramsay, the flag officer commanding Dover, and Lieutenant-General Sir Douglas Brownrigg, who had recently arrived from Boulogne. It was agreed that Nicholson's force, on arrival at Calais, should move at once to the relief of Boulogne.

On reaching Calais, however, Nicholson quickly decided that his first priority was to organize a defence of the port with the forces at his disposal. He also had to put a stop to the chaos that was rapidly building up. Already, the quays were congested with military personnel and civilian refugees, mingled with piles of stores and equipment and with wreckage resulting from sporadic attacks carried out so far by the *Luftwaffe*. Also, in the middle of the afternoon he learned that units of 3 RTR, having set off for St Omer, had run into a strong force of *Panzers* and received a severe mauling, losing twelve of their cruiser tanks. It was fast becoming clear that the enemy now controlled all the major exits from Calais, and this gloomy realization was strengthened when, at 16.00, enemy tanks were seen near the outskirts of the town. An hour later, the first German shells exploded in the harbour area. At 22.00 on 23 May, the destroyer HMS *Verity* arrived at Calais and disembarked Major-General A.G.L. McNaughton, whost 1st Canadian Division was now stationed in England. McNaughton had been sent over by the CIGS to see if it was feasible to keep open the BEF's lines of communication through either Calais or Dunkirk. After a short survey he left by sea for the latter port; it had not taken him long to make up his mind about the future of Calais, and his coded message to the War Office resulted in an urgent signal to Nicholson from Major-General R.H. Dewing, the director of operations. Arriving at 03.00 on 24 May, it stated: 'Evacuation decided in principle. When you have finished unloading your two MT ships commence embarkation of all personnel except fighting personnel who will remain to cover final evacuation.'[8]

One of the piers in the shattered harbour at Calais, scene of much gallantry in May 1940.

General Maxime Weygand, Supreme Commander of the French Armies in the Battle of France.

Vice-Chief of Naval Staff informs me that an order was sent at 2 a.m. to Calais saying that evacuation was decided on in principle, but this is surely madness. The only effect of evacuating Calais would be to transfer the forces now blocking it to Dunkirk. Calais must be held for many reasons, but specially to hold the enemy on its front. The Admiralty say they are preparing twenty-four naval 12-pounders, which with SAP (semi-armour-piercing shells) will pierce any tank. Some of these will be ready this evening.[9]

The first Brigadier Nicholson knew of these pronouncements affecting the future of his command came in the early hours of 25 May, when the destroyer HMS *Wolfhound* – which had been bombarding enemy positions inland together with *Wessex* and *Vimiera* – crept into Calais harbour and disembarked Vice-Admiral Sir James Somerville, commanding the small force of warships that had been sent to lend its support to the defences. Somerville carried the following War Office order addressed to Nicholson:

> In spite of policy of evacuation given you this morning fact that British forces in your area now under Fagalde who has ordered no repeat no evacuation means that you must comply for sake of Allied Solidarity. Your role is therefore to hold on, harbour being at present of no importance to BEF. Brigade Group 48 Div started marching to your assistance this morning. No reinforcements but ammunition being sent by sea. Should this fail RAF will drop ammunition. You will select best position and fight on.[10]

At about the same time, General Maxime Weygand, the French supreme commander, appointed General Fagalde of the French XVI Corps to command all military forces in the Channel ports. Fagalde's first directive in this new capacity was to forbid the evacuation of Calais and to place the French troops there under the command of Brigadier Nicholson. The decision was upheld by Winston Churchill, who later in the day sent the following message to General Ismay of the War Cabinet Secretariat:

The message was, to say the least, worded in a most unfortunate manner, with its demand that Nicholson should sacrifice his men to hold a useless objective. The only glimmer of hope it contained was in its promise of ammunition, which the garrison desperately needed, and in the possibility of relief by the 48th Division. In fact, the 48th Division, then in the Hazebrouck area, had been standing by to march to Calais for some time, but was prevented from doing so by the pressing need to cover the BEF's fighting retreat through Flanders.

At sunrise on 25 May Calais was the scene of desperate fighting, with strong enemy attacks against the Rifle Brigade's positions on the south of the perimeter following a fierce artillery barrage. The brigade had only a handful of scout cars, light tanks and Bren carriers to support it, for most of the 3rd RTR's tanks had been destroyed – many of them deliberately when the earlier order to evacuate was received. Nevertheless, when the enemy infantry came storming over the canals through the dust and smoke of their own shells they encountered withering small-arms fire and recoiled after suffering fearful losses at the hands of troops who were probably the finest marksmen in any army. For several hours they held their own, but in the end the weight of enemy numbers began to tell and the brigade's line was pierced at several points, forcing the British troops to withdraw to a new position between the two dock basins.

Meanwhile, the 60th Rifles – whose main task was to cover the three bridges that linked the old and new towns of Calais – had also been subjected to a formidable artillery barrage, directed by a German observation post in the town hall on the other side of the waterway. Behind the Rifles' right flank was the Citadel, the old fortress into which Brigadier Nicholson had now moved his headquarters and which was occupied by a garrison of 200 Frenchmen and a detachment of Royal Marines, sharing a pair of 75 mm guns. The task of the old town's defenders was made incredibly complicated by the presence of masses of refugees, including several hundred unarmed French and Belgian soldiers, all seeking refuge from the rain of shells.

During the afternoon, after Brigadier Nicholson had received and rejected a German surrender demand, the enemy kept up a steady and accurate mortar barrage on the British positions, causing many casualties and setting fire to a number of buildings until the whole of the 60th's front was obscured by smoke. The British replied with their only two 3-inch mortars, deriving scant comfort from the steady drumroll of naval gunfire they could hear offshore as

Admiral Somerville's destroyers hammered away at the German gun positions west of the town.

Although the harbour at Calais had been subjected to limited attacks by *Luftwaffe* medium bombers at intervals since 19 May, it was only on the 25th that strong formations of Junkers Ju 87 *Stuka* dive-bombers began operating in the area, and at first their principal targets were the troublesome warships offshore rather than the town itself. The *Luftwaffe* unit that carried out the first heavy dive-bombing attack off Calais was *Stuka-Geschwader* 2 (StG 2) under *Major* Oskar Dinort, which had moved up to an advanced base at Guise, east of St Quentin. At 11.00 on the 25th, Dinort led two *Gruppen* of StG 2 – about 40 *Stukas* – against Admiral Somerville's naval force, consisting of the light cruisers *Arethusa* and *Galatea* and the destroyers *Wessex*, *Vimiera*, *Wolfhound*, *Verity*, *Grafton*, *Greyhound* and *Burza*, the latter a Polish ship.

It was the first time that *Stukas* had been used against moving warship targets, and as yet no firm technique had been worked out for this type of operation. It was soon clear to the German pilots that attacks on warships manoeuvring at high speed was going to call for a finer degree of expertise than anything they had encountered so far. Nevertheless, some of their bombs found a target; the *Wessex* was sunk, the *Burza* badly damaged and the *Vimiera* near-missed, sustaining damage that reduced her speed. It was a foretaste of what was to happen a few days later, off the beaches of Dunkirk.

On the following day, with the defensive perimeter in Calais reduced to a tight ring around the Citadel, the final pocket of resistance was subjected to a fierce onslaught by *Stukas*, followed by an artillery barrage that pounded the Citadel for 90 minutes. At noon, a major attack developed against the British positions, and the surviving troops were forced back to the docks area.

The Citadel was now completely isolated, and at 15.00 hours enemy troops supported by tanks broke in from the south. Half an hour later Brigadier Nicholson, his defences completely overwhelmed, was forced to surrender. Sporadic fighting continued until 17.00 as the Germans conducted mopping-up operations; the last to surrender were the battered survivors of a company of the Queen Victoria's Rifles, who were cornered in a schoolhouse in the harbour and shelled into submission by tanks and mortars.

Miraculously, about 200 of the defenders of Calais managed to escape the trap – thanks largely to the efforts of the crews of two Royal Navy yachts, the *Conidaw* and *Gulzar*. The latter rescued nearly 50 men from under the very noses of the Germans in the small hours of 27 May, creeping in to where the soldiers had been seen sheltering under the remains of a pier and getting them away safely.

In all, the Germans took 20,000 prisoners, 3,500 of them British, in the Calais area. Of the sacrifice of 30th Brigade – whose last stand must surely rank as one of the most noteworthy examples of unit gallantry in the history of warfare – Churchill later wrote:

> Calais was the crux. Many other causes might have prevented the deliverance of Dunkirk, but it is certain that the three days gained by the defence of Calais enabled the Gravelines waterline to be held, and that without this, even in spite of Hitler's vacillations and Rundstedt's orders, all would have been cut off and lost.[11]

But how valid was this assessment? German documents released after the war, and the testimony of General Heinz Guderian, commanding XIX *Panzer* Corps, have shown that the capture of Calais was a secondary task. And although the defenders of Calais inflicted such losses on 10th *Panzer's* two infantry regiments

that they took no further part in the campaign in northern France, it may be thought with justification that the brigade deployed to Calais, and in particular its supporting armour, might have been more profitably employed in the defence of the Canal Line on the approach to Dunkirk and should have been shipped to France through that port.

Ironically, the final decision not to relieve the garrison at Calais was not taken until the evening of 26 May. And, in a final stroke of irony, at dawn the next day 21 Westland Lysander army co-operation aircraft from Lympne dropped water and ammunition into Calais. By that time, the defenders were marching into captivity. Three Lysanders were shot down, and all the supplies fell into enemy hands.

The Westland Lysander was the mainstay of the RAF's Army Co-operation squadrons in 1940. This photograph, which shows one lodged in some bushes after a taxying accident, gives a good idea of the aircraft's size.

CHAPTER TWO

Defeated Armies

From the bridge of the destroyer HMS *Wolfhound*, Dunkirk was an awe-inspiring sight. A great column of smoke from the port's blazing oil storage tanks was the first pointer to the destruction that had already been wrought by the *Luftwaffe*. Boiling up from its as yet unseen base over the horizon, its top trailed out on the wind to form a long plume through which the afternoon sun shone fitfully.

A Lockheed Hudson of RAF Coastal Command flies a 'sands patrol' off Dunkirk, with the port's oil tanks ablaze in the background.

The crew of HMS *Wolfhound* had already had a taste of the *Luftwaffe's* fury on this afternoon on 27 May. For fifteen minutes, with Dover scarcely down over the horizon astern, the warship had run the gauntlet of a determined attack by Junkers Ju 87 *Stukas* of *Generalleutnant* Wolfram von Richthofen's VIII *Fliegerkorps*. A combination of good luck and neat evasive action had thrown the dive-bombers off their aim, and as soon as they departed the destroyer's skipper, Captain John McCoy, once again set course at full speed for Dunkirk, conscious that much depended on

the *Wolfhound's* safe arrival. For the ship carried the men whose task it was to organize some order out of the chaos that was even now debouching on Dunkirk and its neighbouring beaches: Captain William Tennant RN and his small command of naval officers and ratings, through whom the evacuation would be channelled.

As the *Wolfhound* approached Dunkirk, Tennant and his officers began to have some idea of the enormity of the task that lay ahead of them. The great pall of smoke seemed to obscure everything, and at its foot the whole waterfront seemed to be ablaze. Flames seethed along the quays from burning warehouses, and as the destroyer drew closer to the harbour a carpet of soot descended on her like black rain.

The *Wolfhound* berthed to the crump of bombs as yet another air raid added to the devastation, which was far greater than Tennant had visualized. The docks, with their five miles of quays, were shattered, the cranes tilted at crazy angles among piles of rubble. The town's railway system had ceased to exist, the tracks ripped apart and twisted by high explosive bombs. Beneath the toppled buildings of Dunkirk, a thousand men, women and children lay dead, victims of the first day of severe air attack.

Tennant was greeted on the quay by Colonel Gerald Whitfield, senior staff officer to General Sir Douglas Brownrigg, Lord Gort's adjutant-general, who briefed him on the extent of the damage and the latest battle situation as far as it was known. Having made his assessment, Tennant issued his orders to his officers, assigning them to their various tasks. Commander Thomas Kerr, one of the naval officers who had accompanied Tennant, later described his personal impression of the situation in Dunkirk and on the surrounding beaches:

> In due course we were marched down through the town to the beach close by and our work began. Such a terrible beach for embarking men because it was practically level and nothing could come in close, not even the boats. We worked without ceasing all the dark hours, restoring order and confidence to the troops. At dawn we withdrew them to the sand dunes for an hour, and afterwards marched them into Dunkirk. We cleared the beach sometime during the afternoon. The Captain in charge, Tennant, reorganized us and said he wanted one officer and party to go to Bray Dunes to embark 5,000 men. There were three of us left and so we cut for it, for it was a poor outlook by the sound of it. Richardson (Commander Hector Richardson) lost, but then said quite rightly that he wanted another officer with him, so he and I set out in a lorry with a party of fifteen.
>
> It took us some time to reach Bray Dunes because the road was badly cratered and we took the wrong turning once or twice, and it was getting dusk when we finally got our party down to the beach. Then we gave a gasp. Five thousand men? Not a bit of it, there must have been 25,000 at the very least. We asked a destroyer to signal this information direct to the Admiralty, then we got busy. What a terrible night that was, for we had got hold of the odds and ends of an army, not the fighting soldiers. There were hardly any officers, and the few present were useless; but our promise of safety, and the sight of our naval uniforms, restored some order to the rabble. Their faith in the Navy was pathetic; we could only do our best. Some we embarked at Bray Dunes, but the remainder we marched in their thousands to Dunkirk; a difficult task in itself, for the sight of just one little dinghy with a queue of 2,000 men waiting to get into it was enough to make them hesitate on the march.
>
> We were all soaked through, because we couldn't persuade the troops to stand on dry sand rather than in the water; every man was afraid that someone else would get in front of him. Towards morning the weather blew up and embarkation from the beach became impossible, so herding them and marshalling them we marched them towards Dunkirk.[12]

During the twenty-four hours between midnight on 26 May and midnight on the 27th, 3,324 British troops were evacuated from Dunkirk and the neighbouring beaches. Added to this figure were 1,250 wounded and 4,000 Frenchmen, the latter all specialists who could play no part in the defence of Dunkirk and whose evacuation had been ordered by *Admiral* Abrial, the C-in-C French Naval Forces in the north. The lifting of troops had been a desperately slow process, and Tennant knew that unless immediate steps were taken to augment the lift the chaos during the next twenty-four hours would become insupportable. The longer the troops had to wait on the beaches, the greater was the likelihood that all semblance of order would break down; and the fighting troops had yet to arrive.

Already, Tennant and his officers had witnessed the appalling spectacle of drunken soldiers roaming the streets of Dunkirk in armed, unruly mobs, looting and pillaging; he himself had confronted one such mob, at no small personal risk, and disarmed its leader. At this show of authority, the first the men had encountered for some time, order was quickly restored – but the worry that the discontent that seethed among the men on the beaches might turn into open mutiny if something was not done quickly was constantly at the back of Tennant's mind. At 20.00 hours on the 27th, after conferring with *Admiral* Abrial and Brigadier Geoffrey Mansergh, senior administrative officer to Lieutenant-General Alan Brooke, commanding II British Corps, he instructed his signals officer, Commander Michael Elwood, to signal Admiral Ramsay in Dover that every available craft must immediately be sent to the beaches east of Dunkirk. Otherwise, evacuation on the 28th might become impossible.

The surface forces committed to the evacuation by Ramsay on this, the first major day of the operation, consisted of one anti-aircraft cruiser – HMS *Calcutta* – nine destroyers and four minesweepers, all of which had been ordered to close the beaches and use their small boats to supplement the lifts being carried out by the cross-Channel steamers and drifters. It was not enough; at low tide the destroyers could approach no closer than a mile inshore, which meant that the crews of their whalers faced a twenty-minute pull to the beaches and when they arrived the boats could take on only twenty-five men at the most. By this method, loading a destroyer to its maximum capacity of 1,000 men could take six hours or more. Additional numbers of small craft would help – hence Tennant's signal to Ramsay – but there was the factor of the weather to be considered. The approaches to the beaches were tricky in ideal conditions, and if the wind, at present blowing from the east, veered to the north, the small-boat operations in the shallows would become extremely hazardous.

The only alternative was to use Dunkirk's East Mole, although it was by no means certain that ships would be able to berth alongside it safely. Nevertheless, it was a risk that had to be taken. At 22.30 on the 27th, a signal was flashed to one of the craft waiting offshore – the personnel vessel *Queen of the Channel* – to come alongside the mole. Cautiously her skipper, Captain W.J. Odell, brought her forward through the darkness until she nudged into position against the mole's wooden structure. For the first time, Tennant saw a glimmer of hope; where one ship had gone, others could follow, and the mole was long enough to accommodate sixteen vessels at a time.

During the early hours of 28 May, five destroyers bore the brunt of the evacuation from Dunkirk. Despatched hurriedly from Dover and other ports along England's south coast, their captains had not had time to receive any briefing other than that they were to proceed to Dunkirk to pick up troops. From the bridge of HMS *Wakeful*, which had been about to refuel at Dover when the order to sail for Dunkirk with all speed was received, Commander Ralph Fisher issued orders to clear the mess decks of all furniture while the ship's cooks prepared cocoa, tea and food. As an afterthought – and fully conscious of the risk involved – he also ordered the crew to offload the destroyer's six tons of torpedoes and 100 depth charges. By reducing weight in this way the ship would be able to lift off an extra 100 men, and her manoeuvrability would be increased if she came under air attack. So, lightened of her war load, *Wakeful* steamed for Dunkirk, to berth by the East Mole before dawn and take on 600 men. Thirty minutes later she was on her way homeward.

Further up the coast, at Bray Dunes, the crew of the destroyer HMS *Codrington* under Captain George Stevens-Guille had been running a shuttle service between the beach and the warship with the latter's whalers when word came through that the East Mole was available. Stevens-Guille lost no time in ordering his boats inboard and setting course for the Mole, where he quickly took on the rest of his quota and followed *Wakeful* back to Dover. Other destroyers were not so fortunate; HMS *Mackay* became grounded on a sand-bank as she felt her way towards the deep-water

Almost home: relieved British troops leaving Dunkirk on the destroyer HMS *Mackay*.

channel off the beaches, which in turn created problems for HMS *Harvester* following close behind. *Harvester* had been despatched to Dunkirk so quickly that there had been no time to take on much essential equipment, including charts; her captain, Lieutenant-Commander Mark Thornton, had simply been ordered to follow *Mackay*, and with the latter now stuck fast he had no alternative but to let his ship drift inshore in the hope that the tide would carry her into the deepest channel. The plan worked, and *Harvester's* boats were soon pulling for the beaches. On board HMS *Sabre*, Commander Brian Dean was also having his problems; he had taken on 800 troops, but his ship was badly overladen and it was touch and go whether she would negotiate the shoals safely. While two seamen clung precariously to small platforms slung out from the ship's sides, chanting the depth soundings, Dean brought the destroyer ahead dead slow. She slipped over the shoals with inches to spare and headed out into the Channel on the 87-mile run home.

Meanwhile at Dover, Admiral Ramsay and his staff were making desperate efforts to assemble the small craft so badly needed by Tennant. So far, they had about 100 at their disposal: 40 craft which had been registered as the result of an Admiralty appeal issued on 14 May, and another 50 or so boats based in and around Dover. But many, many more were needed if even a fraction of the BEF was to be snatched from the beaches.

Early on the 28th, for the first time, the Royal Navy's motor torpedo boats took a hand. They were drawn from the 3rd, 4th and 10th Flotillas based at Felixstowe, and they had already been employed in evacuating servicemen and civilians from Holland.[13] One MTB skipper, Lieutenant Stewart Gould, described the first day's operations at Dunkirk.

We left Dover at 06.35 on 28 May and it was not long before we came under fire from the guns in Calais and Gravelines. The MTBs scattered and eventually reached Dunkirk at 08.30. I took MTB 68 under orders and reported to the Senior Naval Officer. Destroyers were embarking British troops from the East Pier. The town was being bombed and there was a great deal of shelling.

MTB 68 was sent back to Dover with a hand message from the Senior Naval Officer. We (in MTB 16) anchored close inshore and began embarking troops under fire. They were exhausted and still carrying full equipment. Few were able to climb in board and had to be hauled in through the torpedo stern doors. (The early BPB craft launched their torpedoes first from the stern.) Able Seaman Schofield swam voluntarily several hundred yards to save the lives of exhausted men.

We made several trips to and from the beach and transferred over 300 troops to the destroyers. Enemy aircraft attacked and MTB 16's Lewis guns, manned by Able Seaman F. Clark and Telegraphist H.F. McCutcheon, brought down a twin-engined bomber. During one trip inshore we ran aground, damaging the propeller. The centre engine was out of action and the tide was falling. We returned to Commander Maund, who was controlling the evacuation of the beach, and took up duties towing destroyers' whalers. At 21.00 the wind began to freshen and the evacuation continued from Dunkirk itself, to where Maund marched the troops. We left there at 05.50 on 29 May and returned to Dover and Felixstowe for repairs.[14]

The sight of the MTBs – and of other small craft which began to arrive off the beaches during the afternoon of the 28th – heartened the troops considerably, even though towards the end of the day a growing swell meant that the burden of the evacuation had to fall on Dunkirk's East Mole, towards which the columns of fatigued men now tramped. Despite all the problems, 17,804 men were landed in England before midnight on the 28th – double the previous day's total, thanks to the use of the mole and to the prevailing low cloud and drizzle which thwarted the *Luftwaffe*.

So far, German naval activity off Dunkirk had been non-existent, but this situation was not to last. In the early hours of 28 May *Kapitänleutnant* Rudolf Petersen, commanding the 2nd *Schnellboote* Flotilla in Wilhelmshaven, called his officers together and briefed them for offensive operations in the Channel area. Already, on 9 May, Petersen had led four boats of his flotilla in a successful night action north of the Straits of Dover; they had encountered a force of cruisers and destroyers of the British Home Fleet, and in the ensuing brief battle the destroyer HMS *Kelly* had been torpedoed and badly damaged by *Kapitänleutnant* Opdenhoff's S31.[15]

Now, three weeks later, Petersen's orders were simple: the S-boats were to enter the Channel under cover of darkness, lie in wait and strike hard at whatever British vessels they encountered, preferably those homeward bound with their cargoes of troops. Six boats were to undertake the mission, operating in two relays of three, hugging the 200 miles of coast on the outward trip and entering the Channel after dark.

The first three boats slipped out of Wilhelmshaven that afternoon. In the lead was S25, commanded by *Kapitänleutnant* Siegfried Wuppermann, an officer who was later to become one of the German Navy's small ship 'aces' in the Mediterranean. Behind him came *Leutnant* Zimmermann's S30, followed in turn by S34 under *Leutnant* Obermaier. The outward voyage was uneventful, the S-boats entering the Channel on schedule and spreading out, evading the slender screen of MTBs deployed by the Royal Navy from Felixstowe and taking up station, engines off, to the north of Ramsay's cross-Channel routes. Station was kept, from left to right, by S30, S25 and S34, and after ninety minutes of pitching and waiting on the Channel swell it was Obermaier in S34 who made the first contact with the enemy. With the aid of night glasses, he picked out a vessel and identified it as a British destroyer. Starting S34's engines, he closed to action stations and began his attack. At 00.45 on 29 May, he launched four torpedoes at the target.

Among the crew of the destroyer HMS *Wakeful*, the tension of the day's operations was making itself felt. Hardly had the destroyer entered Dover with her first load of troops on 28 May when she was ordered out again, and she had sailed as soon as the soldiers disembarked, still without having refuelled or taken on fresh stocks of ammunition. On her second trip across the Channel she had been attacked by Ju 87s and had sustained a hole in her side from a near-miss, but she had run the gauntlet of the attack and Commander Fisher had brought her back into Dunkirk, taking on another 640 troops. Now he was taking his ship home over Route Y, the most northerly of the evacuation routes, with the light of the Kwinte Buoy visible to port.

There was no time for evasive action. The first of S34's torpedoes passed ahead of the destroyer but the second exploded amidships, tearing *Wakeful* in two. Within thirty seconds she was gone, leaving behind a few islands of wreckage and a handful of survivors, Fisher among them. Over 700 men, mostly troops crammed below decks, went to their deaths with the stricken ship.

Other vessels in the vicinity observed the disaster and closed in to give whatever help they could. The survivors had been in the water for little over thirty minutes when the first arrived: the minesweeper HMS *Gossamer*, closely followed by the Scottish drifter *Comfort*. By 02.00 the destroyer *Grafton*, the minesweeper *Lydd* and the motor drifter *Nautilus* had also reached the scene, their lifeboats joining the search for the remnants of *Wakeful's* crew.

A thousand yards to the east, other eyes were watching the rescue operation. They belonged to *Leutnant* Michalowski and they were glued to the eyepiece of a periscope in the control centre of the submarine U-62. Michalowski now focused on the largest of the English vessels, clearly visible in the periscope's graticule as lights flickered across the water amid *Wakeful's* wreckage. Michalowski quickly checked range, bearing, depth settings and running time, then ordered the launch of a salvo of torpedoes.

The destroyer *Grafton* was lying at rest, her rails crowded with troops who, like her captain, Commander Robinson, were watching the efforts of her lifeboat crews as they continued the search. At that instant U-62's torpedoes struck. One tore away the destroyer's stern; the other sent an explosion ripping through the wardroom, killing 35 officers.

What happened next amounted to panic. The other vessels in the area, their captains aware only that *Grafton* had been subjected to an unexpected attack, began steering in all directions, their gun crews tense and ready to fire at shadows. On the minesweeper *Lydd*, Lieutenant-Commander Haig saw what looked like the silhouette of a torpedo-boat moving south-westwards. *Lydd's* starboard Lewis gun opened fire on it and *Grafton*, which was still afloat, opened up with her secondary armament. It was a terrible mistake; the 'torpedo-boat' was in fact the drifter *Comfort*, carrying survivors from HMS *Wakeful*. Machine-gun bullets raked her decks as the *Lydd* closed right in, cutting the drifter's crew to pieces. Minutes later, *Lydd's* bow sliced into *Comfort's* hull, tearing her apart. There were only five survivors; among them was Commander Fisher, whom *Comfort* had plucked from the sea when *Wakeful* went down. Fisher spent a long time in the water before he was again picked up, more dead than alive, by the Norwegian tramp steamer *Hird* at dawn.

HMS *Grafton*, meanwhile, was finished. At first light the railway steamer *Malines* took off her survivors, and soon afterwards the destroyer *Ivanhoe* put three shells into her waterline. Ten minutes later she turned over and sank. Over the horizon U-62 and Wuppermann's three S-boats were already well on their way back to base; there could be no doubt that the German Navy had won the first round.

By first light on 29 May the number of craft at Captain William Tennant's disposal had grown considerably and the weather continued to favour the evacuation, with fog and drizzle over the beaches. Nevertheless, Commanders Thomas Kerr and Hector Richardson were still sending men back to Dunkirk from Bray Dunes at the rate of a thousand every quarter of an hour, and as yet only about 25,500 had been lifted. Because of the heavy swell along the beaches, it had not proved possible to evacuate the anticipated number of men during the hours of darkness, and there had also been a lot of problems along the East Mole, where ships had to contend with a fluctuation of fifteen feet between high and low tide. In all, seventy vessels had been in operation at Dunkirk and along the beaches during the night of 28/29

May and Admiral Ramsay had promised that more were on their way, although it would be some time before the small craft which were being assembled in the south coast harbours could make their full contribution. As yet, Tennant was unaware of the tragedy that had taken place in the Channel a few hours earlier – or that the ordeal was just beginning.

The evacuation maintained a steady tempo throughout the morning of 29 May. Then, shortly before noon, the mist that had shielded the evacuation from the *Luftwaffe* began to disperse. At 14.00, Dunkirk was attacked by all three *Geschwader* of VIII *Fliegerkorps*, a total of around 180 Ju 87s.

The attack could not have come at a worse time. Eleven ships were berthed at the East Mole, jammed stem to stern, and the French destroyers *Mistral*, *Sirocco* and *Cyclone* were moored alongside in the harbour; all in addition to the host of other craft at work along the nine miles of beach. The *Stukas* concentrated mostly on the harbour and the East Mole, diving through an intense anti-aircraft barrage put up by the warships to deliver their bombs. A 1,000 lb bomb and two 500 lb missiles struck the destroyer HMS *Grenade* in a ripple of almost simultaneous explosions, setting her ablaze from end to end. Her mooring ropes parted and she swung clear of the mole, striking the fishing trawler *Brock* and drifting helplessly into the fairway, a burning hulk. On the mole Commander John Clouston, the piermaster, hurriedly gave orders to another trawler to take the stricken destroyer in tow and drag her clear before she went down, blocking the fairway. The trawler skipper obeyed quickly, pulling *Grenade* out into open water and speedily casting off. A minute later, the destroyer's magazine exploded and the warship disappeared under a mushroom of smoke that was visible from La Panne, ten miles away.

The echoes of the explosion had scarcely died away when another heavy bomb burst on the quayside next to the French destroyer *Mistral*. The blast and chunks of shrapnel scythed away her superstructure, causing severe casualties. Her two sister ships, *Sirocco* and *Cyclone*, were more fortunate; both of them, laden with 500 troops apiece, were near-missed but undamaged. The destroyer HMS *Jaguar* had just got under way when she sustained a direct hit; fearfully damaged, she managed to struggle clear of the harbour, and her captain, Lieutenant-Commander Hine, gave the order to abandon ship. HMS *Verity* succeeded in getting clear, with bombs exploding all around, only to run aground beyond the harbour mouth and suffer damage.

The armed boarding vessel *King Orry* arrived in the middle of the attack, steaming past the wreck of the *Grenade* which by a miracle was still afloat. Within minutes the *King Orry* was also hit, a bomb tearing away her steering gear so that she swung out of control and ripped a great gap in the mole, putting it temporarily out of action. Then, as the water poured into her, the *King Orry* heeled over and went down. Berthed beside the mole, the trawlers *Calvi* and *Polly Johnson* both received direct hits. A bomb hurtled down *Calvi*'s ventilation shaft and exploded deep in her vitals, blowing out her bottom. As she began to settle, still upright, her crew scrambled on to the deck of a neighbouring trawler, the *John Cattling*.

Hour after hour, or so it seemed to the dazed, blast-rocked soldiers and sailors, the onslaught went on. Like the *King Orry*, the paddle minesweeper *Gracie Fields* took a hit on the stern that wrecked her steering gear she circled helplessly until she eventually sank, the minesweeper *Pangbourne* taking off her survivors. The personnel ship *Fenella*, with 600 soldiers on board, survived a near miss only to have a bomb rip through her deck and burst in her engine room; a shattered hulk, she had to be abandoned.

At 15.30 the air attacks were taken up by the twin-engined bombers of *Luftflotte* 2: Heinkel He 111s, Dornier Do 17s and Junkers Ju 88s, the latter from *Kampfgeschwader* 30 at Antwerp and *Lehrgeschwader* I from Düsseldorf. The Ju 88s attacked the biggest merchant vessel to be used in the Dunkirk evacuation, the 6,900-ton Glasgow freighter *Clan MacAlister*, which was laden with

landing craft. The bombs shattered her, setting her on fire and killing a third of her crew as well as many of the soldiers who had recently boarded her. Once again the *Pangbourne* came to the rescue, taking survivors from the crippled freighter before she went down.

Six miles west of Dunkirk, Heinkels caught the Southern Railway ferry *Normannia* in the open sea off Mardyck; torn apart by bombs, she settled to the bottom on an even keel. Her sister ship, the *Lorina*, suffered a similar fate minutes later, while the minesweeper *Waverley* went down in that same cauldron, blown to pieces in a 30-minute attack by a dozen Heinkels. Hard by the beaches, the old Thames river paddle-steamer *Crested Eagle*, filled to capacity with troops and the survivors of the *Fenella*, was hit by a single bomb and burst into flames. A white-hot furnace, with screaming, burning men leaping overboard into the oily water, she slowly approached the beach under the direction of her skipper, Lieutenant-Commander Booth. At last she grounded and the survivors threw themselves into the shallows, away from the fearful heat, while the ship flared like a beacon behind them.

Such was the awful toll of 29 May; and, in addition to the ships sunk, many others had been seriously damaged. They included the sloop *Bideford*, her stern a mass of tangled wreckage; the crippled destroyer *Jaguar*, which somehow refused to sink; and the destroyers *Gallant*, *Greyhound* and *Intrepid*, among the Royal Navy's most modern warships of this kind. Yet despite all the destruction, despite the chaos and loss of life, the embarkations had continued even through the worst of the air raids, the vessels' captain taking incredible risks to get the men away – like Lieutenant Edwin Davies, commanding the paddle-minesweeper *Oriole*, who deliberately grounded his ship to provide a kind of jetty over which 2,500 men scrambled to other waiting boats, then managed to free her and set course for home with 600 troops of her own on board.

As dusk fell on 29 May, the scene off the beaches at Dunkirk was one of utter carnage; the whole sea seemed to be littered with blazing ships. Nevertheless, 47,310 men had been lifted off during the day, 33,558 of them from the East Mole – a fact that underlined that structure's vital importance. Yet now the mole was unusable, its lifeline broken by the luckless *King Orry*, and as the hours dragged by Tennant's anxiety increased; there was no sign of the ships that should have arrived to continue the evacuation after dark. By 21.00 only four trawlers and a yacht had appeared, and the horizon was empty.

Tennant had no way of knowing that the First Sea Lord, Admiral Sir Dudley Pound, seriously alarmed by the day's losses, had already issued orders for the Navy's eight most modern destroyers to be withdrawn from Operation DYNAMO. This meant that the burden of the evacuation would now fall on the fifteen elderly destroyers still at Ramsay's disposal, and these would be capable of lifting not more than 17,000 men in the next 24 hours.

There was, by this time, bitter resentment among the men on the beaches over the apparent absence of RAF fighters over Dunkirk and its environs. In fact, RAF Fighter Command was doing its utmost to provide the necessary protection, a matter that was not fully appreciated until years after the event. British fighter cover over Dunkirk was provided by a total of sixteen first-line fighter squadrons drawn from Air Vice-Marshal Keith Park's No. 11 Fighter Group, deployed on its south-eastern airfields: Biggin Hill, Manston, Hornchurch, Lympne, Hawkinge and Kenley, to name the principals. This standing cover of sixteen squadrons was frequently rotated, those which suffered a high rate of attrition being sent north for a rest and replaced by fresh units drawn from Nos 12 and 13 Groups, so that in all 32 RAF fighter squadrons participated in the nine days of Operation DYNAMO. No more than sixteen, however were committed at any one time, for Air Chief Marshal Sir Hugh Dowding, the C-in-C Fighter Command, knew that the real test would soon come in the skies over southern England and was anxious to preserve what remained of his fighter strength to meet it. Losses so far in the Battle of

France had been fearfully high, the equivalent of six squadrons of Hurricanes.

On 27 May – a day on which the *Luftwaffe* carried out twelve major attacks on Dunkirk, using a total of 300 bombers, flying 550 escort fighter sorties, dropping 15,000 high explosive and 30,000 incendiary bombs – AVM Park's sixteen fighter squadrons, with 287 serviceable aircraft at their disposal, carried out 23 patrols over Dunkirk, the patrols varying in strength from nine to twenty aircraft. During the day fourteen Spitfires and Hurricanes were lost; the RAF claimed 38 enemy aircraft, but in the heat of battle this was greatly exaggerated.

Despite poor weather conditions on 28 May No. 11 Group flew eleven squadron patrols in the Dunkirk sector during the day, with 321 individual fighter sorties. The RAF claimed the destruction of 23 enemy aircraft for the loss of thirteen of their own number. Again, the RAF claim was exaggerated, losses being about equal. On the 29th, the day of heavy attacks on Dunkirk, the RAF carried out nine patrols, with formations of between 25 and 44 fighters providing cover over the Dunkirk sector. They succeeded in intercepting three out of the five major attacks launched by the *Luftwaffe* that day, but all the German raids were heavily escorted by fighters and the RAF could not succeed in breaking them up. The score at the end of the day was marginally in the *Luftwaffe*'s favour, with sixteen British fighters shot down against fourteen German aircraft. There is little doubt that the *Luftwaffe*'s losses on 29 May would have been higher, and the damage to Allied shipping correspondingly less, if the 3.7-inch anti-aircraft guns of the British 2nd Anti-Aircraft Brigade had been in action. The Brigade was responsible for the defence of Dunkirk, but due to an unfortunate miscarriage of orders all its guns had been deliberately put out of action on the evening of 27 May, leaving only the Bofors of the 51st Light Anti-Aircraft Regiment – effective only up to 4,000 feet – and the guns of warships to defend the port.

The night of 29/30 May passed with agonizing slowness. Dawn broke at last to reveal a welcome sight for Captain Tennant and his hard-pressed staff: the whole length of the beaches shrouded in a chill, dank fog that had rolled in from the Channel overnight.

Under its sheltering veil, the rescue armada patiently assembled over the past days crept out at last from England's south coast ports, coves and estuaries; almost a thousand craft, destroyers, minesweepers, sloops, yachts, ferries, cockle boats, drifters, barges, trawlers, schuits and pleasure boats – all bound for the cauldron of Dunkirk, all with a single purpose: to bring salvation to the waiting thousands, clustered like dark clouds on the sands from La Panne to the burning port. More were coming, too, small craft for the most part, together with volunteers to man them; volunteers such as Lieutenant-Commander Archie Buchanan, RN (Retired), who – not disclosing his previous naval service – signed on as a motor boat engineer at Lowestoft in response to a BBC radio appeal the previous evening. At nine o'clock in the morning of the 30th he was deep in the bowels of his assigned craft, the six-berth estuary cruiser *Elvin*, going over her two Highlander Fordson 25 hp engines enthusi-astically. Together with three other cruisers, she was to sail for Dunkirk 24 hours later.

The first wave of small craft arrived off the beaches, still under their blanket of fog, to find a light wind blowing from the east and the surf that had hampered operations on the previous day gone. At intervals engineers were hard at work building improvised jetties from lorries and whatever spare planks and gratings they could find; small craft could lie alongside these, which meant that in some cases troops no longer had to wade out often neck-deep into the sea. Larger craft also attempted in some cases to berth alongside these flimsy structures, with disastrous results; the makeshift piers crumpled under the strain and the engineers had to start all over again.

As the fog persisted, the evacuation received an unexpected boost: the First Sea Lord decided to lift his restriction on the use of the Royal Navy's most modern destroyers. The lifting of the ban

The troops made jetties from abandoned lorries to reach the craft offshore. This *Luftwaffe* photograph of the beach at La Panne was taken after the evacuation.

was supposed to be temporary, but in the event the demands of Operation DYNAMO were to become so pressing over the next 24 hours that the destroyers remained committed to the end.

Some of the hardest-worked vessels off the beaches on this Thursday, 30 May, were the minesweepers. They were able to come much closer inshore than the destroyers, and consequently their loading took place at a higher frequency – which in turn often meant more cross-Channel trips.

No ship had a prouder record off Dunkirk than HMS *Locust*, which, together with her sister ship *Mosquito*, was based at Sheerness as part of the Thames Estuary Defence Flotilla. Both vessels had sailed for Dunkirk on 29 May in company with the Thames paddle-steamers *Golden Eagle* and *Crested Eagle*; the rumour circulating round the lower deck was that they were bound for Le Havre to evacuate women and children. Then, as they altered course around the North Foreland, the crews saw for the first time the enormous pall of black smoke that rose from the oil tanks at Dunkirk. As they approached, each ship broke out her battle ensign; the crews knew for certain now that this was something deadly serious.

HMS *Locust*, the minesweeper that had as proud a record as any ship during the Dunkirk evacuation.

On the morning of 30 May, after taking on troops during the night, *Locust* was given the task of towing the sloop HMS *Bideford* – minus her stern, which had vanished in the explosion of the bomb that had hit her and of her own depth charges. The job was accomplished with great difficulty, the tow home taking 30 hours. As she cleared the French coast, *Locust* came under heavy fire from enemy guns at Gravelines, but she got clear under cover of a smoke screen laid down by two destroyers.

HMS *Bideford* had just completed the loading of her troops when she was hit. One of the soldiers, F.G. Hutchinson, a signals despatch rider with the 42nd East Lancashire Division, later paid tribute to the calm efficiency of the sailors of both *Bideford* and *Locust*:

Down below conditions were fairly chaotic; the accommodation was packed and the gun on the deck above was making a fearful racket. Suddenly, above all the noise there was an almighty crash and *Bideford* seemed to lift right out of the water and then sink back, shuddering. After recovering from the shock those of us below made a scramble for the companionway leading to the deck, the general impression being that we were sinking. However she remained alfoat, for by good fortune her bulkheads held even though forty feet had been blown off her stern. A petty officer stopped the rush on deck; he told us that we were in no immediate danger of sinking and that we were to stay put until a vessel arrived to take us off. By this time casualties started coming down, and we were saddened to learn that the sailors had suffered badly. I estimated that there had been about fifty casualties, most of them fatal.

A short while later, we learned that the minesweeper HMS *Locust* had drawn alongside and was going to take us off, so we formed a queue at the foot of the companionway leading to the deck. I was quite far back in the queue and decided that I would just have time to make it to the galley and collect my uniform, which I had taken off to dry out; all my personal possessions were in my jacket pocket, including my paybook. On returning to the queue, which by this time was quite small, I was dismayed to learn that the *Locust* had filled to capacity and could take no more. Those of us who were left remained on *Bideford*, knowing that with the coming of daylight all hell would be let loose again; then we learned that *Locust* was going to try to take us in tow.

After several abortive attempts, it became obvious that we were firmly lodged in a sand-bank. At one stage during the attempts to move us, all available men were formed up on one side of the ship and on the command we all ran to the other side in an effort to rock her free. We eventually floated clear when the tide came in, and in the small hours, towed by the faithful *Locust*, we limped away from Dunkirk. During all this time a surgeon had been working non-stop below, operating where possible on the wounded. I found a hammock and enjoyed the most perfect sleep I can ever remember.

Even then our troubles were not over, for some time later I was awakened by a petty officer who told me that some French colonial troops on board were expressing strong doubts about our intention of taking them to England, and were insisting on being landed in France. Most of them were armed, and the PO instructed us that in the case of mutiny we were to make our way to the bow of the ship where arms would be issued. Fortunately nothing came of this, and we limped on our way towards Dover.[16]

If the men of HMS *Locust* were in the dark as to their destination when they sailed from England, the crews of the Grimsby-based 4th Minesweeping Flotilla were left in no doubt, as W.T. Elmslie, then a seaman aboard the fleet minesweeper HMS *Dundalk*, remembered:

On 28 May 1940 our flotilla, MS4, was berthed in Harwich on a rest day. During the forenoon divisions were held on the quay and the commanding officer of MS4 addressed all hands, advising them that Britain was passing through one of the blackest pages of her history and that very soon we would be called upon to do something which we had never been called upon to do before. It would be dangerous; but he had no doubt that every man would do his duty.

On the following Thursday, 30 May, HMS *Dundalk* – which was now at Grimsby – sailed from that port independently and proceeded south. During the voyage the crew were advised that we were making for the beaches of Dunkirk to evacuate the BEF, and shortly afterwards all battle ensigns were hoisted.

We arrived off the beaches on Thursday evening and were detailed to proceed to La Panne, bringing off as many soldiers as possible. The scene on the beaches at La Panne at this time was very depressing, with dark groups of soldiers huddled together in small parties. Through the twilight we could see the oil tanks burning in the distance, and occasional flashes of gunfire lit up the horizon. The boats were lowered, each manned by one sailor; they were towed to the beach by a motor launch and filled to capacity, the troops manning the oars and pulling back to the ship.

The process went on all night. Just before dawn a boatload of wounded came in; as soon as the men were taken aboard one of them, an officer of the Durham Light Infantry, came up to our first lieutenant and asked him to be put back ashore, as there were more wounded to be looked after. 'Jimmy' told him that he was very sorry; the ship had taken on her full quota, with every inch of space occupied above and below, and the sooner *Dundalk* could unload her troops in England the sooner she would be back. The army officer pleaded, but to no avail. Suddenly, he turned and wandered away, past the 12-pounder which I was manning. He looked all in and utterly dejected. Then, from round the stern, came the putt-putt of a motor-boat. The officer hailed it; it came quietly round the stern and he took a flying leap into it from the afterdeck. The boat disappeared into the night and I never saw him again. As he went I looked at the beach, at the burning oil tanks and the flashing of guns; and I knew that I would not have had the courage to do what that man did that night.[17]

Not all the officers were of the same calibre as this one. Among the hundreds of dedicated men, from subalterns to brigadiers, who brought their

men back to Dunkirk and shared their agony with them to the end, there were the inevitable rotten eggs – officers who deserted their own troops, or who had not sufficient will and authority to control exhausted, rebellious men, or who simply broke under the strain and gave up. Such things are inevitable in war, particularly among those who have not experienced combat before. Nevertheless, the sight of officers losing their heads, with the consequent breakdown of disciplined, is the most damaging blow to morale that can happen in a habitually disciplined army, and it happened at Dunkirk. Sometimes, as a result, what should have been an orderly procession to the waiting boats degenerated into a wild scramble.

For the crews of many of the small craft that arrived off the beaches on this Thursday – stunned as they already were by the holocaust that unfolded before their eyes – the sight of dirty, wild-eyed men rushing through the surf towards them was an unnerving experience. Time and again, boats were capsized by the onrush of troops laden with field equipment, equipment that dragged them down to a choking death in the water. Yet in the great majority of cases the embarkation proceeded in good order, despite the fact that the fighting troops who now came pouring into the beach-head through the perimeter were often crazed with hunger and thirst, every instinct urging them to break ranks and forage in wild bands for water to slake their caked throats and for food, however meagre, to ease the cramps in their stomachs.

It was during the afternoon of 30 May that the Navy's modern destroyers returned to the operation. Ships bearing proud names – *Harvester, Havant, Icarus, Impulsive, Ivanhoe, Javelin* – they steamed at full speed from their south coast ports across the narrow seas, heading for the beaches at La Panne. Meanwhile the destroyer *Esk* had also arrived post-haste off the beaches, bringing with her a personality who, on the orders of the First Sea Lord, was to co-ordinate the movements of the rescue ships: Rear-Admiral Frederick Wake-Walker. With him came 80 officers and ratings, including Vice-Admiral Gilbert Stephenson, who was to take control of the evacuation at La Panne, and Vice-Admiral Theodore Hallett, who was to be responsible for the Bray Dunes sector. Wake-Walker himself set up his HQ at Malo-les-Bains; from here, with incredible energy, he moved among the rescue craft, transferring his flag no fewer than six times to different ships in the space of 24 hours. Captain William Tennant and his exhausted team certainly had some big guns on their side now.

One of the vessels from which Wake-Walker temporarily flew his flag was the destroyer HMS *Worcester*. Later that day she sailed for England bearing two VIPs: Lieutenant-Generals Alan Brooke and Sir Ronald Adam, their task at Dunkirk over. Brooke's departure had been preceded by a moving scene: heartbroken in the belief that his II Corps was to be sacrificed so that the rest of the BEF might escape, he had wept bitterly as he bade farewell to his old friend General Bernard Montgomery, commanding III Corps. Now, as fatigue swept over him in waves, he collapsed into a bunk on board *Worcester* and slept.

Meanwhile, Wake-Walker's primary concern had been to get the East Mole operational once more. By 20.30 hours on 30 May, following hasty repairs, he judged that the mole was once again fit for use by destroyers and sent a signal to that effect to Admiral Ramsay in Dover. With ships once again working from the mole the number of troops lifted off increased substantially during the evening; by midnight the day's total had reached 53,823, of whom some 30,000 had been taken from the beaches.

On Friday 31 May the task of the evacuation personnel increased a hundredfold, for now the decision had been taken to lift off French troops in equal numbers – and already the evacuation fleet had suffered badly, from collisions, groundings and mechanical troubles as much as from enemy action. Moreover, navigation on the approaches to Dunkirk was becoming extremely hazardous because of sunken wrecks, and to make matters worse the wind had risen to force three, seriously complicating the task of the small craft in the shallows. Many small boats, laden to the gunwales with troops, set out for home – a move which Wake-Walker urgently tried to stop, for every small craft would be needed that night to ferry men to the ships waiting offshore. For a time, towards noon, boat work off the beaches became virtually impossible, and enemy bombing and artillery fire had become so intense that larger ships could not use the port. The crisis seemed grave: and then, in the afternoon, both enemy activity and the swell decreased, and by the time the day ended no fewer than 68,014 men had been taken off – the highest daily total of the whole operation.

And still the small boats were coming – although for some, it was not easy, as Lieutenant-Commander Archie Buchanan of the *Elvin* testified,

> Skipper Noble took the boat to Ramsgate without any charts, just his memory to go on. He seemed to be able to judge by the look of the water where the banks and the deeps were and if there was enough water to cross a bank. We arrived at Ramsgate about 4 pm on the 31st and Noble went ashore to report to the senior naval officer. To Noble's amazement and fury we were ordered back to Lowestoft, and when he asked about charts he was told: 'You got here without charts – you can go back without them!'
>
> On arrival back at Oulton Broad I went ashore and rang up my wife Ruth at the farm. She said that she had just had a telephone call to say that we were to return to Ramsgate. I asked her to bring my rifle and some other things down with her. We drew charts and provisions for forty-eight hours and had fuel for about thirty-six hours. Ruth brought the rifle and then dashed off to get some Beechams pills, which she dropped into the cockpit as we went under the bridge at Mutford Locks on our way from Oulton Broad to the sea at Lowestoft.
>
> On arrival at Ramsgate about 10 am on 1 June I went ashore with Noble to report to the SNO and we were ordered to go alongside the South Wall – I had the distinct impression that this was where the boats that were not going to be used were sent, and I got into conversation with a Sub-Lieutenant Coates RNVR who told me that his naval motor cutter had broken down and the crew had refused to do another trip in her, so I suggested he took *Elvin*. I collected a spare battery and four rifles and

ammunition from store – the latter somewhat unlawfully. As I was walking away, I heard the lieutenant-commander in charge protest to the storeman 'Surely you are not issuing rifles to *civilians!*'

In the late afternoon Coates came along and told us that there was an operation taking place that night, so we took him on board. We were fairly well jammed in by other boats, until a kindly trawler skipper gave a kick ahead on his engines to take the lot clear and let us out. We went alongside the East Wall where boats were given their orders. Coates went ashore to report but the commander in charge was very reluctant to let us go – civilian crew, too slow, Red Ensign and so on. Eventually we just took matters into our own hands, letting go fore and aft; as we moved out there came a shout from the petty officer up top and the commander turned away in apparent disgust. A shower of first-aid kits fell into our cockpit and we were on our way.

We had no idea what the operation was, or what we were supposed to do. With our boat darkened, we just followed the general flow of traffic across and then steered straight for the fires of Dunkirk.[18]

The morning of 1 June dawned brilliantly clear, and at first light the *Luftwaffe* arrived over the beaches with murderous intent, 40 *Stukas* of VIII *Fliegerkorps* launching a violent attack on the evacuation fleet. As they were turning for home 28 Hawker Hurricanes of RAF Fighter Command arrived and were soon engaged in a fierce battle with the Messerschmitt 109s of *Jagdgeschwader* 51 and the Messerschmitt 110s of *Zerstörergeschwader* 26.

Bill Elmslie, back off La Panne in HMS *Dundalk* after replenishing in Dover, recalled that even before the arrival of the first wave of bombers, small-craft operations off the beaches were complicated by a heavy swell. Coming away from the makeshift jetty in one of *Dundalk*'s whalers with eleven soldiers on board, the boat suddenly capsized and Elmslie and his passengers went headlong into the sea. Somehow they managed to hang together and drifted back to the beach, where they righted the boat, baled her out and set off once more for *Dundalk*. As they pulled away for a second time Elmslie caught sight of something that made a lasting impression on him: an Army padre, moving up and down the column of patient men on the jetty, directing, helping, encouraging, selecting soldiers for the boats, his

The Battle of France brought some curious aircraft to Britain's south coast airfields, including Vought 156s of the French Navy; these aircraft attacked German armoured columns advancing on Dunkirk.

complete calm an inspiration to all. Elmslie returned to the minesweeper with his boatload, and it was while he was waiting to hook on that the *Luftwaffe* swept out of the sky.

I glanced back at the beach and saw a German fighter streaking across the sands, his machine-guns cutting through those columns of soldiers like a reaper slicing through corn. Our own guns were hammering away furiously. One dive-bomber came hurtling straight at us and we were convinced he was going to hit us, but at the last moment he swerved and his bomb went wide. I think this was due to the efforts of a seaman manning one of our twin Lewis guns, who sent up some very accurate fire against the enemy aircraft.

That morning of 1 June was one I shall remember for a long time. Not very far from us lay HMS *Skipjack*, an oil-burning fleet sweeper and a member of our flotilla. She was lying at anchor, still taking on troops, when she took the full delivery from a dive-bomber and went up in a terrific explosion. When the smoke cleared she had vanished; there was simply nothing there any more.[19]

Skipjack went down with 275 troops on board; there were very few survivors. The bombers now turned their attention to the big fleet destroyer HMS *Keith*, to which Admiral Wake-Walker had recently transferred his flag. The *Keith*'s gunners were down to their last 30 rounds of ammunition, and there was little the warship's captain could do except take violent evasive action. The first attack on her came while she was turning under full port helm and no fewer than nine bombs exploded in a pattern close to her starboard side, throwing her over on her beam ends and causing severe damage to her hull. She careered in a tight circle, her rudder jammed, and then the second attack came in. This time a heavy bomb went down her aft funnel and exploded in her boiler room, while near misses caused further damage. She lost way rapidly, enveloped in clouds of steam, and wallowed to a stop with a 20-degree list to port. Wake-Walker was taken off by an MTB and transferred his flag to another vessel; shortly afterwards the *Keith* was hit yet again by the *Stukas* and the warship turned turtle and sank.

Meanwhile the dive-bombers had hurled themselves on another destroyer, HMS *Basilisk*, hitting her aft and killing eight men. She survived another attack and began the long struggle back to Dover, but she later had to be abandoned and her survivors were taken off by trawlers, among them the French *Jolie Mascotte*. The shattered hulk of the *Basilisk* continued to float until it was sent to the bottom by a torpedo from the destroyer *Whitehall*.

The massacre went on unabated. Some vessels, in the act of taking on troops, were powerless to take evasive action; other captains – like Lieutenant-Commander Kirkpatrick of the *Dundalk* – suspended operations and kept their ships on the move, zig-zagging down the coast amid the hail of bombs. On *Dundalk* Bill Elmslie witnessed an unforgettable sight; the fleet destroyer HMS *Havant* forging out into the Channel with so many troops on board that her entire superstructure seemed to be covered in khaki. The next instant a salvo of bombs hit her, killing all her engine room staff. Immediately, two minesweepers closed alongside and and the troops poured from the stricken ship on to their decks. The *Havant* had taken two bombs through her engine room and a third exploded as she passed over it; the minesweeper HMS *Saltash* tried to take her in tow, but it was hopeless. At 10.15, after further air attacks, she sank with the loss of 34 hands.

Other ships were more fortunate. The destroyer HMS *Ivanhoe* had a bomb rip through her forward funnel and explode in the boiler room; terror-stricken soldiers scrambled from her lower decks and on to the minesweeper *Speedwell*, which came alongside. Despite her damage the destroyer remained afloat and was taken in tow by the tug *Persia*.

As the vicious air attacks died away, the ships returned to the beaches and the mole at Dunkirk to carry on with the embarkation. It was a brief respite. At 13.00 the *Luftwaffe* returned, the Stukas plummeting down on the French destroyer *Foudroyant*. Three direct hits and a deluge of near misses reduced her to tangled wreckage, and she went down within three minutes. As her survivors struggled in the water, a defiant voice began to sing *La Marseillaise* and soon they were all singing as they drifted with the tide amid the islands of debris and pools of oil.

Not only the warships suffered, although these were the *Stukas'* primary targets. The old *Brighton Queen*, a paddleboat converted for minesweeping, had just set out for Dover with 700 French troops on board when the *Stukas* pounced; a 550-lb bomb hit the boat's afterdeck, causing fearful casualties. The survivors were taken off by the minesweeper *Saltash* before the *Brighton Queen* sank. There were casualties, too, on the personnel vessel *Prague*, which was steaming away from Dunkirk with 3,000 French troops on board when she was hit and damaged; her sister ship, the *Scotia*, was also hit while carrying 2,000 French troops, many of whom were drowned when they panicked and rushed the boats. The destroyer HMS *Esk* took off most of the survivors. The *Scotia*, of 3,454 tons, was the largest merchant ship to be lost that day.

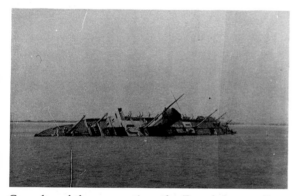

Casualty of the evacuation: the French luxury liner *Champlain* sunk by a mine off the coast.

On some ships that managed to limp back to Dover the casualty toll was frightening. The old destroyer HMS *Worcester* was relentlessly attacked for thirty minutes by flight after flight of dive-bombers, sustaining damage that reduced her speed to a mere ten knots; yet she limped across the Channel with her pitiful cargo of 350 dead and 400 wounded. During the late

afternoon, the French naval vessels off Dunkirk once again came in for severe punishment; at 16.00 *Stukas* fell on a convoy of French auxiliaries, sinking three of them – the *Denis Papin*, *Venus* and *Moussaillon* – within five minutes.

RAF Fighter Command carried out eight squadron-strength patrols during the course of the day, claiming the destruction of 78 enemy aircraft – a figure that was later officially reduced to 53. However, *Luftwaffe* records admit the loss of only nineteen bombers and ten fighters for 1 June, with a further thirteen damaged; and since the Royal Navy claimed ten aircraft destroyed and French fighters another ten, the actual score must remain in doubt. What is certain is that Fighter Command lost 31 aircraft during the air battles of 1 June, and that the evacuation fleet lost 31 vessels of all types sunk – including four destroyers – and eleven damaged. Most of the stricken vessels fell victim to air attack, but it was the German Navy that had the last word. Shortly before midnight, *Leutnant* Obermaier, making yet another sortie into the Channel in *Schnellboot* S34, sighted two ships and attacked with torpedoes, sinking both. They were the trawlers *Argyllshire* and *Stella Dorado*.

Despite the losses, the evacuation fleet lifted off 64,429 British and French troops on 1 June. Since the last stretches of beach still in Allied hands, and the shipping offshore, were now being heavily shelled, Admiral Ramsay planned to lift as many men as possible in a single operation on the night of 1/2 June. It had originally been planned to complete the evacuation on this night, but this was no longer feasible; there could be no question of abandoning the French troops who had fought so hard on the perimeter, and through whom the British had passed on their way to the beaches. Ramsay therefore decided to concentrate all available ships after dark in the Dunkirk and Malo areas, from where the maximum lift might be obtained. For this purpose he had at his disposal some 60 ships, together with the many small craft still involved in the operation; the French could provide ten ships and about 120 fishing craft.

One of the little craft which arrived off the beaches that night was the *Elvin*, with Archie Buchanan on board.

We lay off the entrance until first light. We could hear gunfire to the eastward and saw a great pall of smoke over the town and flashes in the inner harbour. As soon as we could see we went alongside the eastern pier where a column of soldiers was drawn up. An officer called out *'Combien de soldats?'*, and as I could not remember the French for twenty-five I replied *'Trente,'* but before we could take on the thirty that had been detailed by the officer the sub rushed up from below and said that we were full.

Alongside the pier there was a small open motor boat with an RNR sub in charge and a whaler in tow. He looked to me as if he was taking on a bit more than he could handle. I nipped over to him and asked him what he was going to do with his lot and he told me that he was going to put them on a ship outside the harbour and come back for more. This seemed a good idea and we decided to do the same.

The destroyer had gone when we got outside the harbour, so we chased after some French minesweepers to westward hoping to put our soldiers on board, but they were unable to take them so we decided to set course back to Ramsgate. We had no idea where the swept channel was, but as we drew only three feet six inches and it was not low water we didn't think that there was much danger from mines. This conclusion may have been fortified by memories of the Dover Patrol in 1917, when it used to be said that British mines were so safe that they never went off. I think a large lump of wood would have been far more dangerous.[20]

As *Elvin* made her way back to Ramsgate with her weary passengers – all soldiers of the French 28th Infantry Regiment – the big lift went on. There was no question now of taking off any but walking wounded; stretcher cases took up too much room, and the urgency to evacuate the thousands of fit men still on the beaches was too pressing. Captain Tony Steede of the Green Howards, himself badly wounded in the leg by a mortar bomb, remembered that:

There were so many wounded that they could not be accommodated in the château; stretcher cases were lying all around the ground in the open air. I personally was in an ambulance, with a dying Hurricane pilot in the bunk above me. It was far from pleasant. Then we got a message that the last boats would soon be leaving Dunkirk, and that anyone who could walk was to make his way down to the beaches. Some managed it, struggling along on improvised crutches made from broom handles, but they were very few. The rest of us knew with terrible finality that we had no hope. All we could do was lie there and wait, and the waiting was bad enough; the French had placed a light anti-aircraft gun in the château grounds, and this drew a lot of artillery fire.[21]

By midnight on 2 June a further 26,256 soldiers had been evacuated from Dunkirk. The last British battalion to leave was the 1st King's Shropshire Light Infantry, which had covered the withdrawal of the 1st Division the previous evening. At 23.30, Captain Tennant informed Admiral Ramsay that the BEF had been evacuated. Then Tennant, together with General Alexander, commanding the 1st Division, boarded a motor torpedo boat and set off to make a reconnaissance of the beaches. Sighting no further British troops, they set course for England.

There remained the French: some 30,000 of them, whose resistance continued throughout 3 June. The last great effort of Ramsay's evacuation fleet therefore had to be made during the night of 3/4 June, and the resources available to accomplish the task were seriously depleted. Of the 41 destroyers originally assigned to Operation DYNAMO only nine were left, and only five of the 45 personnel vessels. Nevertheless, at 22.15 on 3 June these set out across the Channel, together with a couple of dozen smaller craft, and the last lift began. The ships probed into Dunkirk harbour, lifting men from both the east and west moles, while boats cruised along the beaches, their crews hailing any groups of French troops that were sighted. Among the vessels which took part in this final evacuation was the little gunboat *Locust*, whose crew during the evening had the unhappy task of placing demolition charges on their sister ship, the gallant little *Mosquito*, sunk inshore with her decks awash a few hours earlier.

Amid all the devastation, amid the tightly-packed columns of battle-weary French troops on the East Mole, one of *Locust*'s company saw something that touched his heart: a tiny pup, only a few days old, in danger of being trampled underfoot. He rescued it and brought it aboard – and, aptly named 'Dunkirk', it remained the ship's mascot for a year until it found a new berth in a petty officer's home in Gillingham, where it lived out its days.

'Dunkirk', the little dog that became HMS *Locust*'s mascot after a crew member rescued it.

By 0400 on 4 June Operation DYNAMO was almost over; almost, but not quite. The last French troops capable of being lifted off before dawn had filtered down through Dunkirk, and the last boats were moving in. An hour earlier *Admiral* Abrial and General Fagalde, the latter commanding the French XVI Corps, had both been taken off, and it was left to the French III Corps commander, General Fournel de la Laurencie – who had earlier refused an order from the French High Command to lay down his arms and surrender, and instead had brought his men back to Dunkirk in good order – to conduct a final, moving ceremony. It

was described by Commander H.R. Troup, RN, who had been supervising the final embarkation.

> About a thousand men stood to attention four deep about halfway along the pier, the General and his staff about thirty feet away; and after having faced the troops whose faces were indiscernible in the dawn light, the flames behind them showing up their steel helmets, the officers clicked their heels, saluted and then turned about and came down the boat with me, and we left at 03.20.[22]

The last ship to leave the mole in the dawn light was the old destroyer HMS *Shikari*, and her load brought the total for the night to 26,209, all but seven of them French troops. Some of the men, as they marched down to the harbour, had stooped to scoop up a handful of earth, which they placed reverently in a tunic pocket. It would be more than four years before they trod the soil of France again. Many would never return.

At 09.00 on 4 June, the French troops remaining in Dunkirk – between 30,000 and 40,000 men – formally surrendered to the Germans, and at 14.23 the Admiralty announced the completion of Operation DYNAMO. In nine days of incredible achievement 198,284 British troops had been brought away; counting the 26,402 non-combatants taken off before the start of the evacuation proper, this made a grand total of 224,686 men of the British Expeditionary Force, of whom 13,053 were wounded. The number of Allied troops evacuated rose to 141,445, making a combined total of 366,131.

The cost of Operation DYNAMO, however, had been terribly high for the seaborne forces engaged. Of the British ships committed, 226 had been sunk out of a total of 693, 56 of them large craft such as destroyers, minesweepers and personnel craft. Out of the total of 168 Allied ships involved – mainly French, with a few Polish, Dutch and Belgian – seventeen were lost.

Enemy action against ships at sea and the beaches resulted in the deaths of some 3,500 British troops out of the total of 68,111 killed, wounded and taken prisoner during the retreat to Dunkirk. No firm figures for French personnel

Souvenir of a miracle: the destroyer HMS *Mackay*, with troops on board and evacuation battle honours inscribed on the photograph.

of the disaster that had overwhelmed the BEF and the French and Belgian armies in Flanders. Only in the principal south coast ports – and in particular Dover, where base troops and wounded were being landed almost continuously from 20 May – did the populace have an inkling that the Allies might be suffering an overwhelming defeat.

Prior to the main evacuation a joint agreement had been working out between the Royal Naval Sick Quarters at Dover and neighbouring authorities, both military and civil, for the reception and treatment of casualties. All resources were to be pooled in case of a serious emergency. The first casualties had arrived on 11 May, the day after the German invasion of the Low Countries; they were sailors from HMS *Whitshed*, which had come under air attack while evacuating personnel from Holland. On the fourteenth, 37 casualties were landed from HMS *Wivern*; this was the first large batch of wounded to arrive at Dover and it revealed many of the difficulties encountered in dealing with casualties in small ships, such as the inaccessibility of the wounded and the ingenuity required in getting them on to stretchers and transferring them to ambulances on the quayside.

The report of Captain A.P. Fisher, the Senior Naval Medical Officer Dover, provides an illuminating insight not only into the reception of casualties, but also into the extent and frequency of the cross-Channel traffic that built up during the nine days of Dunkirk:

> By 25 May it was necessary to obtain additional medical staff, two additional ambulances being obtained and a converted motor bus loaned from Chatham. By this time the RAMC had established a medical transport office at the Dover Marine Station, and had organized a service of hospital trains and convoys of motor ambulances. Up to this time we have endeavoured to deal with all naval casualties ourselves, but owing to the fact that all landing stages were being used at the same time this was found impracticable and an arrangement was made with the RAMC that they would deal with all

losses were ever issued, but they were high. Witness the sinking of the French destroyer *Bourrasque*, with 300 drowned out of 800; the destruction of the destroyer *Sirocco*, with 750 men; the loss of 400 on the *Emile-Deschamps*, 300 on the *Brighton Queen* and 300 of the 2,000 on the *Scotia*. It seems likely that the actual combined loss through enemy action may have been in the region of 6,000 troops, and this figure takes no account of those accidentally killed or drowned or of the substantial naval casualties.

On 27 May, the day on which the main evacuations from Dunkirk began, few people in Britain as yet had any real idea of the magnitude casualties at the Admiralty Pier, and the naval staff with those at all other landing stages.

During this period (25 May – 5 June, 1940) 180,982 troops were landed in Dover; of this number 6,880 were casualties requiring hospital treatment. 31 May was the peak day; during this twenty-four hours 34,484 troops were landed in Dover from the following ships: 25 destroyers, 12 transports, 14 drifters, 14 minesweepers, 6 paddle minesweepers, 5 trawlers, 16 motor yachts and small vessels, 12 Dutch schuits, 4 hospital ships, and 21 miscellaneous vessels. Amongst these troops were approximately 1,200 casualties. Disembarkation went on throughout the twenty-four hours, but was most intense in the middle and morning watches.

All ships carrying wounded were met by one ambulance with a medical officer and two sick berth ratings. The medical officer would board the vessel, ascertain the number of casualties, estimate the amount of ambulance transport required, render first aid when required to the more seriously injured. Injuries of almost every variety were met with and it was impossible to lay down any definite rules for treatment; this depended on the discretion of the man on the spot. Generally speaking, it was deemed expedient to transfer the most serious cases – such as multiple wounds, wounds of the abdomen, chest and head – to hospital without delay. Morphia injections were given, and dressings applied with as little disturbance of the patient as possible, but ensuring the complete covering of all wounds. No elaborate bandaging was used. The patient was kept warm and protected from the elements with blankets.

In the ships attended, some form of first aid had usually been attempted. Destroyers and larger transports carried medical officers, and in these the standard of first aid was usually high, though in many cases the medical officer had not had time to attend all cases, particularly when the ship had been subjected to enemy air attack during the passage, fresh casualties occurring. In the smaller ships the first aid carried out was necessarily more rudimentary, though it was rare to find a wounded man who had not had some sort of dressing applied.

Blood transfusion was never attempted on the quayside. On one occasion, however, in response to a destroyer medical officer's signal the apparatus was taken to Admiralty Pier, but was not used as the patient, who had had an amputation of the leg, was

in satisfactory condition and was immediately transferred to hospital. This patient, a petty officer of fine type, after his wound had been treated in hospital overheard the medical officer say that he required plenty of fluid. He asked for a bottle of beer and dispatched it, and an hour later had the other half. Next day he assured me that bottled beer was a better lifesafer than blood transfusion any day.

Casualties arrived in Dover in every sort of vessel which, in the vast majority of cases, were berthed at one of the many landing stages. On a few occasions casualties had to be removed from ships moored in the harbour; also medical assistance was sometimes asked for by ships lying off Dover. The removal of casualties from the ships could not commence until the troops had been disembarked. The medical officer of the ship could usually give an approximate number of casualties, and information as to the more serious ones requiring instant removal to hospital. About sixty per cent of the ships went to Admiralty Pier. This position was the most suitable as ambulances could be parked close by. The hospital trains were in station about 200 yards away, and large squads of stretcher bearers were constantly in attendance.

Our work was chiefly concerned with the outlying landing stages. At most of these, steep brows and slippery steps had to be negotiated, the patients being either manhandled or conveyed to the quayside in Neil Robertson stretchers. From these most cases were transferred to Field Service or ARP stretchers and placed in an ambulance. Carrying wounded from the ships to the landing stages, and thence to the ambulances, proved a great physical strain and it was very gratifying to see how eager the sailors were in helping to carry their wounded mates and also the keenness of the ambulance drivers to assist.

One hospital train was kept at the Marine Station, and one in a siding in reserve and a third at a station twelve miles inland. Their accommodation varied from 150 to 250, with a medical officer and nursing staff. All types of casualties, except those urgently in need of surgical attention, were transported by train. This method saved the nearby hospitals from total submersion. In all, 4,646 were transported in the trains.

The Royal Naval Sick Quarters, HMS *Sandhurst* Sick Bay and Dover Patrol Sick Bay worked at high pressure during the Dunkirk evacuation. I cannot give even an approximate figure of the number of cases that received first aid here, but 200 cases were admitted for the night. The cases were not all wounded, but included cases of immersion and nervous exhaustion. The cases were only detailed for one or at the most two nights, and were then either discharged to the rest camp or hospital as requisite. The value of the sick bays was particularly demonstrated in the nervous cases. On one occasion twenty ratings from one crew were accommodated in HMS *Sandhurst*; they all appeared anxious and generally 'jittery'. A bath, a hot meal, a dose of bromide and a good sleep enabled all except two of these to resume duty next day.

Amongst the casualties brought into Dover there were approximately 600 naval casualties, including fifty-four dead . . . The casualties included wounds of every description met with in warfare. The main causative agents were high explosive bombs, high explosive shells, Messerschmitt cannon shells, machine-gun bullets, burns from incendiary bombs, ignited cordite and ignited oil fuel. In addition when ships were sunk those in the water were exposed to concussion injuries due to the explosion of bombs, mines and depth charges. Bomb splinter wounds, machine-gun bullet wounds were commonest in that order.[23]

For most of the troops who came away from Dunkirk, the passage homeward across the Channel remained at best a vague memory. The majority collapsed into the sleep of utter exhaustion the moment they found a space on the crowded deck of one of the rescue ships. For Gunner Tom Collins of the 35th Field Battery, Royal Artillery, sharing the experience of the many thousands of others, the sweetest words he would ever hear in his life were, 'Wakey, wakey, lads, come on, you're at Dover!' Fatigue shrugged off, he and his comrades scrambled to the deck of the destroyer that had brought them over and poured on to the quay, pausing only to let the wounded be taken off first.

Unwashed, unshaven, very prominent in our rags and tatters, we were welcomed it seemed by people from all walks of life; but those were were top of the league in my books were the crew who had brought us back, the men who had attended the sick and

wounded – and the WVS, who gave every man a mug of tea, a piece of cake and a cigarette. After we settled down in the waiting train, something happened that has stuck in my mind ever since: a soldier got to his feet and said, 'Boys, I'm thanking God I'm home. Now let's give a thought for the boys we left behind.' And we, all strangers from different units, held a minute's silence in that compartment; and as we travelled through the green fields, I thought that England wasn't such a bad place after all.[24]

For others, the journey to England had the never-to-be-forgotten quality of a nightmare. Bill Elmslie, on HMS *Dundalk*, saw Frenchmen staring at the receding coastline of their homeland, tears streaming down their faces, not knowing when or if they would see France again; and a French officer, passing among the crew and solemnly shaking hands with each man as he murmured broken words of thanks. He saw, too, a young Royal Fusilier slumped on the deck and weeping as though his heart would break, sobbing over and over again that his brother was still in there, somewhere beyond the smoke and flames of Dunkirk . . . And the fifteen other Royal Fusiliers, exhausted beyond description, who nevertheless fell in on the quay at Folkestone and marched away in regimental order with rifles at the slope, their officer at their head.

The port of La Pallice burning after a German air attack.

They were an exception. Although the vast majority of troops who arrived back in England retained their rifles – a not inconsiderable tribute to the British Army's standard of discipline –

three weeks of battle and immersion in water had reduced their clothing to a pitiful state. Many had no uniform left at all, and came ashore dressed in whatever nondescript rags they had managed to pick up *en route*. Private Peter Pring of the 1/6th South Staffords, who landed at Folkestone, remembers one soldier who shared his train compartment wearing the black-and-white striped trousers of a French farmer's best Sunday suit, a sack with holes cut in it for the neck and arms, and – the crowning glory – a silk top hat.

For those without items of clothing, the people of the debarkation ports pitched in with whatever spare items they had available. The British people opened their hearts to the homecoming soldiers and sailors, as Commander Thomas Kerr describes:

We landed at Margate . . . and reported to Dover. The people were so good to us; they tried to fit us out with boots, fitted up the sailors and fed them. Richardson and I fed at the pub and had a rough wash, then we were given a lorry to take us to the station. The rest of the party got off at Chatham, their depot, and I went on to London. Somewhere around eight o'clock we arrived at Victoria. There were crowds and crowds, with policemen keeping open a lane. I toddled down in my tin hat and bedroom slippers, haversack and revolver still strapped around me. Someone shouted 'Good old Navy!' and a woman kissed me on the cheek. They cheered and I wanted to cry. Then a man got hold of me and said: 'Where do you want to go? I'll look after you.' He led me to a taxi, brought me to the Admiralty and paid the cab off.[25]

Peter Pring, trundling through the countryside in his troop train towards Aldershot, was as puzzled as the other men in his compartment to see suburban gardens festooned with slogans: 'Welcome Home, Brave Lads'. 'Well Done, Our Heroes'. To men who had just suffered the most crushing defeat in the history of the British Army, it took some time for the significance to sink in. 'Christ!' said someone in an awed voice. 'They mean *us*!'

The memory of this battered army coming home was to remain strong in the minds of those civilians who witnessed it. One of them, W.E.

Williamson, then a railway clerk at Weymouth in Dorset, later wrote:

Slowly they came, bewildered and shocked, yet the faces of the hundreds showed the great joy of once again being on dry land, above all their homeland. Even the troops of other nations accepted thankfully the greeting and helping hand from those waiting on the quayside. The bedraggled army was marshalled by Army and Navy personnel, the local Home Guard, the Salvation Army, the Red Cross, coach drivers, police, railwaymen and every possible local organization. Fearing air attack, the troops were encouraged to disperse temporarily in the streets, away from the sea front. They sat on the pavements with their backs to railings and garden walls; men, women and children brought out jugs of tea and plates of food, spared from their own meagre rations. Sodden and bloodstained uniforms were gratefully exchanged for trousers, jackets, shirts and dressing gowns.

The railway station staff were now in top gear. Trains were being marshalled, instructions were issued, control points and railway junctions to other regions were in direct contact, arranging the reception of troop specials and their dispatch to secret destinations. We were all part of this huge effort to get the army away from the coast: railwaymen and RTOs with their red caps and armbands were working together as one team, shepherding the men into railway sidings and yards prior to getting them away.

With some of my railway colleagues, I handed out blank Great Western Railway postcards to the troops. They were asked to write just two words – 'Am Safe' – adding their Christian name and home address. The cards were sent off that day, with no postmark or stamp. I remember we ran out of cards and ransacked cupboards in the stock room for blank railway truck labels. In three days we sent off several thousand, most of them with their messages scribbled by railway staff and other helpers. Many of the troops were dead beat with exhaustion, and we had to lift hundreds into the carriages. A lot of scheduled trains were cancelled to provide extra rolling stock and engine power for the massive movement.[26]

Throughout the southern counties, and Kent in particular, thousands of volunteers, mainly women, worked tirelessly by day and night to

St Jean de Luz, the last French port to be evacuated during Operation AERIAL.

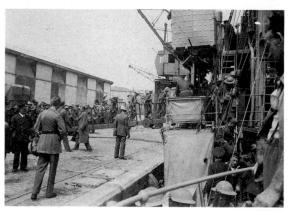

A lot of evacuation work remained to be done after Dunkirk. These photographs show HMS *Mackay* at Brest.

supply food and drink to the troops at stations where their trains halted. The whole of Kent was literally ransacked in a gigantic bid to collect all available supplies of food and cigarettes, collection centres being set up at Redhill, Tonbridge, Faversham and Headcorn. Many firms and individuals donated supplies and money in this spontaneous voluntary gesture.

The gratitude of the soldiers was overwhelming. Private Mons Trussler of the 4th Royal Berkshire Regiment – his first name having been bestowed upon him by a father who had survived that other famous fighting retreat of the First World War – safe in Folkestone Hospital after being carried ashore with other wounded, recalled 'dear old ladies coming in with huge plates of bread and butter, cut very thin, which we devoured like wolves. They looked on in amazement as we cried, every last man of us.'

At Margate, Reg Rushmere of the Royal Signals '. . . had a marvellous reception. There were people handing out oranges, and when we got on the train they came to the carriages with fruit and whatever we wanted.' J.F. Duffy of the 52nd Heavy Regiment RA aso remembers the people of Margate with affection:

'I had no boots and was still soaked. Single-decker buses were awaiting us on the quayside, and we were taken to Margate railway station. It was such a wonderful sight to see the WVS giving out cups of tea and sandwiches . . . we knew now that we were home.'

At camps and reception centres all over the country, military and civilian personnel had been standing by to receive the incoming thousands. There could be no attempt to sort out the men into their units at the debarkation ports; that task would be undertaken later, when the urgency was over. As far as the railways were concerned, the second phase of Operation DYNAMO began when the troops were rested and refreshed and redistributed to regular depots, where units were reorganized and re-armed. This second phase did not begin until 6 June, 48 hours after the last troops had been brought back from Dunkirk.

The complete withdrawal from France, however, was to last considerably longer. Between 4 and 25 June 1940, British ships carried out a whole series of evacuations beginning at Le

Evacuation completed: a troop-laden warship about to leave Brest harbour.

Division, trapped with its back to the sea at St Valéry between Dieppe and Le Havre, was frustrated by fog and the premature surrender of the French commander.

In some ways, AERIAL provided an even more convincing demonstration of the effectiveness of sea power than Operation DYNAMO; but it was the evacuation from Dunkirk, with all its valour and human drama, that caught the attention of the free world.

> So long as the English tongue survives, the word Dunkirk will be spoken with reverence. For in that harbour, in such a hell as never blazed on earth before, at the end of a lost battle, the rags and blemishes that have hidden the soul of Democracy fell away. There, beaten but unconquered in shining splendour she faced the enemy. This shining thing in the souls of free men Hitler cannot command or attain or conquer . . . It is the great tradition of Democracy. It is the future. It is Victory.'
>
> *New York Times*, 1 June 1940.

Havre, moving west to the Gulf of St Malo, the Channel Islands and Cherbourg, round Ushant to Brest, and finally from Bayonne and St Jean de Luz near the Spanish frontier. These operations, collectively known under the code-name of AERIAL, resulted in the rescue of an additional 191,870 fighting troops and 35,000 civilians. The biggest loss incurred during these operations was at St Nazaire, when the troopship *Lancastria* was sunk with 3,000 on board. Only on one occasion did the Royal Navy fail in its task to any appreciable extent, and that was when the planned evacuation of the 51st Highland

The port of La Rochelle, with a destroyer's twin Lewis AA guns in the foreground, pictured during Operation AERIAL.

CHAPTER THREE

Breathing Space

Despite the emotion – and, indeed, the hope – that Dunkirk had stirred in the hearts of the English-speaking peoples, there seemed every possibility that victory would be Hitler's, and soon at that. Yet in June 1940, throughout the British Isles – and nowhere more than on the threatened south and east coasts – there was a curious sense of relief. Britain no longer had allies to deceive her or let her down. She stood alone to face the direst threat she had known in a thousand years, and somehow it seemed right that it was so. Such optimism, though, was not shared by others.

After I had seen with my own eyes what the military men were calling their "defences" on the beaches at Dover and Brighton, I marvelled at their confidence. Except for some mangy barbed-wire barricades and some concrete anti-tank constructions, I saw little that would delay an invader. Yet the military spokesman kept reassuring me (so they thought) with such commands as "We still have our Navy, Mr Reynolds" and "The Channel will stop Hitler" – the Channel that a month before had not stopped a thousand English small boats from bringing the beaten armies to safety. Hearing what I heard, seeing what I saw, I found time to wonder at British sanity.

Quentin Reynolds, US War Correspondent, late June 1940.[27]

Indeed, it seemed to many observers, including some British military commanders, that after the traumas of Norway and France the Germans seemed capable of anything. From the end of May, to the average Briton, it seemed that invasion might come at any time. The British Chiefs of Staff, however, knew otherwise, thanks to the priceless gift of ULTRA – the most secret organization at Bletchley Park whose task it was to break the enemy's high-grade cyphers, and in particular to decrypt the general-purpose German ENIGMA code. The ENIGMA cypher of the *Luftwaffe* had been broken regularly since 22 May, and a fortnight later intelligence acquired in this way was instrumental in dispersing the invasion panic. Decrypts of signals passing between the *Luftwaffe* and the German Army revealed, first, that Hitler intended to finish off the campaign in France, south of the Somme, before making further strategic moves; and, secondly, more ENIGMA decrypts revealed that, after the renewal of the German offensive on 5 June, French resistance was crumbling too fast to be stopped. This strengthened the Chiefs of Staff to resist French requests for the despatch of further air reinforcements to France, a move that brought great relief to the C-in-C RAF Fighter Command, Air Chief Marshal Sir Hugh Dowding, who did not have access to ULTRA and its secrets.

So, thanks to ULTRA, the Chiefs of Staff knew that they had an invaluable breathing space, although how long it would last was anyone's guess. With the thousands of men newly returned from France scattered all over the country – the evacuated divisions would not begin to reassemble in coherent form until the end of June – the defence of the United Kingdom rested on fifteen infantry divisions, of which four were training formations. Eight of the divisions were employed for coastal defence, the remainder being deployed further inland to meet the threat of an airborne assault. The only formed armoured assets were the 2nd Armoured Division, with 180 light tanks, and the 8th Battalion Royal Tank Regiment with 50 Mk I Matildas. The total inventory of tanks in Britain at the beginning of June 1940 was actually 963, but most of these were obsolete; the most modern armour, such as the Matilda Mk II with its 40mm two-pounder gun, had been sacrificed in France. What remained included 132 Vickers Medium Mk II tanks of 1920s vintage, 110 'Infantry' tanks, 103 cruisers and 618 light tanks, mostly scattered among training units.

The French campaign had cost the British Army nearly 700 tanks of all types. It had also cost 880 field guns, 310 heavier artillery pieces, 500 anti-aircraft guns, 650 anti-tank guns, 6,400 anti-tank rifles and 11,000 machine-guns, along with thousands of tons of ammunition. In the whole of the United Kingdom, whether on issue to units or in store, there were only 54 anti-tank guns, barely enough to equip one division, and 2,300 Bren light machine-guns, enough for one division and one brigade. There were 420 field guns, most of them obsolete, with 200 rounds per gun, and 153 medium and heavy guns with 150 rounds each.[28]

Five of the available infantry divisions were responsible for guarding the English coastline from the Wash to Selsey Bill. All were under strength and short of weapons of every calibre, especially heavy weapons. The five divisions should have had a combined total of 360 artillery pieces; instead, they had only 101 between them. Of these, 48 were 4.5-inch howitzers and 24 were 18-pounders, all dating from 1918. Only 31 were relatively modern 18/25-pounders. Perhaps most serious of all, the five divisions could muster only twelve 2-pounder anti-tank guns between them; their total establishment, on paper, was 240. Even that almost completely worthless weapon, the .55-inch Boyes anti-tank rifle, was in critically short supply.

At this time, General Sir Edmund Ironside, who had been commanding the Home Forces

since late May, and his planning staff expected that any major German seaborne invasion would take place in the area of the Wash, with diversionary landings to the north and south. A small airborne landing on the Isle of Ely was also anticipated, followed by a major airborne assault in the quadrilateral Birmingham–Wolver-hampton–Shrewsbury–Ludlow. In fact, although tentative planning for an invasion of England had been undertaken by the German Naval Staff in the autumn of 1939, no firm plans for such a venture yet existed.

As a mobile reserve with which to meet the expected threat, Ironside had at his disposal three infantry divisions; 1st Canadian, 53rd, and 52nd (Lowland), deployed in a line from Aldershot to Northamptonshire. In East Anglia there was also an understrength, under-equipped second-line Territorial division, 2nd London, later to be re-designated 47th Division. The 2nd Armoured Division was in Lincolnshire, ready to move against an invasion in the Wash area. On 8 June, however, this reserve was stripped of two of its best formations, the 52nd Division landing at Cherbourg to support the French campaign in the south and the first units of 1st Canadian Division going ashore at Brest a few days later. Within three weeks, both divisions had been evacuated and were on British soil once more.

On 25 June, Ironside's mobile reserve was re-organized and split in two, with 2nd Armoured and 43rd Infantry Divisions deployed north of the Thames to reinforce East Anglia. The other half, comprising 1st Canadian Division (less one brigade which had lost its transport in France), two New Zealand brigades and the 1st Armoured Division, which had been hurriedly reformed and equipped with 81 cruiser and 100 light tanks, formed a second corps that was based in the Aldershot area for the support of south-east England.

Meanwhile, on 20 June, a strip of land twenty miles wide from Rye to the Wash was declared a Defence Zone which could not be visited by anyone, including British nationals, without a permit. On 29 June this restriction was extended to the whole of the east coast, and on 3 July all beaches from Brighton to Selsey Bill were closed to the public. By this time, the divisions that had been evacuated from Dunkirk were being re-organized, re-equipped and inserted into key coastal defence areas: priority was given to General Bernard Montgomery's 3rd Division, which was emplaced near Brighton. Winston Churchill visiting it at the beginning of July, was concerned over a number of shortcomings, and sent one of his famous 'Action this Day' missives to the Secretary of State for War.

'I was disturbed to find the 3rd Division spread along thirty miles of coast, instead of being, as I had imagined, held back concentrated in reserve, ready to move against any serious head of invasion. But much more astonishing was the fact that the infantry of this division, which is otherwise fully mobile, are not provided with the buses necessary to move them to the point of action. This provision of buses, waiting always ready and close at hand, is essential to all mobile units, and to none more than the 3rd Division while spread about the coast.

'I heard the same complaint from Portsmouth that the troops there had not got their transport ready and close at hand. Considering the great masses of transport, both buses and lorries, which there are in this country, and the large numbers of drivers brought back from the B.E.F., it should be possible to remedy these deficiencies at once. I hope, at any rate, that the GOC 3rd Division will be told today to take up, as he would like to do, the large number of buses which are even now plying for pleasure traffic up and down the sea front at Brighton.'[29]

While the Army strove to make good the attrition it had suffered in France, and to fortify England's beaches against the expected invasion, the Royal Navy also strove to organize a strong destroyer defence force of four flotillas – 32 destroyers – based on Harwich, Dover, Portsmouth and Plymouth. It was a desperately difficult task, for most of the destroyers that had survived the Dunkirk evacuation had been dispersed for repairs and the others were still engaged in evacuating British personnel from the Biscay ports.[30]

Fortunately, the German Navy, having sustained serious losses during the Norwegian campaign, was in no position to offer a serious challenge. In June 1940 the Germans had only one flotilla of large destroyers, two flotillas of smaller destroyers and many fast motor torpedo craft, the S-boats. It was the latter that would prove to be the biggest thorn in the Royal Navy's side, especially now that they were able to operate from the newly-captured French harbours. On the night of 24/25 June, the S-boats struck their first blow against Channel traffic when the S36 torpedoed and sank the tanker *Albuera* off Dungeness, and the S19 sank the coaster *Kingfisher*. By this time, a flotilla of five MTBs (MTB 18, 67, 70 and 71) was operating from Dover with the task of countering the S-boat threat, but it was to be some time before they became available in sufficient numbers to make any real impact on the marauding enemy craft. In any case, the S-boats were faster, bigger and better armed than the British craft, and it needed considerable skill and judgement to get the better of them.

On 28 June, the *Luftwaffe* mounted a heavy attack on the Channel Islands, and the next day German forces began landing there. By 4 July, the occupation of the Channel Islands was complete.

The first week of July 1940 saw one of the more unhappy events of the Second World War: the destruction of the French Fleet by warships of the Royal Navy at its Mediterranean bases. The French Navy's *Force de Raid* included several large, powerful and modern battleships and cruisers which had been evacuated from French ports before the final collapse, ironically with the assistance of the Royal Navy. Churchill was convinced that the Germans would do their utmost to secure these powerful forces as a prelude to the planned invasion of Britain, and as the French were unwilling either to join the British fleet or to neutralize their warships, the destruction of them by force remained the only alternative.

In parallel with operations in the Mediterranean, steps were taken to secure the French warships which had reached British ports. There were about 200 small French craft in British harbours, while the old battleships *Courbet* and *Paris* were at Portsmouth and Plymouth respectively. The large, ocean-going submarine *Surcouf* was also at Plymouth; her crew offered resistance to the take-over and there were four casualties, three British and one French.

On 4 July, for the first time, the *Luftwaffe* attacked a Channel convoy in strength. The convoy, code-named OA178, consisted of fourteen heavily-laden merchantmen outward bound from the Thames across the Atlantic. The convoy passed Dover, and was off Portland when it was hit by two *Stukagruppen* of StG 2 at about 13.00. In the next few minutes the *Stukas* bombed and sank four freighters, the *Britsum* (5,255 tons), the *Dallas City* (4,952 tons), the *Deucalion* (1,796 tons) and the *Kolga* (3,526 tons). Six more ships were damaged. That night, the survivors were attacked by S-boats, which torpedoed and sank the *Elmcrest* (4,343 tons) and damaged the *British Corporal* (6,972 tons) and the *Hartlepool* (5,500 tons).

Nor was that all. Also on 4 July, the *Stukas* dive-bombed Portland harbour, where they sank the tug *Silverdial* and the anti-aircraft ship *Foylebank*,

The first air-sea rescue of the war: on 18 September 1939, the tramp steamer *Kensington Court* was torpedoed 70 miles west of the Scillies. The crew of 34 were picked up by Sunderlands of Nos 204 and 228 Squadrons, one of which is seen circling here.

as well as damaging the freighters *East Wales* (4,358 tons), *William Wilberforce* (5,004 tons) and *City of Melbourne*. The loss of life was considerable, not least on the *Foylebank*, where 60 men were killed.

As a result of these devastating attacks, no more large freighters would be despatched into the Atlantic via the English Channel. Only small coastal convoys would continue to venture into that dangerous waterway, and then under an escort of at least six fighter aircraft.

In the week that followed the destruction of OA178, the *Luftwaffe* made a number of other, smaller-scale attacks on traffic in the Channel. On 7 July, Heinkel He 111s attacked Portland harbour, sinking a moored lighter and damaging the minesweeper *Mercury*. Bombs also near-missed the steamer *British Inventor*, killing one crew member. Two days later, Heinkels hit and damaged the freighter *Aegean* and the 1,546-ton coaster *Kenneth Hawksfield*.

The destruction of British shipping during and after Operation DYNAMO seemed to reinforce a growing belief that the Germans were waging a one-sided war, and Winston Churchill, impatient as ever for action, was concerned to find ways and means of taking the war to the enemy. One obvious method was to use RAF Bomber Command; in June 1940 the Command had carried out a number of long-range attacks against targets in northern Italy, which had declared war on Britain and France when the collapse of the latter seemed imminent, but then the bombers had been able to uplift fuel in the Channel Islands, a facility that was now denied to them. In July, Bomber Command was pre-occupied in stepping up its attacks on enemy shipping and port facilities, and was marshalling its resources to strike at enemy invasion craft assembling in the occupied Channel ports.[31]

Another means of striking at the enemy, and one much favoured by Churchill, involved the use of the recently-formed special forces – the Commandos. A beginning of sorts was made on the night of 24/25 June, when Commandos of No.

Before the Battle of Britain, British air-sea rescue was poorly organized, with few specialist craft available. As the battle progressed, the system became tighter and better co-ordinated. Here, a high-speed ASR launch works in conjunction with a Lysander in the English Channel.

11 Independent Company carried out Operation COLLAR; setting out from Ramsgate and Dover in RAF Crash Boats, they landed on the French coast near Hardelot, Boulogne and Merck to carry out a reconnaissance and, if possible, capture some Germans. In the event the raid was abortive; only one group, landing at Merlimont Plage, had a brush with the enemy in which two Germans were killed. The other groups saw nothing, although the Hardelot party came under fire while re-embarking.

On 2 July, following the enemy occupation of the Channel Islands, Churchill – still fired by the notion of special raiding parties – wrote in a memorandum to General Ismay, head of the Military Wing of the War Cabinet Secretariat:

'If it be true that a few hundred German troops have been landed on Jersey or Guernsey by troop-carriers, plans should be studied to land secretly by night on the islands and kill or capture the invaders. This is exactly one of the exploits for which the Commandos would be suited. There ought to be no difficulty in getting all the necessary information from the inhabitants and from those evacuated. The only possible reinforcements which could reach the enemy during the fighting would be by aircraft-carriers, and here would be a good opportunity for the Air Force fighting machines. Pray let me have a plan.'[32]

By 'aircraft-carriers', of course, Churchill – for whom military terminology was never a particularly strong point – meant transport aircraft.

The plan that emerged called for 140 men of No 3 Commando, under Major John Durnford-Slater, and No. 11 Independent Company to be put ashore on Guernsey with the object of destroying German aircraft and facilities on the airfield there. On 7 July, a reconnaissance was made by 2nd Lt Nicolle, who was landed on Guernsey by the submarine H43 (Lt G.R. Colvin); Hubert Nicolle was formerly of the Royal Guernsey Militia, so knew the area well.

The main operation, code-named AMBAS-SADOR, was launched on the night of 14/15 July. The plan was to land at three separate points on the south coast of the island, the men being taken across the Channel by the destroyers HMS *Saracen* and HMS *Saladin* and then transferred to seven RAF crash boats.[33] While the landings took place, two Avro Ansons of RAF Coastal Command were to fly overhead to drown the noise of the launches' engines. One party was to head for the airport from Point de la Moye; the second was to land further east at Petit Port on the Jerbourg peninsula to attack a German machine-gun post and billets at Telegraph Bay, reported by 2nd Lt Nicolle; and the third was to go in at Le Jaonnet Bay, midway between the other two, to intercept any German troops sent from St Peter Port or Fort George.

The convoy set out from Dartmouth at 18.45, arriving off the Guernsey coast in poor visibility, with mist and drizzle. The three parties transferred to the crash boats and set off, but the two belonging to No. 11 Independent Company failed to locate their beaches and abandoned the mission, one being picked up by HMS *Saladin* and the other returning to Dartmouth independently. Only the 40 men of No 3 Commando under Major Durnford-Slater reached their correct beach at Petit Port and set off for Telegraph Bay, but found nothing at all there, so they decided to re-embark. This proved an unexpectedly difficult operation, as neither launch could get close inshore; the men had to be ferried to the craft by a naval rating manning a dinghy, three at a time. Unfortunately the dinghy capsized, and several men had to be left behind on the beach. They were subsequently

captured, and one man was lost when the dinghy overturned.

Although AMBASSADOR had been a dismal failure, it was embellished by the British propaganda machine and proved a valuable morale-booster to the general public. Some valuable lessons were learned, not least of which was that future coastal raiding forces would need purpose-built landing craft. It was also clear that future Commando operations would need far more planning if they were to have a hope of succeeding, and that the men would have to be better trained. Those left ashore on Guernsey had had no choice; not a man of them could swim.

Meanwhile, German plans for the invasion of England were beginning to take on a firmer aspect, even though the Army and the Navy held widely diverging views on how they should be implemented. Admiral Raeder, the Germany Navy C-in-C, and his staff had few illusions regarding the difficulty and danger of carrying a large army over stormy, tide-swept seas over which they did not possess adequate maritime control, and on 11 July Raeder outlined the perils of the project, attempting to persuade Hitler that an invasion should be attempted only as a last resort. The Army, also lukewarm to the idea of an invasion at first, had begun to change its attitude after the close of the French campaign, and on 12 July General Alfred Jodl, Chief of Operations at the *Oberkommando der Wehrmacht* (OKW) sent in a memorandum expressing the opinion that an invasion might succeed if it took the form of a 'river crossing on a broad front' provided that the *Luftwaffe* assumed the role of artillery, the Navy secured an impenetrable sea lane in the Dover Straits, and the first wave of assault troops was very strong.

It was a particularly naive assessment, but it was followed the next day by an operational plan, prepared by the *Oberkommando des Heeres* (OKH), the Army High Command. An ambitious document, it envisaged landing thirteen divisions in three days – six from Army Group A between Ramsgate and Bexhill, four more from Army Group A between Brighton and the Isle of Wight, and another three, from Army Group B, farther west in Lyme Bay. This initial assault force would be supplemented by 28 other divisions, including armoured, motorized, and airborne.

The task of the Army Group A divisions was to establish a continuous bridgehead, extending between thirteen and nineteen miles inland, and then roll forward on a broad front to form a line extending from Gravesend to Southampton. After reinforcement, the Army Group would push on to form a second line from Maldon, on the Essex coast, to the Severn estuary at Gloucester. London would be by-passed, encircled and isolated, to be reduced to submission later by air attack and starvation. Meanwhile, the divisions of Army Group B would cut off the south-west by advancing from Lyme Bay to Bristol. Having secured most of southern England, the OKH believed, somewhat optimistically, that the rest of the country would succumb within a month. The operation was to bear the code-name *SEELOWE* – Sea Lion.

While the Germans laid their plans, the British defences re-armed at a furious pace. Many of the desperately-needed weapons came from the United States, a fact that tends to be overlooked.

Although President Roosevelt had proclaimed the neutrality of the United States upon the outbreak of war, and had placed an embargo on the shipment of arms to amy of the belligerents, this embargo had been ingeniously side-stepped in November 1939, when what became known as the 'Cash and Carry' scheme came into force. Under this scheme, belligerents could buy arms from non-governmental armaments companies, as long as they paid in dollars and provided their own shipping to transport the goods across the Atlantic. In practice, the scheme – which became law by a narrow Congressional vote on 4 November 1939 – was of benefit only to the Allies.

Within a matter of days, a British purchasing commission was established in the United States and was buying up material on a massive scale. Since the United States was forbidden to sell arms directly to a belligerent government, the United States Steel Export Company was nominated to handle the deal. Deliveries were initially slow, and with the urgency that followed the German victories in France and the Low Countries Winston Churchill made a plea to President Roosevelt for the release of reserve arms stocks

As the war progressed, dedicated ASR search squadrons were formed. This photo shows a Hurricane of No. 279 Squadron fitted with long-range fuel tanks.

that were surplus to the requirements of the US War Department.

The call for action went out from the White House, and within 48 hours a list of surplus equipment was being prepared. During the first ten days of June, after loading at arsenals all over the country, freight trains were converging on Gravesend Bay, New York, and it was from there that the first laden cargo ship, the SS *Eastern Prince*, sailed for England on 13 June. In her holds she carried 48 crated 75mm field guns, 28,000,000 rounds of .30 calibre ammunition, 15,000 machine guns and a batch of 12,000 rifles. A further dozen freighters with similar loads sailed for Britain before the end of June, followed by fifteen more in July.

No matter that the weapons were old, or that they had been packed in grease for the past twenty years. When the grease was boiled off the elderly P-14 rifles and 1917-pattern Colt .45

pistols, the majority worked well. And among the shipments were some excellent close-quarter weapons: .45 calibre Thompson sub-machine guns, the 'Tommy Guns' of the pre-war gangster movies.[34]

Many of the rifles went to the Home Guard, formed in mid-May 1940. Its original title was the Local Defence Volunteers, the initial letters of which lent themselves readily to the quickly-acquired nickname 'Look, Duck and Vanish.' The LDV became the Home Guard on 14 July, by which time more than a million men had volunteered.

But the fate of the free world would not be decided by volunteers armed with ancient rifles, nor by the better-equipped regular divisions strung out along the Channel coast. It would be decided by a handful of young men whose average age was twenty. In the weeks to come, they would achieve immortality.

CHAPTER FOUR

The Channel Air War: Summer 1940

After Dunkirk, the rhetoric of Prime Minister Winston Churchill made it seem as though the fighters of the Royal Air Force had snatched a victory out of the overall tide of defeat that had swept away the British Expeditionary Force. The reality was somewhat different; the losses sustained by RAF Fighter Command and the *Luftwaffe* during the evacuation phase were about even, while the French campaign as a whole had cost Air Chief Marshal Dowding's Command 453 Hurricanes and Spitfires.

While Fighter Command strove to make good its losses during June 1940, Bomber and Coastal Commands both stepped up their offensive operations against enemy targets. In Coastal Command's case, this involved intensifying

attacks on enemy shipping, with particular reference to convoys, off the Dutch coast; night attacks were also made by Lockheed Hudsons on Dutch oil targets and harbour installations. Bomber Command, while concentrating on attacking communications and oil targets in Germany, and on minelaying activities, also carried out limited attacks on coastal targets in the Channel area; on the night of 13/14 June, for example, Handley Page Hampdens bombed the docks at Boulogne and Dunkirk.

From 5 June, the *Luftwaffe* was also active, small numbers of bombers attacking 'fringe' targets on the east and south-east coasts of England. These attacks caused little significant damage; their main purpose was to provide the German

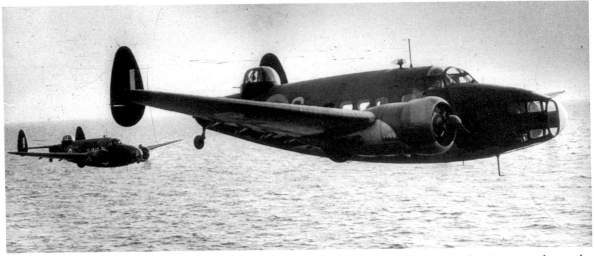

As a maritime patrol aircraft, the Lockheed Hudson was a far better proposition than the Anson, and was the backbone of RAF Coastal Command in 1940–41.

bomber crews with operational and navigational experience. On both sides, great care was exercised in avoiding damage to civilian property and loss of life. As one Junkers 88 pilot, *Kapitän* Hajo Herrmann, later recorded:

'We were allocated important strategic and military targets off the east coast of England, the oil refineries at Thames Haven and the nitrogen works at Billingham (the latter in the north-east of England – author). We dive-bombed them under a full moon, with strict instructions either to bring our bombs home or look for shipping targets if we were unable to identify our main target quite clearly. I always

flew on ahead and gave the others clearance to attack only after I had recognised the target positively and had put down one or two benzol bombs.'[35]

Many coastal reconnaissance and minelaying operations were undertaken in the Channel area during this phase by Heinkel He 115 floatplanes.

On 30 June, the C-in-C *Luftwaffe*, *Reichsmarschall* Hermann Göring, issued a general directive setting out the aims of the planned air assault on Britain. The *Luftwaffe*'s main target was to be the Royal Air Force, with particular emphasis on its fighter airfields and aircraft factories; as long as Fighter Command remained

Bombing-up a Handley Page Hampden. The Hampden was to play an important role in the offensive against the enemy-occupied Channel ports.

unbeaten, the *Luftwaffe*'s first priority must be to attack it by day and night at every opportunity, in the air and on the ground, until it was destroyed. Only then would the *Luftwaffe* be free to turn its attention to other targets, such as the Royal Navy's dockyards and operational harbours, as a preliminary to invasion.

On 3 July the *Luftwaffe* carried out its first daylight attacks on the English coast. Among other targets, the forward airfield at Manston, in Kent, was attacked by a small force of Dornier Do 17s, which came in at low level and dropped anti-personnel bombs on the landing area. The only damage was to a lawnmower. On the following day the Germans began flying fighter sweeps over south-east England. Dowding and the Air Officer Commanding No. 11 Group Air Vice-Marshal Keith Park, refused to be drawn, and it was not until 7 July that there was serious skirmishes, the RAF losing six aircraft and the *Luftwaffe* five. Three of the aircraft were Spitfires of No 65 Squadron from Hornchurch, bounced by Messerschmitt 109s.

On the morning of 10 July – the date generally accepted as marking the start of the Battle of Britain – a Dornier Do 17P reconnaissance aircraft of 2/*Fernaufklärungsgruppe* 11 sighted a large coastal convoy off the North Foreland, heading south-west for the Straits of Dover. Although escorted by Me 190s of I/JG 51, the Dornier was attacked and severely damaged by Spitfires of No. 74 Squadron from Manston, eventually crash-landing near Boulogne with the loss of three of its four crew. But the damage had been done, and the Germans were now fully alerted to the passage of the convoy, code-named BREAD.

At about 10.30, a *Staffel* of Me 109s appeared over the Channel, sweeping parallel to the Kentish coast. Nine Spitfires were scrambled from Biggin Hill to intercept them and, in a brief but inconclusive engagement, one Spitfire of No. 610 Squadron was hit in the port wing and had to make an emergency landing at Hawkinge.

The main action began after 13.30, when the Chain Home radar station at Dover detected a build-up of considerable size behind Cap Gris Nez and passed on the information to HQ No. 11 Group at Uxbridge. As the enemy force – consisting of 24 Dornier 17s of KG 2, closely escorted by 20 Me 110s of ZG 26 *Horst Wessel*, with a similar number of Me 109s of JG 51 flying top cover – was plotted leaving the enemy coast, five squadrons of Hurricanes and Spitfires were scrambled to intercept. In the battle that followed, one Me 109 was shot down into the Thames Estuary and two more crash-landed in France after sustaining damage. The twin-engined Me 110 *Zerstörer*, which had performed well against inferior opposition over Poland and France, suffered heavily; ZG 26 lost three aircraft over Folkestone and two more were damaged by RAF fighters as they fled across the Channel. Of KG 2's Dorniers, two were destroyed – one when a Hurricane of No. 111 Squadron collided with it – and three others were damaged.

The RAF's only combat loss during the action was Hurricane P3671 of No. 111 Squadron, which collided with the Dornier whilst under attack by a 109 of JG 51, losing a wing. The pilot, Flying Officer T.P.K. Higgs, baled out but was killed. Three other 111 Squadron Hurricanes were damaged, one by friendly fire; three Spitfires of No. 74 Squadron also received damage, and although some of the RAF fighters had to make crash-landings their pilots were unhurt and all the aircraft were repairable.

The determined RAF fighter attacks, together with some accurate anti-aircraft fire – especially at Dover, where the barrage was radar-directed – had made it impossible for the Dorniers to make a co-ordinated attack on the convoy, although they did succeed in sinking one small ship.[36] Away to the west, however, the *Luftwaffe* enjoyed better fortune.

While the attack on the BREAD convoy was still in progress, 63 Junkers Ju 88s of *Luftflotte* 3 approached the Cornish coast from the west, confusing the radar controllers at Dry Tree, on Lizard Point. Splitting up, the enemy force attacked Falmouth and Swansea, its bombs falling on railways, ships at anchor and a munitions factory, causing 86 casualties. It was a

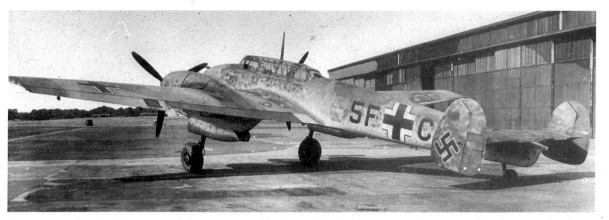

The Messerschmitt 110 was completely outclassed by the RAF's fighters, and suffered appalling losses in the Battle of Britain. As a night-fighter, later in the war, it was a success.

grim foretaste of what the population of southern England would suffer in the weeks to come, and to make matters worse the raiders escaped unscathed. Because of the radar confusion, Spitfires of No. 92 Squadron were not scrambled from Pembrey in time to make an interception; in fact, the only RAF pilot to come near the Ju 88s was Wing Commander Ira ('Taffy') Jones, the First World War ace with 40 victories. Taking-off from a training airfield in an unarmed Hawker Henley target tug, he chased a Ju 88 out to sea, firing Very flares at it and doubtless cursing his lack of guns and ammunition. Jones's exploit reinforced the view of many Fighter Command pilots that the Henley – originally developed as a fast light bomber, but never used in that role – might have been used to good effect against enemy bombers if fitted with machine-guns. Capable of nearly 300 mph, it would at least have taken some of the strain from the hard-pressed Spitfire and Hurricane squadrons. About 200 were in service in 1940.

Thursday, 11 July, saw more fierce fighting over the Channel; when the day ended the *Luftwaffe* had lost fifteen aircraft to the RAF's six. It was on this day that the Junkers Ju 87 dive-bomber entered the battle, with aircraft of *LG* 1 and *StG* 2 attacking Portland. Two *Stukas* were shot down, and the inferiority of their escorting Me 110s was again demonstrated in dramatic fashion when

four were shot down by RAF fighters, two off Portland and one of the Ney Breakwater. The fourth crash-landed at Grange Heath near Lulworth after being attacked by pilots of Nos. 238, 87 and 601 Squadrons, in that order. All the Me 110s belonged to 9/*ZG* 76.

Not all the successes of 11 July belonged to Fighter Command. Early in the morning, an Avro Anson of No. 217 Squadron, based at St Eval in Cornwall, was on patrol over the Channel when the Coastal Command crew sighted a Heinkel He 59 floatplane, the type used by the German air-sea rescue service. It was also found suspiciously close to British coastal convoys from time to time. This example, belonging to *Seenotflugkommando* 1 and bearing the civil registration D-ASOU, was damaged by the Anson and forced down into the Channel. Its four-man crew took to their dinghy and were later picked up drifting near the Channel Islands; the aircraft was retrieved by the Royal Navy and beached at Walmer Harbour, Kent.

Actions against south coast targets and Channel shipping also resulted in the loss of several Heinkel He 111s on 11 July. *I/KG* 1 lost two aircraft and had a third damaged during night operations against coastal towns on 10/11 July, and in the early evening RAF fighters destroyed two Heinkels of *KG* 55 in an attack on Portsmouth, damaging a third so badly that it was a write-off.

The *Luftwaffe* also lost two Dornier 17s and a Ju 88 during the day's operations.[37]

The Heinkels suffered even more heavily on 12 July, five being shot down and a sixth damaged beyond repair. All the Heinkels except one, which belonged to *KG 26* and was shot down over Aberdeen, were engaged in attacks on convoys off Aldeburgh and Orfordness. Two Dornier 17s and a Ju 88 were also shot down. The fight, however, was not all one-sided; return fire from the bombers – especially the Do 17s – was very accurate, accounting for two Hurricanes destroyed and a number damaged.

Saturday, 13 July, was hailed as a major success for the Hurricanes of No. 56 Squadron from North Weald, which intercepted a force of Ju 87s and their fighter escort over Portland. The Hurricane pilots claimed the destruction of seven *Stukas*; in fact, all the enemy dive-bombers returned to base except two which made forced landings in France. One of the Me 110 escorts was shot down and three suffered heavy damage. Elsewhere, Hurricanes of No. 238 Squadron shot down a Dornier 17 reconnaissance aircraft off

Chesil Beach, while Spitfires destroyed an Me 109 south of Dover. In the day's action, No. 56 Squadron lost two Hurricanes and No. 238 Squadron one.

During this phase, Air Chief Marshal Dowding, anxious to preserve his fighter strength, committed the Hurricanes and Spitfires to convoy protection work in relatively small numbers; fighter cover was only increased when a convoy reached the perilous waters of the Dover Straits, although the forward coastal airfields of Fighter Command were reinforced on 19 July, when an improvement in the weather brought expectations of greater enemy activity. In fact, this day proved a black one for the Command, which lost ten fighters against four *Luftwaffe* aircraft shot down. Six of the RAF aircraft were the hapless Boulton Paul Defiants of No. 141 Squadron from West Malling, which were bounced by the Me 109s of III/JG 51 off Dover and shot down in flames one after the other. Ten of the squadron's pilots and air gunners were lost.

There were several major engagements over the Dover Straits during the last days of July, and

An Avro Anson of No. 224 Squadron on patrol over a coastal convoy. The Anson was worthless in the anti-submarine role, being armed only with bombs. Two 'German' submarines attacked in the English Channel by Ansons soon after the outbreak of war were in fact British. Luckily, they escaped.

The Junkers Ju 87B *Stuka* was used with success against the Channel convoys, but suffered heavy losses against determined fighter opposition.

the entry in the war diary of No. 32 Squadron, operating out of Biggin Hill, is fairly typical of an 11 Group unit during this period.

> 20 July 1940. Convoy escort, 10 miles east of Dover. At 17.58 hours with 610 Squadron, intercepted a raid on the convoy by about fifty Junkers Ju 87s and Messerschmitt 110s, escorted by Messerschmitt 109Es. Led by S/L Worrall the Squadron shot down six of the enemy (3 Me 110s, 2 Me 109s and one Ju 87) and damaged four others (all Me 109s). One Hurricane was lost but the pilot, F/Lt Bulmer, is reported to have baled out near North Foreland. Sgt Higgins was slightly wounded in the face by splinters from bullets striking his protecting armour.[38]

Also typically, the claims in the above report are wildly exaggerated. In all probability, No. 32 Squadron scored no success that day. No Me 110s were lost on operations, and the five Me 109s confirmed as destroyed were attributed to other fighter squadrons. Nor did the *Luftwaffe* lose any Ju 87s, although four made forced landings in France with varying degrees of damage. In all, the Germans lost fourteen aircraft on 20 July, the RAF nine fighters.

On 25 July the *Luftwaffe* adopted a change of tactics, sending out strong fighter sweeps to draw the RAF fighters into battle before launching its bomber attacks. As a consequence, 60 Ju 87 *Stukas* were able to bomb a convoy with impunity while the fighters of No. 11 Group were on the ground refuelling. Later in the day, the convoy was attacked by 30 Ju 88s, escorted by about 50 Me 109s. The attacks continued until 18.30; fifteen of Dowding's fighter squadrons were engaged in the course of the day, destroying sixteen enemy aircraft for the loss of eight of their own, all Spitfires.[39]

In four weeks of operations over the English Channel, the *Luftwaffe* had sunk 40,000 tons of British shipping, including three destroyers. Combat losses during the month's air fighting were *Luftwaffe* 190, RAF Fighter Command 77, of which 46 were Hurricanes – the aircraft which had borne the brunt of the fighting, and would continue to do so. Fifty RAF fighter pilots were killed or missing, and with German preparations for the invasion of England clearly under way, the loss was serious. It was already apparent that such a continued rate of attrition would be extremely hard, if not impossible, to make good.

There followed a comparative lull lasting a week. Then, on 8 August, Hurricanes were at the forefront of a furious air battle that developed when large formations of Ju 87s, under strong fighter escort, attacked a 250-ship convoy code-named PEEWIT off the Isle of Wight. One of the Hurricane squadrons involved was No. 145 from Westhampnett, led by Squadron Leader J.R.A. Peel. The RAF pilots were about to engage a *Stuka* formation when they were themselves bounced by 109s and forced on the defensive. Two of the squadron's Hurricanes, one of them Peel's, were shot down; the CO was rescued from the sea off Boulogne. That day's fighting cost the RAF fifteen

Hurricanes and Spitfires against 21 enemy aircraft destroyed; it was the biggest loss sustained by Fighter command since the offensive began. The RAF's losses for 8 August included a number of aircraft destroyed in air actions over Dover and the Thames Estuary, when six squadrons of Hurricanes and two of Spitfires intercepted two heavy raids carried out under strong fighter escort. Six Hurricanes were lost in these battles, the others claiming six enemy aircraft.

The PEEWIT convoy, meanwhile, had lost six ships, three sunk by *Schnellboote* before dawn and the others by air attack. Several more were damaged. It was the first convoy to attempt a passage through the straits in daylight since 25

A convoy in the western approaches to the English Channel, photographed from a Sunderland. The ships are making one of their frequent course changes to confuse U-boats.

At a later date, long-range ASR aircraft were fitted with airborne lifeboats. Photographs show one being installed in the bomb-bay of a Wellington, and being dropped to the crew of a USAAF B-17 ditched in the Channel.

July, in the day of furious action when S-Boats and bombers had sunk or badly damaged eleven out of 21 ships, mostly colliers. PEEWIT was unfortunate in that the enemy had been alerted to its presence by a newly-completed coastal radar station at Wissant (Ushant), one of several experimental stations that were being set up

along the arc of coast from the Friesian Islands to the Cherbourg Peninsula. It was to be some time before the British became aware that radar – or radio locations, as it was still known – was no longer their sole monopoly.[40]

Bad weather frustrated operations on 9 and 10 August, the latter originally scheduled as ADLERTAG – Eagle Day, the start of the air offensive proper – but on the 11th four heavy air attacks were launched on Dover and Portland. The Dover raids were intercepted by the Hurricanes of Nos 1, 17, 32, 56, 85 and 111 Squadrons, which claimed eleven enemy aircraft for the loss of nine of their own, and by the Spitfires of Nos 64, 65 and 74 Squadrons, which claimed five for the loss of three. Five of the shot-down Hurricanes belonged to No. 111 Squadron, which could claim only one Messerschmitt 109 in return, and worse than the loss of the aircraft was the fact that four of the pilots were killed. The attack on Portland, carried out by Ju 88s with an escort of Me 110s, was broken up by sixteen Hurricanes of Nos 87. 213 and 218 Squadrons, together with ten Spitfires of Nos 152 and 603; nine enemy aircraft

The Messerschmitt 109 was a serious opponent as long as its pilots were given a free hand to sweep ahead of the bombers, drawing the RAF's fighters into combat.

were shot down for the loss of five RAF fighters. There were more skirmishes in the afternoon as the Germans attempted to bomb a convoy, and the day ended with 35 enemy aircraft destroyed for the loss of 30 Hurricanes and Spitfires. Since the beginning of July the *Luftwaffe* had lost 274 aircraft, the RAF 124.

On 12 August, the *Luftwaffe* switched the weight of its attacks to the coastal radar stations and the forward airfields of Manston, Lympne and Hawkinge. That morning, 24 hours before the main offensive was due to begin, 21 Messerschmitt 109s and 110s took off from Calais-Marck airfield and set course out over the Channel. They belonged to *Erprobungsgruppe* 210; the only unit of its kind in the *Luftwaffe*, its aircraft had all been fitted with racks enabling them to carry 500- and 1,000-lb bombs. On the previous day the *Gruppe* had tried out the idea operationally for the first time when 24 Messerschmitts dive-bombed convoy BOOTY off the Harwich–Clacton coastline, setting two freighters on fire. The German aircraft had been intercepted by the Spitfires of No. 74 Squadron, but all had returned to base.[41]

On this morning of 12 August, *Erprobungsgruppe* 210's targets were the radar stations at Dover, Pevensey and Rye. At 11.00, Me 110s dropped eight 1,000 lb bombs on the Pevensey station, while the remainder of the *Gruppe* attacked the masts at Rye and Dover. Although the bombs causes some damage, all three stations were operational again within three hours.

It was a different story at Ventnor on the Isle of Wight, where the radar station was attacked 30 minutes later by fifteen Junkers 88s of KG 51 and KG 54. Their bombing was extremely accurate and the station was damaged beyond repair. To cover up the dangerous gap created by the loss of the Ventnor station, the British transmitted a false signal on the wrecked transmitter's frequency; the German listening-posts on the other side of the Channel believed that Ventnor was still fully operational. In fact it was only after eleven days of non-stop work that another station was brought into action on the Isle of Wight.

While Ventnor was under attack, around 75 more Ju 88s dive-bombed Portsmouth harbour, Portland, and industrial targets in Portsmouth and Southampton, including the Supermarine

Spitfire production plant at Woolston. The Ju 88s made their attack through the balloon barrage and intense anti-aircraft fire put up by shore batteries and ships in the harbour. Their bombs caused substantial damage, especially in Portsmouth, and 100 or so casualties. But the attack cost the *Luftwaffe* dearly; ten Ju 88s failed

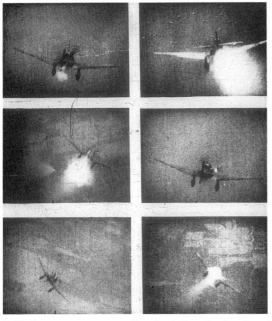

Stills from a camera-gun film depicting the demise of a *Stuka* over the Channel, July 1940.

to return, falling victim either to the anti-aircraft barrage, the Spitfires of No. 152 Squadron or the Hurricanes of No. 213. Five Me 110s and an Me 109, escorting the bombers, were also destroyed.

At noon, the CHL radar station at Foreness, untouched by the morning's attacks, reported 50 plus hostiles off North Foreland. They were Junkers Ju 87s, and they were searching for two Channel convoys, AGENT and ARENA. The attack on the latter was successful, the escorting fighters keeping the Spitfires and Hurricanes at arm's length, and several vessels were sunk or damaged, but the attack on AGENT was beaten off, albeit at the cost of four Hurricanes destroyed. All the Ju 87s returned to base.

In parallel with these attacks, a force of Dornier 17s of KG 2 raided the airfield at Lympne with showers of 100-lb bombs, causing some damage to the hangars, tarmac and buildings. Then, at 13.30, it was once again the turn of *Erprobungsgruppe* 210; twenty Messerschmitts swept across the airfield at Manston and dropped their bombs just as a flight of Spitfires of No. 65 Squadron was preparing to take-off. The Spitfires got airborne amid the exploding bombs and climbed for altitude, but the raiders had gone. Manston was temporarily put out of action. Later that afternoon the German bombers struck at Hawkinge and again at Lympne; both airfields were heavily damaged, and all through the night personnel worked like slaves to repair the cratered runways.

By nightfall on 12 August the *Luftwaffe* had despatched 300 bombers, with as many escorting fighters, against British targets. The Germans had lost 27 aircraft, the RAF 20; and the main offensive had yet to develop.

There was a significant development on 12 August and it had nothing to do with the air battle. Soon after the *Luftwaffe* completed its attack on the radar stations, heavy-calibre shells from a German long-range battery across the Channel exploded in Dover. It was the town's first experience of such an attack, but it would not be the last.[42]

During the night, the *Luftwaffe* carried out several harassing attacks on coastal targets, including the docks at Bristol. During this raid, a Heinkel He 111 of KG 27 crash-landed at Sturminster Marshall, near Wimborne, Dorset, after being abandoned by its crew, who were all taken prisoner. The Heinkel had been attacked by a Blenheim night-fighter equipped with highly secret, and still very experimental, AI radar.

At 07.30 the next morning the *Luftflotten* stood ready to launch the first attacks of ADLERTAG, but at the last minute H-Hour was postponed because of bad weather. The Dornier 17s of KG 2, however, failed to receive the signal in time; they took off in fog and rain and set course for the English coast without fighter escort. The 55

Balloon cable-cutting equipment was tested over the British Isles by the Heinkel He 111s of KG 54, but proved too cumbersome to be a success.

Dorniers were tracked by radar and AVM Park scrambled two squadrons of Hurricanes and a squadron of Spitfires, dividing them between the damaged airfields at Hawkinge and Manston and a convoy in the Thames Estuary. He also ordered most of a squadron of Hurricanes to patrol between Arundel and Petworth, leaving behind one section to cover their home base of Tangmere, near Chichester. Lastly, a squadron of Hurricanes orbiting over Canterbury could be called upon to support any of the other units engaging the enemy. Further west the Air Officer Commanding No. 10 Group, AVM Quintin Brand, scrambled a squadron of Hurricanes to patrol the Dorset coast. Another squadron and a half of Hurricanes were held on immediate readiness at Exeter.

Flying in tight information, just under the cloud base, the Dorniers passed over Eastchurch airfield and unloaded their bombs on the runways, hangars and parked aircraft. At that moment the raiders were attacked by the Spitfires of No. 74 Squadron from Hornchurch, led by Squadron Leader A.G. Malan. One of the Dorniers was shot down and the remainder scattered, climbing

Streams of tracer from an RAF fighter converge on a Heinkel He 111.

towards the clouds. The battle was then joined by the Hurricanes of No. 151 Squadron, under Squadron Leader E.M. Donaldson, followed a few minutes later by the Hurricanes of No. 111 led by Squadron Leader J.M. Thompson, and a fierce air

RAF fighter pilots dash for their Hurricanes after receiving the call to scramble.

battle developed over the Thames Estuary. By the time the bombers reached the shelter of the clouds four more had been destroyed.

At 11.30, 23 Me 110s of *Zerstörer-Lehrgeschwader* 1 took off from their airfield near Caen with orders to patrol the English south coast near Portland. Although they were picked up by radar as they crossed the French coast near Cherbourg, and although their strength was correctly reported as 'twenty plus bandits', the radar could not tell what type of aircraft they were. Since Dowding had given orders that his Spitfires and Hurricanes were to avoid combat with enemy fighters if possible (a fact that had been known to the Germans since late July, thanks to *Luftwaffe* signals intelligence, which had intercepted transmissions between RAF Sector Controllers and patrolling fighters) the controllers of No. 11 Group would probably not have scrambled any fighter squadrons had they known the identity of the enemy aircraft. In the event three squadrons took off from Tangmere, Warmwell and Exeter to intercept the enemy, and in so doing fell into the very trap that Dowding had been trying to avoid. The Germans planned that when their bombers eventually arrived they would catch the Spitfires and Hurricanes on the ground as they refuelled and re-armed.

The Hurricanes engaged the Me 110s over the coast and the German fighters immediately adopted a defensive circle. Three Hurricanes were forced to break off the action with battle damage, but five Me 110s went down into the sea, and five more returned to France severely hit. The action once again highlighted the heavy, twin-engined Me 110's vulnerability in combat with lighter, more manoeuvrable fighters, and to make matters worse ZLG 1's mission had failed. The unit had drawn three British fighter squadrons on to itself so that the bombers could slip through according to plan – but the bombers did not come for another three hours, by which time the RAF fighter squadrons were ready for them once more.

At 15.00, 52 Junkers 87s of StG 2 took off from their base at Flers to attack RAF airfields in the Portland area. They were escorted by the Me 109s of JG 27. However, southern England was hidden under a blanket of cloud, making a dive-bombing attack out of the question, and the *Stukas* circled over the coast in search of a target. Within minutes their fighter escort was being hotly engaged by a strong force of Hurricanes from Exeter and Middle Wallop, while fifteen Spitfires of No. 609 Squadron attacked the bombers. Five of the *Stukas* were quickly shot down; the remainder jettisoned their bombs and fled for home.

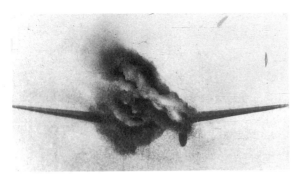

A Heinkel He 111 explodes in mid-air, disintegrating in a cloud of debris.

High above southern England, vapour trails criss-cross the sky as RAF fighters engage the *Luftwaffe*.

The next wave of bombers, approaching the coast a few minutes later, ran into the hornets' nest stirred up by StG 2. They were the Ju 88s of KG 54, and they used the cloud cover to good advantage. One formation dropped its bombs on Southampton harbour, while others dived on the airfield at Middle Wallop, one of Fighter Command's vital sector stations. The bombs caused only light damage, but severe damage was inflicted by another Ju 88 formation at Andover, a few miles away. Three Ju 88s were shot down and eleven returned with battle damage, some making crash-landings.

Meanwhile, over Kent, No. 11 Group was having a hard time. General Bruno Loerzer's II *Fliegerkorps* has sent in both its *Stuka-Geschwader*, as well as a third from VIII *Fliegerkorps*, preceded by the Me 109s of JG 26. The Messerschmitts were able to beat off a flight of Spitfires from Kenley, allowing the 86 Junkers 87s to proceed unmolested to their target, the airfield of Detling near Maidstone. Fifteen minutes later the airfield lay in ruins; the hangars were burning, the operations room was wrecked, the station commander was dead and twenty British aircraft were destroyed. It was a brilliant attack, and in terms of its execution was highly successful. But there were no RAF fighters at Detling; it was a Coastal Command station. Nevertheless, among the aircraft destroyed were eight Blenheims of No. 53 Squadron, recently deployed there to carry out attacks on the enemy-held Channel ports.

At the close of ADLERTAG the *Luftwaffe* had flown 485 sorties, mostly against RAF airfields; three had been badly damaged, but none was a fighter base. The cost to the *Luftwaffe* was 34 aircraft; the RAF lost thirteen aircraft and seven pilots. On 14 August, operations against the British Isles were hampered by bad weather. Nevertheless, attacks by small numbers of aircraft on Manston, Dover, Middle Wallop and Sealand cost the *Luftwaffe* eleven bombers and six fighters, while the RAF lost five Hurricanes and a Spitfire, together with three Blenheim fighters of No. 600 Squadron destroyed on the ground during an attack on Manston by Me 110s of *Erprobungsgruppe* 210.

At 10.30 on 15 August patches of blue sky began to show through the grey overcast which had stretched from horizon to horizon since dawn, and by 11.00 the clouds had broken up completely. A few minutes later, 40 *Stukas* of II *Fliergerkorps*, escorted by a similar number of Me 109s, crossed the French coast near Cap Blanc Bez. Their targets were the airfields of Lympne and Hawkinge. As they approached the English coast they were met by the Spitfires of No. 64 Squadron and the Hurricanes of No. 501, but these were held at bay by the 109s and the *Stukas* caused severe damage at Lympne, putting the airfield out of action for two days. The damage was less severe at Hawkinge, where one hangar was hit and a barrack block destroyed.

The Operations Room at Fighter Command HQ, Stanmore. Fighter Command's command and control system was undoubtedly the finest in the world.

The battle now shifted to the north, where two *Geschwader* of *Luftflotte* 5, operating from bases in Norway and Denmark, attempted to attack airfields and industrial targets in the Tyne–Tees area and in Yorkshire. The raids were intercepted by seven RAF fighter squadrons, which destroyed eight Heinkel 111s, six Junkers 88s and eight escorting Me 110s for the loss of one Hurricane. In mid-afternoon the battle flared up again in the south, when a major raid was mounted by the Dornier 17s of KG 3 from St Trond and Antwerp-Deurne, in Belgium. Over the coast they made rendezvous with their fighter escort, the Me 109s of JG 51, 52 and 54. The German formation was detected by radar as it assembled over Belgium and northern France, and as it headed across the Channel eleven RAF fighter squadrons – about 130 Spitfires and Hurricanes – were scrambled. Such was the diversity of the incoming raid plots, however, that the fighters were shuttled to and fro by the sector controllers with no real co-ordination. For example, the Hurricanes of No. 17 Squadron were

patrolling the Thames Estuary when they received an urgent recall to their base at Martlesham Heath, north of Harwich. While still a long distance away the pilots could see columns of smoke rising from Martlesham, and when they arrived overhead they found that the airfield had been badly hit. Unnoticed and without any opposition, *Erprobungsgruppe* 210's 24 bomb-carrying Messerschmitts had slipped in at low level, bombed, and got clear before anyone had a chance to fire a shot. It was 36 hours before the field could be made serviceable once more. Meanwhile, the Dorniers of KG 3 had split into two waves, one heading for Eastchurch and the other for Rochester. At the latter target their bombs caused severe damage to the Short aircraft factory, setting back production of the Stirling bomber by several months.

So far, Kesselring's *Luftflotte* 2 had been attacking across the Straits of Dover. Now it was the turn of Sperrle's *Luftflotte* 3; 120 miles to the south-west, his units were forming up over their airfields. At 16.45 the Junkers 88s of LG 1 began taking off from Orleans, followed fifteen minutes later by the Ju 87s of StG 1 from Cherbourg. The bombers rendezvoused with the Me 109s of JG 26 and JG 53 and the Me 110s of ZG 2, and the whole armada of more than 200 aircraft set course for the English coast.

The Germans, however, had thrown away their tactical advantage. The time elapsing between the raids had enabled Air Vice-Marshals Park and Brand to take adequate countermeasures, and to meet the attackers they were able to put up fourteen fighter squadrons – a total of 170 aircraft, the biggest number of fighters the RAF had so far committed to the battle at any one time.

The Spitfires and Hurricanes met the bombers over the coast and concentrated on the Ju 88s, destroying nine of them in a matter of minutes and breaking up the enemy formation. Of the fifteen aircraft of II/LG 1, only three managed to break through to their target, the Fleet Air Arm base at Worthy Down, north-east of Southampton. The others jettisoned their bombs and turned for home, under continual attack. II/LG 1 lost two Ju 88s, and IV/LG 1 three aircraft out of seven. I/LG 1 was more fortunate. Its twelve Ju 88s had been the first to cross the coast, and had managed to achieve an element of surprise. They dived on Middle Wallop, just a fraction too late to catch two fighter squadrons on the ground. The last Spitfires

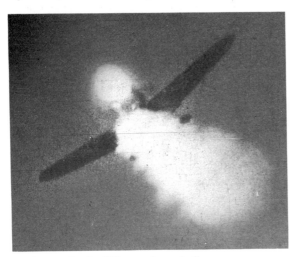

A Messerschmitt 109 goes down in flames.

of No. 609 Squadron were just taking off when the bombs exploded among the hangars. It was the third raid on Middle Wallop in three days. During the attack the German pilots had the impression that they were bombing Andover; apparently they still did not know that Middle Wallop was a much more important sector station.

The fact that the Ju 88s bore the brunt of the RAF fighter attacks probably saved the vulnerable Ju 87 *Stukas* from a severe mauling. Even so, six were shot down. But it was the Messerschmitt 110 that suffered the worst attrition of the day. While I and III/ZG 76 had been detached to escort the northern attacks, losing eight of their number, the *Geschwader*'s other units had been operating in support of the cross-Channel operations, during which they lost twelve aircraft. Together with the destruction of an aircraft of ZG 2 over the Channel, this brought Me 110 losses during the morning and afternoon to 21 aircraft, and the day was by no means over.

At 18.30, fifteen Me 110s and eight Me 109s of *Erprobungsgruppe* 210 set out over the Channel, escorted by the Me 109s of JG 52. Their target was Kenley, south of London, but they made a navigational error and bombed Croydon by mistake, destroying 40 training aircraft, killing 68 people and injuring 192, mostly civilians. As they were carrying out their attack they were intercepted by the Hurricanes of Nos 32 and 111 Squadrons and four Me 110s were quickly shot down. The remainder ran for the Channel, but near the coast they were attacked by the Spitfires of No. 66 Squadron and two more were destroyed, together with an Me 109.

As night fell on 15 August, both sides retired to lick their wounds and assess their losses and victories. The *Luftwaffe* had flown 1,270 fighter and 250 bomber sorties during the day, and the Germans had lost 71 aircraft, mostly bombers and Me 110s. The RAF's loss was 31.

On 16 August the *Luftwaffe* returned in force and struck at Brize Norton, Manston, West Malling, Tangmere, Gosport, Lee-on-Solent, Farnborough and Harwell. Forty-six training aircraft were destroyed at Brize Norton, and the

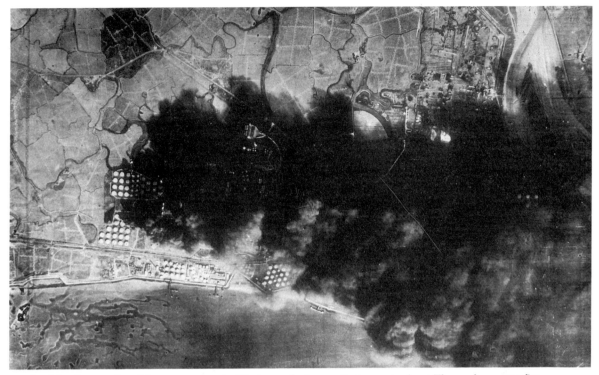

Much of the German bombing was accurate. Photograph shows oil storage tanks at Thameshaven on fire.

radar station at Ventnor on the Isle of Wight was bombed once more. In the afternoon the weather clamped down again, and although *Luftflotte* 2 sent out a force of bombers to attack the fighter airfields of Debden, Duxford, North Weald and Hornchurch the raiders were forced to turn back, unable to find their targets under a thick blanket of cloud. Despite the sporadic nature of the fighting, air combats during the day cost the *Luftwaffe* 44 aircraft and the RAF 22. It was on this day that Flight Lieutenant J.B. Nicholson of No. 249 Squadron, patrolling near Southampton in a Hurricane, was attacked by a Me 110. Cannon shells wounded Nicholson in the leg and eye and set his aircraft on fire, yet he remained in the blazing cockpit and managed to shoot down his attacker before baling out, severely burned. He was awarded the Victoria Cross, the only one to be won RAF Fighter Command.

On Sunday, 18 August, following another spell of bad weather, the Germans launched a series of heavy attacks on the sector stations of Kenley and Biggin Hill. These attacks were carried out mainly by the Dornier 17s of KG 76, which, despite their fighter escort, suffered heavily, losing six aircraft with several more damaged. Two Ju 88s operating with KG 76 (the *Geschwader* was in the process of re-equipping with the new type) were also destroyed. The most fearful German loss of the day, however, was sustained by the Ju 87 *Stukas* of StG 77, which set out to attack the airfields at Ford, Gosport and Thorney Island, together with the radar site at Poley on the south coast. They were intercepted by the Hurricanes of No. 43 Squadron and the Spitfires of No. 152, which destroyed no fewer than eighteen of the dive-bombers and damaged five more. It was the last time that the *Stuka* appeared in British skies.

StG 77 was not the only *Luftwaffe* formation to suffer heavily that day: ZG 26, flying escort missions, lost fifteen Me 110s to RAF fighters, while the single-engined fighter *Geschwader* lost

Hurricanes of No. 601 Squadron on patrol over southern England. Note the fifth aircraft weaving below and astern. This kind of tight formation cost Fighter Command many lives before better tactics were evolved.

The Hurricane could absorb tremendous battle damage, as this photograph of a No. 615 Squadron aircraft reveals.

sixteen Me 109s between them. KG 53, attacking North Weald, lost four Heinkel 111s. The total *Luftwaffe* loss for 18 August was 66 aircraft; the RAF lost 35 fighters.

From 19 to 23 August inclusive, air action was confined to skirmishing as both sides rested and regrouped. During this period the *Luftwaffe* lost 27 aircraft, the RAF eleven fighters. 23 August saw the radar station at Ventnor back in operation again. The weather continued to improve steadily, and the *Luftwaffe* resumed its attacks on RAF ground installations. The next day, 24 August, North Weald was heavily

Douglas Bader, who commanded the Tangmere Wing in 1941.

bombed, together with Hornchurch, Manston and Portsmouth naval base. By noon Manston had ceased to function, although Hornchurch escaped with relatively light damage. The airfield attacks cost the Germans seven Ju 88s and four He 111s. In all, the *Luftwaffe* lost 30 aircraft during the day, and Fighter Command twenty. Among the latter were four Boulton Paul Defiants of No. 264 Squadron, shot down during an engagement over the Channel. Three more Defiants were damaged.

That night, during attacks on targets in the London area, some bomber crews made a navigational error and dropped bombs on London itself – an act that was to have a far-reaching effect on the future conduct of the battle. On the night of

During the Battle of Britain period the Germans strengthened their coastal anti-aircraft defences considerably, as this photograph – taken during a night raid – shows.

25/26 August, following a day that had seen heavy German raids on Portland, Weymouth, Warmwell and Dover, RAF Bomber Command attacked Berlin for the first time, aiming at industrial targets in the city by way of reprisal for the previous night's raid on London. The attack was hampered by thick cloud. Of the 81 aircraft despatched (Wellingtons, Whitleys and Hampdens of Nos 3, 4 and 5 Groups) 29 claimed to have bombed Berlin. Six aircraft, all Hampdens, failed to return; three ditched in the sea and their crews were rescued.

From 11.00 on 26 August, fighters of No. 11 Group fought a running battle between Canterbury and Maidstone by 50 bombers escorted by 80 fighters. In this action, No 616 Squadron lost five out of twelve Spitfires, No. 264 Squadron lost three more Defiants, and No. 1 (Canadian) Squadron three Hurricanes, but an attempted raid on Biggin Hill was broken up. All available squadrons were committed to intercept a further attack by 40 Dornier 17s of KG 2 and KG 3 on Debden and Hornchurch airfields, escorted by 120 fighters; the latter were compelled to withdraw through lack of fuel and the bombers suffered heavily, eleven Dorniers being shot down. A third major attack, by 50 Heinkel 111s of KG 55 escorted by 107 fighters, was intercepted by three RAF squadrons and four bombers were destroyed. The *Luftwaffe*'s total losses on this day

A typical dispersal scene during the Battle of Britain. Hurricanes of No. 111 Squadron, possibly at Croydon.

added up to 34 aircraft, and KG 3 had suffered so much attrition that it took no further part in the battle for three weeks.

But the RAF had also suffered heavily, losing 28 fighters and sixteen pilots, RAF Fighter Command was now under immense strain, and it was a relief when the weather closed in again on 27 August, bringing a brief respite. There were scattered combats between Fighter Command and the *Luftwaffe*, but most were interceptions of reconnaissance aircraft. The Germans lost two Dornier 17s and a Heinkel 111 over the British Isles, the latter shot down by AA during the night raid on Coventry. The RAF lost one Spitfire through enemy action.

Luftwaffe attacks resumed on 28 August, two heavily-escorted bomber formations crossing the Kent coast soon after 09.00. Eastchurch airfield was badly damaged. During the morning's action the luckless No. 264 Squadron lost three more Defiants, with another three damaged, which brought its losses in three operational sorties to twelve aircraft and fourteen aircrew. After this, the Defiant was withdrawn from daylight operations. Later in the day, Rochford was damaged in an attack by 30 Dorniers. Fighter Command accounted for 26 enemy aircraft during the day for the loss of fifteen of its fighters, one of which was shot down by friendly fire, and on the following day, when the Germans launched 700 fighter sorties over southern England in an attempt to draw Fighter Command into battle, the score was twelve German aircraft against nine British.

The refusal of Fighter Command to be drawn into action on 29 August encouraged the Germans in the belief that they were well on the way to achieving air supremacy, but although the fighter defences were seriously weakened, they were not worn down nor compelled to withdraw on any large scale from their forward airfields in southern England. The *Luftwaffe* was still a long way from attaining its primary objective, which was to put Fighter Command out of action in the potential invasion area. Meanwhile, *Luftflotte* 3 had switched to night bombing on the night of 28/29 August, launching 340 sorties against Merseyside and targets on the south coast. These attacks brought the total number of night sorties mounted against the British Isles so far to 600, during which the *Luftwaffe* had lost only seven aircraft. It seemed a far more attractive option than the costly daylight raids.

By day, the Germans continued to attack the RAF airfields lying in a defensive semi-circle before London: Kenley, Redhill, Biggin Hill, West Malling, Detling, Manston and Gravesend to the south-east, and to the north-east Hornchurch, Rochford, Debden and North Weald. On 30 August Biggin Hill was completely wrecked, with 65 personnel killed and wounded, and on the following afternoon this target was hit again.

Despite the damage to the air defences, the oft-quoted thesis that the British fighter defences would have broken down if German air attacks on fighter installations had continued for fourteen days longer than they actually did, exaggerates the effects of the German bombing attacks and disregards the overall potential available on either side. As a last resort, Fighter Command could have withdrawn its units from airfields in the south-eastern coastal area to bases out of range of German single-engined fighters, or No. 11 Group's fighters could have been reinforced by the fighters of the other three groups. In either case, the Germans would never have achieved numerical fighter superiority over the southern coastal area because of a simple arithmetical fact: fighter production in Britain was more than double that of Germany.[43]

Hurricanes, now armed with 20mm cannon, joined Spitfires on early CIRCUS operations over France. Photo shows aircraft of No. 3 Squadron.

In fact, the crisis facing Fighter Command as September opened revolved around a shortage of aircrew, rather than a shortage of aircraft. The Command had lost about 300 pilots in the Battle of France, and was still short of 130 pilots at the beginning of August. During that month losses exceeded replacements, the deficit growing to 181. Had the battle not taken place over British soil, the situation might have become critical. From 19 August to 6 September Fighter Command suffered a total loss of 290 aircraft and 103 pilots, while the *Luftwaffe*, whose aircraft did not go down over friendly territory when hit, lost 375 aircraft and 678 aircrew.

There was no doubt that the strain, and the growing number of relatively inexperienced aircrew being committed to the battle – some with as little as 20 hours' experience on Spitfires or Hurricanes – was beginning to tell on Fighter Command during the last days of August and

Pilots of Yellow Section, No. 72 Squadron, at Gravesend in October 1941. Jim Rosser (see p.82) is on the left.

71

Spitfires of No. 72 Squadron at RAF Acklington, Northumberland, winter 1940–41. In the summer of 1941 this squadron formed part of the famous Biggin Hill Wing and took part in many CIRCUS operations.

Spitfires of No. 72 Squadron climbing over Holy Island Sands, August 1940. This squadron, with others, shattered the attack on northern England by *Luftflotte* 5 on 15 August 1940.

into September, as the deficit between British and German losses narrowed. To make matters more difficult, the Germans were tightening up their fighter escort procedure. On 1 September, when the Heinkels of KG 1 attacked the docks at Tilbury, its eighteen bombers were escorted by three *Jagdgeschwader* – roughly four fighters to every bomber. All the German aircraft returned to base, having been virtually unmolested by the RAF. The day's operations cost the RAF fifteen fighters, including four Hurricanes of No. 85 Squadron, against the *Luftwaffe*'s nine. The losses contrasted sharply with those sustained during a series of savage air battles on 31 August, when the RAF lost 24 aircraft and the *Luftwaffe* 28.

The scores were again close on 2 September, when several airfields, including Biggin Hill, Lympne, Detling, Eastchurch (three times), Hornchurch (twice) and Gravesend were heavily attacked, together with the aircraft factory at Rochester and Brooklands aerodrome, adjacent to the vital Hawker and Vickers factories. Fighter Command maintained standing patrols over its sector airfields during the day and lost 23 aircraft against the *Luftwaffe*'s 26, seven of which were Messerschmitt 110s.

On 3 September the airfield attacks continued, North Weald being very severely damaged, and in the day's fighting the RAF and *Luftwaffe* each lost sixteen aircraft. Meanwhile, across the Channel, events were taking a new and dramatic turn.

That morning, *Reichsmarschall* Göring summoned his *Luftflotten* commanders, Kesselring and Sperrle, to a conference at The Hague. The main item on the agenda was the feasibility of a 'reprisal' attack on London; the *Luftwaffe* Operations Staff had ordered *Luftflotten* 2 and 3 to prepare such an attack on 31 August, even though there still existed in order from Adolf Hitler forbidding bombing raids on the capital.

A lack of documentary evidence makes it hard to reconstruct the process leading to the decision to attack London. Hitler's desire for reprisals following RAF attacks on Berlin, themselves a consequence of the erroneous raid on London in August, certainly played its part, but this is not the

whole of the story. Bombing attacks on targets in the London area had been at the core of a plan originated by II *Fliegerkorps* before the start of the air offensive, the idea being to wear down the British fighters by bringing them to battle over the city, which was within the range of German single-engined fighters. That was one valid reason for attacking the city, although it hinged on another, far less valid one. This was the belief of *Luftwaffe* Intelligence that Fighter Command only had been 150 and 300 aircraft left to it early in September, so that the final blow could be delivered to it over London. The head of *Luftwaffe* Intelligence, *Oberst* Josef Schmidt, had arrived at this conclusion by simply deducting the wildly exaggerated figures of German combat claims from the originally

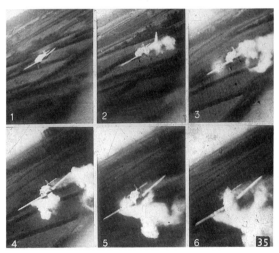

The end of a Messerschmitt 109F, shot down over France.

assumed British fighter strength, at the same time underestimating British fighter production. It was one of the most incredible misconceptions of wartime German intelligence, and yet it was supported by both Göring and Kesselring. It was not supported by *Feldmarschall* Hugo Sperrle of *Luftflotte* 3, nor by *Luftwaffe* Signals Intelligence, which had compiled far more accurate figures for Fighter Command's strength.[44]

On 4 September, Hitler declared in public that he now wanted to 'erase' British cities, and on the

London's burning: in September, the *Luftwaffe* switched the weight of its attacks to the capital, bringing respite to Fighter Command's battered airfields.

following day he gave the order to attack London and other major cities by day and night. The assault on London was to begin in the afternoon of 7 September, and was to be directed mainly against the docks. The city was to be attacked by *Luftflotte* 2 by day and *Luftflotte* 3 by night. Simultaneous attacks were to be conducted against armament factories and port installations. Thirty aircraft and armament factories were selected, and attacks on these began on 4 September, in parallel with continuing raids on Fighter Command's airfields. But from now on, London was the key target, and on that decision rested the outcome of the Battle of Britain.

While the young pilots of Dowding's Fighter Command fought and died over the Channel and the harvest-fields of southern England, RAF Bomber Command had been waging its own war against the enemy in the Channel and North Sea areas. On 13 July 1940, Bomber Command switched a major part of its efforts to the German invasion preparations in the ports, anchorages and harbours stretching from Delfzijl in the north of Holland to Bordeaux in south-west France. These ports were to be attacked frequently during the four years that were to pass before the Allied invasion of Europe, but the most intensive phase of the air offensive against them – the 'Battle of the Barges', directed against the armada of small

craft assembled by the Germans for the thrust across the Channel – lasted until the end of October 1940.

Aircraft of every Bomber Command Group, as well as Coastal Command and the Fleet Air Arm, took part in this nightly offensive, the importance of which has to a great extent been eclipsed by the massive air battle that dragged its vapour trails over the skies of southern England during that

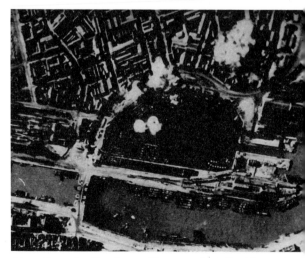

Aircraft of Bomber Command attacking a concentration of invasion barges at Cherbourg. Attacks such as this caused great destruction among the invasion craft.

long summer. But the Battle of Britain was, in the broad sense, a victory for the British bombers too; for although the Hurricanes and Spitfires of Fighter Command denied the Germans the air superiority necessary for a successful invasion, the attacks mounted on the invasion ports were so effective that, even if the *Luftwaffe* had succeeded in obtaining temporary mastery of the air over southern England, Hitler's invasion fleet would have been in no position to sail on the planned date.

This was clearly substantiated by the Germans themselves on several occasions. On 12 September, for example, only three days before Operation SEALION was scheduled to take place, HQ Navy Group West sent the following signal to Berlin:

> Interruptions caused by the enemy air forces, long-range artillery and light naval forces have, for the first time, assumed major significance. The harbours at Ostend, Dunkirk, Calais and Boulogne cannot be used as night anchorages for shipping because of the danger of English bombing and shelling. Units of the British fleet are now able to operate almost unmolested in the Channel. Owing to these difficulties further delays are expected in the assembly of the invasion fleet.

With the invasion thought to be imminent, Bomber Command launched a maximum effort offensive against the enemy-held ports. On the night of 13/14 September the bombers sank 80 barges in Ostend harbour, and the following night severe damage was inflicted on concentrations of enemy craft at Boulogne. This raid was carried out by the Fairey Battles of the newly-formed Nos 301 and 305 (Polish) Squadrons, flying their first operational mission. The Battles of Nos 12, 103, 142 and 150 Squadrons – at full strength again after the losses they had suffered in France – also carried out attacks on the enemy ports during this period. It was the Battle's swan-song as a first-line aircraft; in October it was withdrawn from operations and replaced by Wellingtons and Blenheims.

On 14 September, Hitler issued a Supreme Command Directive postponing the launch of

The Handley Page Halifax was the second four-engined heavy bomber to enter RAF service. The photograph shows a Mk I of No. 35 Squadron, which took part in Bomber Command's offensive against the French Atlantic ports.

Operation SEALION until 17 September. On the morning of the 16th, however, the German Naval War Staff once again reported that the invasion ports had been subjected to heavy bombing:

> In Antwerp considerable casualties have been inflicted on transports. Five transport steamers in the port have been heavily damaged; one barge has been sunk, two cranes destroyed, an ammunition train has blown up, and several sheds are burning.

There was worse to come. On the night of 16/17 September, only hours before the crucial German Supreme Command conference that was to decide whether or not the invasion would take place, a force of Blenheims and Battles surprised a strong concentration of enemy landing craft in the open sea off Boulogne. Several barges and two transports were sunk, with heavy loss of life. The vessels had been engaged in an invasion training exercise. German bodies, washed up on the English Channel coast later, gave rise to rumours that an invasion had actually been attempted.[45]

On that same night the RAF also struck at the whole coastal area between Antwerp and Le Havre, and this prompted the German Naval Staff to report the following day that:

Bombing-up a Wellington of No. 3 Group before an attack on Brest. Unescorted Wellingtons suffered heavily on such daylight operations.

'The RAF are still by no means defeated; on the contrary, they are showing increasing activity in their attacks on the Channel ports and in their mounting interference with the assembly movements.'

This statement was underlined by Bomber Command on the night of 17/18 September when, in full moonlight conditions, every available aircraft pounded the Channel ports and caused the biggest damage so far to the invasion fleet. Eighty-four barges were sunk or damaged at Dunkirk alone, while elsewhere a large ammunition dump was blown up, a supply depot burned out and several steamers and MTBs sunk. The next day, the Naval Staff report made gloomy reading:

The very severe bombing, together with bombardment by naval guns across the Channel, makes it necessary to disperse the naval and transport vessels already concentrated on the Channel and to top further movement of shipping to the invasion ports. Otherwise, with energetic enemy action such casualties will occur in the

course of time that the execution of the operation on the scale previously envisaged will in any case be problematic.

On 19 September, four days after the great air battle over London and southern England that would henceforth be marked as Battle of Britain Day, and which cost the *Luftwaffe* 56 aircraft, Hitler ordered the invasion fleet assembled in the Channel ports to be dispersed so that 'the loss of shipping space caused by enemy air attacks may be reduced to a minimum.' Operation SEALION had been postponed indefinitely, and Hitler's preoccupation now was with the projected attack on the Soviet Union.

Between 15 July and 21 September, according to German naval sources, the British air offensive sank or damaged 21 transports and 214 barges in the Channel ports, about twelve per cent of the total invasion fleet. These figures should be treated with some reservation, as even at this stage of the war the Germans were in the habit of playing down their actual losses in confidential reports to the Supreme Command. The actual loss, in terms of both men and material, was probably higher, but even the figure of twelve per cent is sufficient testimony that the bombing effort during those crucial weeks was far from wasted.

Nevertheless, the effectiveness of the effort against the Channel ports was grossly underestimated by the War Cabinet. Churchill in particular expressed disappointment at the results of the attacks, as revealed by air reconnaissance, in a minute to the Air Minister, Sir Archibald Sinclair, on 23 September:

> What struck me about these (reconnaissance) photographs was the apparent inability of the bombers to hit very large masses of barges. I should have thought that sticks of explosive bombs thrown along these oblongs would have wrought havoc, and it is very disappointing to see that they all remained intact and in order, with just a few apparently damaged at the entrance.[46]

Churchill did not take into account the fact that many of the barges, although apparently intact, had been made unseaworthy by damage that the photographs did not show. The bomber crews who were over the ports night after night knew that they were sinking the barges faster than anyone had thought possible. The only question in their minds was whether they were sinking them fast enough to thwart the invasion if Fighter Command were annihilated.

The ports were easy to find, but they were not an easy target. Light flak was plentiful and losses were heavy. The anti-aircraft defences were particularly strong around Antwerp, and it was while attacking this target on the night of 15/16 September 1940, that Sergeant John Hannah, one of the crew of a Hampden of No. 83 Squadron, carried out an act of great courage that won him the Victoria Cross. The citation tells the story.

> On the night of 15 September 1940, Sergeant Hannah was the wireless operator/air gunner in an aircraft engaged in a successful attack on an enemy

barge concentration at Antwerp. It was then subjected to intense anti-aircraft fire and received a direct hit from a projectile of an explosive and incendiary nature, which apparently burst inside the bomb compartment. A fire started which quickly enveloped the wireless operator's and rear gunner's cockpits, and as both the port and starboard petrol tanks had been pierced there was a grave risk of fire spreading. Sergeant Hannah forced his way through to obtain two extinguishers and discovered that the rear gunner had had to leave the aircraft. He could have acted likewise, through the bottom escape hatch or forward through the navigator's hatch, but remained and fought the fire for ten minutes with the extinguishers, beating the flames with his log book when these were empty.

During this time thousands of rounds of ammunition exploded in all directions and he was almost blinded by the intense heat and fumes, but had the presence of mind to obtain relief by turning on his oxygen supply. Air admitted through the large holes caused by the projectile made the bomb compartment an inferno and all the aluminium sheet metal on the floor of this airman's cockpit was melted away, leaving only the cross bearers. Working under these conditions, which caused burns to his face and eyes, Sergeant Hannah succeeded in extinguishing the fire. He then crawled forward, ascertained that the navigator had left the aircraft, and passed the latter's log and maps to the pilot.

This airman displayed courage, coolness and devotion to duty of the highest order and by his action in remaining and successfully extinguishing the fire under conditions of the greatest danger and difficulty, enabled the pilot to bring the aircraft to its base.[47]

The Royal Air Force was not alone in its campaign against the German invasion forces that were assembled mainly in the ports of Dunkirk, Ostend, Calais and Boulogne. Whenever possible, even though operating conditions in the Channel had become very difficult because of air attack, the Royal Navy took the opportunity to strike at shipping movements off the enemy coast. On 8 September 1940, for example, three motor torpedo boats, MTB 14, MTB 15 and MTB 17, set out from Dover to attack a German convoy of about 30 small vessels approaching Ostend. Two of the boats, MTBs 15 and 17, entered Ostend harbour under cover of darkness and an RAF aid raid and launched their torpedoes, hitting two vessels. Exactly what they hit was never established, but it was the first successful MTB torpedo attack of the war.

On the night of 10/11 September, a striking force comprising the destroyers *Malcolm*, *Veteran* and *Wild Swan* set out to patrol the Channel off Ostend, which was again under air attack, when radar contact was made with an enemy convoy. Soon afterwards, the destroyers made visual contact with the enemy, aided by the light of flares dropped by the RAF, and opened fire, sinking an escort vessel, two trawlers that were towing barges, and a large barge.

Offensive sweeps of this kind were a regular feature during September 1940, when the threat of invasion was at its height, the naval forces usually operating from Harwich or Portsmouth; the Dover destroyer force had been dispersed, having suffered substantial damage through air attack. At the same time, aircraft of the Fleet Air Arm, operating from bases in south-east England, joined the RAF in maintaining pressure on the enemy invasion ports.

The biggest guns the Navy could bring to bear on the enemy coast were mounted in two warships of World War One vintage, the battleship *Revenge* and the monitor *Erebus*. Both mounted 15-inch guns, the *Erebus* being fitted with a twin turret bearing her main armament and also with four twin 4-inch and two single 3-inch AA guns. She carried a crew of 300. On

ML347 at Portsmouth, February 1942. An experimental magnetic minesweeping skip is seen on the right of the photograph.

20 September she set out from Sheerness to bombard the German gun battery at Cap Gris Nez, but the sortie had to be abandoned because of bad weather. On 30 September, however, she fired seventeen rounds into a concentration of invasion craft in the Calais docks area, the fire being directed by a Fairey Swordfish spotter aircraft. On the following day, the German battery at Wissant fired precisely the same number of rounds at Dover by way of retaliation.

On 10 October it was the turn of HMS *Revenge*, the old battleship – armed with eight 15-inch guns – sailing from Plymouth with a screen of 5th Flotilla destroyers: the *Jackal, Kipling, Jupiter, Jaguar, Kashmir* and *Kelvin*. The cruisers *Newcastle* and *Emerald* were also at sea, protecting the western flank, while a flotilla of six MTBs sailed from Portland to provide a screen against S-boats. *Revenge*'s target was Cherbourg, and for eighteen minutes, beginning at 03.33 on 11 October she laid a barrage of 120 15-inch shells across the crowded harbour, to which was added a total of 801 4.7-inch shells from the seven escorting destroyers. The resulting conflagration could be seen 40 miles out to sea. The British force reached Spithead at 08.00 without damage, despite being shelled for the best part of ten miles by a German heavy battery.

On 16 October HMS *Erebus*, escorted by the detroyer *Garth* and *Walpole*, again bombarded the French coast in the vicinity of Calais with the aid of spotter aircraft. Forty-five salvoes were fired, beginning at 01.00, before the British force withdrew. Neither the *Erebus* nor the *Revenge* made any further sorties of this kind, even though the British heavy gun defences on the Channel coast in October were still pitifully weak. The pre-war heavy gun strength on the Straits of Dover, comprising two 9.2-inch and six 6-inch guns, had been reinforced during the summer by one 14-inch, two 6-inch and two 4-inch guns, all Naval weapons, together with a pair of 9.2-inch guns on railway mountings; and in October these were further reinforced by two 13.5-inch guns from the old depot ship *Iron Duke*, also on railway mountings, and a battery of four

5.5-inch guns from HMS *Hood*. Further heavy gun batteries, at Fan Bay, South Foreland and Wanstone, would not become operational until a much later date, by which time the invasion threat had passed.

While the British strove to disrupt enemy invasion plans, German destroyers were extremely active in the Channel area during September and October 1940, laying minefields to protect the flanks of their projected cross-Channel invasion routes and also making hit-and-run sorties against British shipping. One particularly successful sortie was undertaken on the night of 11/12 October by the German 5th Flotilla from Cherbourg, comprising the destroyers *Greif, Kondor, Falke, Seeadler* and *Wolf*. They sank the armed trawlers *Listrac* and *Warwick Deeping* with gunfire and torpedoes, and shortly afterwards destroyed the Free French submarine chasers CH6 and CH7, manned by mixed French and Polish crews. The German ships withdrew safely; although they were engaged by the British destroyers *Jackal, Jaguar, Jupiter, Kelvin* and *Kipling*, the latter achieved nothing more spectacular than several near misses. Another inconclusive action was fought between British destroyers of the 5th Flotilla, supported by the light cruisers *Newcastle* and *Emerald*, and enemy destroyers off Brest on 17 October, with no damage suffered by either side. The British warships came under air attack during the operation, the most serious threat coming from a flight of very determined RAF Blenheims whose crews had clearly not been trained in warship recognition!

November 1940 saw a resurgence of air attacks on British shipping by Junkers Ju 87 *Stukas*, which had been standing by at their airfields in the Pas de Calais to lend tactical support to Operation SEALION, now postponed. Their area of operations was the Thames estuary, where British convoys were assembling, and between 1 and 11 November they sank one merchant vessel and damaged six more. On 14 November they attacked targets in the Dover area, destroying a drifter and damaging three more vessels, but these missions marked the *Stuka*'s swansong over the British Isles.

There was a further destroyer action on 27/28 November 1940, when the British 5th Destroyer Flotilla intercepted an enemy flotilla from Brest. In the ensuing engagement the destroyer HMS *Javelin* was hit by two torpedoes, which blew off her bows and stern and detonated the ammunition in her magazine, destroying her superstructure as well as killing three officers and 43 ratings. Amazingly, she remained afloat and was towed into harbour, to spend thirteen months in dock being virtually rebuilt. She eventually returned to operations and went on to survive the war.

Notwithstanding actions such as these, it was enemy mines that accounted for the highest proportion of British shipping losses in the closing months of 1940. Of the 42 Royal Navy vessels lost in the Channel area between 1 September 1940 and the end of the year, 28 were sunk by mines.

The threat of invasion had receded, and Hitler's eyes, by the end of 1940, were turned towards the east. But the question must be asked whether Operation SEALION might have succeeded, had it gone ahead. All the accumulated evidence suggests that it would not. The matter is summed up admirably by the official Royal Navy historian.

We who lived through those anxious days may reasonably regret that the expedition never sailed; for, had it done so, it is virtually certain that it would have resulted in a British victory comparable for its decisiveness to Barfleur or Quiberon Bay; and it can hardly be doubted that such a victory would have altered the entire course of the war. It is indeed plain today that, of all the factors which contributed to the failure of Hitler's grandiose invasion plans, none was greater than the lack of adequate instruments of sea power and of a proper understanding of their use on the German side. Britain, on the other hand, not only possessed the necessary ships and craft, but they were manned by devoted crews who were imbued with a traditional and burning desire to come to grips with the enemy invasion fleet. Finally, we may remark how the events of the summer of 1940 emphasised once again what many other would-be conquerors of Britain had learnt in turn – namely, that an overseas expedition cannot be launched with any prospect of success without first defeating the other side's maritime forces, and so gaining control of the waters across which the expedition has to pass.[48]

In conflict, with a centuries-old maritime power, there is little doubt that Hitler, had he launched his invasion, would have learnt, too late, the landsman's lesson.

CHAPTER FIVE

Cross-Channel Sparring, 1941

The Battle of Britain was over: Operation SEALION had been postponed indefinitely. The *Luftwaffe*'s bombers now came at night, striking at Britain's cities in the cold, interminable darkness of the war's second winter.

It was time for RAF Fighter Command to turn from defence to offence. On 20 December 1940, two Spitfires of No. 66 Squadron, flown by Flight Lieutenant G.P. Christie and Pilot Officer C.A.W. Brodie, took off from Biggin Hill and set course across the Channel under a low cloud base. Crossing the enemy coast at Dieppe, they swept down on Le Touquet airfield and shot up several installations. There was no opposition from either flak or fighters and both Spitfires returned safely to base.

During the next few days, Spitfires and Hurricanes from other squadrons, operating in twos and threes, made short dashes into enemy territory. Their pilots reported that the *Luftwaffe* was absent from the sky. Encouraged, Fighter Command decided to try something bigger. On 9 January 1941, in brilliant sunshine and perfect visibility, five fighter squadrons penetrated thirty miles into France. There was no sign of movement on the snow-covered airfields they flew over; not a single Messerschmitt took to the air to intercept them.

The following day, the RAF decied to stir up a hornets' nest. That morning, six Blenheims of No. 114 Squadron, escorted by six squadrons of Hurricanes and Spitfires, attacked ammunition and stores dumps in the Foret de Guines. This time, the *Luftwaffe* took the bait, but only to a limited extent. There was some skirmishing, in the course of which one Hurricane was shot down. Two battle-damaged Spitfires crash-landed on return to base, one of the pilots being killed. It was an inauspicious end to the RAF's first combined daylight bombing raid and fighter sweep, known as CIRCUS No. 1.

Nevertheless, offensive sweeps were carried out whenever the weather permitted during the early weeks of 1941, and *Luftwaffe* opposition gradually increased. It was clear that the Germans, adopting the policy of the RAF before the Battle of Britain, were reluctant to commit their fighter defences in strength. There was also another reason: in January 1941, several first-line *Luftwaffe* units on the Channel coast had begun to re-equip with an improved model of the Messerschmitt, the 109F-1, but early in February three 109Fs were lost when the complete tail assembly broke away, and the remainder had to be withdrawn for structural modifications.

By March 1941, fighter sweeps over the continent were becoming organized affairs, with the Spitfire and Hurricane squadrons operating in Wing strength. A Fighter Command Wing consisted of three squadrons, each of twelve aircraft. There were Spitfire Wings at Biggin Hill, Hornchurch and Tangmere, mixed Spitfire and Hurricane Wings at Duxford, Middle Wallop and Wittering, and Hurricane Wings at Kenley, Northolt and North Weald.

The Biggin Hill Wing, in the spring and summer of 1941, comprised Nos 72, 92 and 609 Squadrons, all of which had achieved impressive records in the Battle of Britain. It was led by Wing Commander A.G. Malan, a redoubtable South African with eighteen confirmed victories to his credit, a DSO and two DFCs. Known to all and sundry as 'Sailor' because of his pre-war service in the Merchant Navy, he was one of the RAF's foremost air combat tacticians, and his famous *Ten Rules of Air Fighting* were displayed on crew-room walls throughout Fighter Command.

Malan was not a talkative man. His business was killing the enemy, and the basic skills of this trade were hammered home hard to those who found themselves under his leadership. During the Battle of Britain, when he first rose to fame, the popular Press did its best to surround him with an aura of glamour. War reporters found him uncommunicative, and on the few occasions when he did open up his forthright manner often shocked them. Once, he was asked how he went about shooting down a German bomber.

> I try not to, now, I think it's a bad thing. If you shoot them down they don't get back, and no-one over there knows what's happening. So I think the right thing to do is let them get back. With a dead rear gunner; a dead navigator, and the pilot coughing up his lungs as he lands. If you do that, it has a better effect on their morale. Of course, if you just mean to shoot them down – well, what I generally do is knock out both engines.'[49]

The pilots of the Biggin Hill Wing were proud to belong to what was generally recognized as an élite formation. One of them was Sergeant (later Flight Lieutenant) Jim Rosser of No. 72 Squadron, who flew his first sweeps in the spring of 1941 and whose experiences were typical of many young pilots.

> We would cross the Channel in sections, line astern, climbing all the time. We always climbed into the sun, which was absolute hell; your eyes felt as though they were burning down into your head and within a few minutes you were saturated in sweat. It might have been just a coincidence, but on every sweep I flew we always seemed to head for Lille, which we hated. It was our deepest penetration at that time, and there was flak all the way.
>
> I will never forget my first operation. Seventy-two Squadron was flying top cover; I was 'Yellow Two', in other words the number two aircraft in Yellow Section, and quite honestly I hadn't a clue what was going on. We flew a sort of semi-circle over France,

still in sections line astern, and then came out again. I never saw a single enemy aircraft; but we must have been attacked, because when we got home three of our Spits were missing.[50]

Number 72 Squadron's commanding officer was an Australian, Desmond Sheen, who had begun his operational career with the Squadron before the war. In April 1940 he had been posted to No. 212 Squadron and during the next few months had flown photo-reconnaissance sorties all over Europe in specially-modified Spitfires, returning to No. 72 Squadron just in time to take part in the Battle of Britain. He was to lead the squadron on sweeps over occupied Europe for eight months, from March to November 1941.

Sheen's opposite number with No. 92 Squadron was Squadron Leader Jamie Rankin, a Scot from Portobello, Edinburgh, who had originally joined the Fleet Air Arm but later transferred to the RAF. When he was appointed to command No. 92 Squadron in March 1941 it was the top-scoring unit in Fighter Command, and its score increased steadily under Rankin's leadership. Rankin himself opened his score with No. 92 by destroying a Heinkel He 59 floatplane and damaging an Me 109 on 11 April. This was followed by another confirmed 109 on the 24th, and in June – a month of hectic air fighting over France – he shot down seven more 109s and claimed another probably destroyed.

It was Jamie Rankin who provided Jim Rosser with the latter's first Me 109. Rosser was now commissioned, with the rank of pilot officer.

> We didn't always fly operationally with our own squadron. On this occasion Jamie Rankin was leading the Wing and I was flying as his number two, which was a considerable privilege. The *Luftwaffe* was up in strength and there was an almighty free-for-all during which the Wing got split up. I clung to Jamie's tail like grim death, and as we were heading for the Channel he suddenly called up over the R/T and said: 'There's a Hun at two o'clock below – have a go!' I looked down ahead and to the right and there, sure enough, was a 109, flying along quite sedately a few thousand feet lower down. I dived after him, levelled out astern

and opened fire. He began to smoke almost at once and fell away in a kind of sideslip. A moment later, flames streamed from him.[51]

Leadership of this kind emerged in more than one way during that spring and summer of 1941.

Once, – Jim Rosser remembers – we were on our way back home after a sweep, heading for Manston as usual to refuel, when the weather clamped down. I knew Manston well by this time, and I just managed to scrape in, together with four or five other pilots. Many of the others, however, were relatively new boys and they were in trouble. Then one of our 72 Squadron flight commanders, Ken Campbell, came up over the radio and told everybody to get into a circle and stay put above the murk. One by one he guided them down, wingtip to wingtip, until they were safely on the ground. When he eventually landed, I don't think he had enough fuel left to taxi in. More than one pilot owed his life to Ken that day.[52]

By May 1941, 56 squadrons of fighters and fighter-bombers were regularly taking part in offensive sweeps over Europe. Of these, 29 Squadron still flew Hurricanes, but the earlier Mk Is had now been almost completely replaced by improved Mk IIAs and IIBs. Before the end of the year, however, the Hurricanes were to assume the role of fighter-bomber, the fighter sweeps being undertaken exclusively by Spitfires. In June, the Spitfire II began to give way to the Mk V, which was to become the most numerous of all Spitfire variants. The majority were armed with two 20 mm cannon and four machine-guns, affording a greater chance of success against armour plating. However, the Spitfire V was essentially a compromise aircraft, rushed into service to meet an urgent Air Staff requirement for a fighter with a performance superior to the latest model of Messerschmitt. The début of the Spitfire V came just in time, for in May 1941 the *Luftwaffe* fighter units on the Channel coast had begun to receive the Messerschmitt 109F, its technical problems now resolved. On 11 May, a group of bomb-carrying Me 109Fs attacked Lympne and Hawkinge, and one of them was shot down by a Spitfire of No. 91 Squadron. The Spitfire V failed

to provide the overall superiority Fighter Command needed so badly; at higher altitude, where many air combats took place, it was found to be inferior to the Me 109F on most counts, and several squadrons equipped with it took a severe mauling during that summer.

Several notable RAF pilots flew their last sorties in a Spitfire V. One of them was the near-legendary Douglas Bader, who flew with artificial legs as the result of a pre-war flying accident. In 1941 Bader commanded the Tangmere Wing, which comprised Nos 145, 610 and 616 Squadrons, all flying Spitfires, and by the end of July his personal score stood at 22 enemy aircraft destroyed. Bader had an aversion to cannon armament, believing that it encouraged pilots to open fire at too great a range, so his personal aircraft was a Spitfire VA wth an armament of eight machine-guns.

Handling the large fighter formations which were being pushed across the Channel that summer called for a high degree of skill on the part of the controllers, whose vital role is all too often ignored, or rather eclipsed, by headier tales of air combat. And by July 1941 CIRCUS operations were very large affairs, with as many as eighteen squadrons of fighters covering a small force of bombers. Getting six Wings of Spitfires airborne, to the rendezvous at the right time and place, and shepherding them into and out of enemy territory, was something of a nightmare for everyone concerned, and it began on the ground. Three squadrons of Spitfires – 36 aircraft – might make an impressive sight as they taxied round the perimeter of an airfield, but with propellers revolving dangerously close to wingtips and tails it was all too easy to make a mistake. A late starter would add to the problems as its pilot edged around the outside of the queue, trying to catch up with the rest of his squadron.

Making rendezvous with the bombers, usually over Manston, was another critical factor. A Spitfire's tanks held only 85 gallons of petrol, and every minute spent in waiting for the Blenheims to turn up reduced a pilot's chances of getting home safely if he found himself in trouble over

France. And over enemy territory the *Luftwaffe* always seemed to have the advantage. No matter how high the Spitfires climbed, the 109s usually managed to climb higher, ready to pounce on the 'tail-end Charlies' of the fighter formations and pick them off. There was no dog-fighting in the original sense of the word; the Messerschmitts fought on the climb and dive, avoiding turning combat with the more manoeuvrable Spitfires wherever possible, and the difference between life and death was measured in no more than seconds.

One of the biggest fighter sweeps of 1941, CIRCUS 62, was mounted on 7 August, when eighteen squadrons of Spitfires and two of Hurricanes accompanied six Blenheim bombers in an attack on a power station at Lille. The whole force made rendezvous over Manston, with the North Weald Wing, comprising the Hurricanes of No. 71 Squadron and the Spitfires of Nos 111 and 222 Squadrons providing close escort for the bombers. Behind and above, as immediate top cover, came the three Spitfire squadrons of the Kenley Wing: Nos 452 (Australia), 485 (New Zealand), and 602. High above this 'beehive' of nearly 80 fighters and bombers came the target support Wings, flying at 27,000 feet. There was the Biggin Hill Wing, with Nos 72, 92 and 609 Squadrons; the Hornchurch Wing, with Nos 403 (Canadian), 603 and 611 Squadrons; and Douglas Bader's Tangmere Wing, with Nos 41, 610 and 616 Squadrons. The target support force's task was to assure air superiority over and around Lille while the attack was in progress.

On this occasion, however, the *Luftwaffe* stubbornly refused to be drawn into battle in large numbers. Six weeks earlier, the Germans had invaded the Soviet Union, and many fighter groups had been transferred from the Channel area to the Eastern Front. Those that remained, seriously outnumbered in the face of Fighter Command's growing strength, had been ordered to conserve their resources. The 109s stayed well above the Spitfire formations, shadowing them. From time to time, small numbers of Messer-

schmitts broke away and darted down to fire on a straggler, always disengaging when the rest of the Spitfires turned on them. The 109s shot down one of No 41 Squadron's flight commanders.

The bombers, meanwhile, had found Lille obscured by cloud, so had turned back towards the Channel to attack a concentration of barges at Gravelines. A fierce air battle was already in progress over the coast, where two Polish squadrons of the Northolt Wing – Nos 306 and 308 – had been waiting to cover the Blenheims during the first phase of their withdrawal. Number 308 Squadron was suddenly bounced by about eighteen Messerschmitts, and lost two Spitfires. The Blenheims made their escape, but the rear support Wing, comprising Nos 19, 257 and 401 Squadrons, was attacked and lost two Spitfires and a Hurricane. The RAF had therefore lost six aircraft, a result which, set against a claim of three Me 109s destroyed, could hardly be considered favourable, in view of the far smaller number of enemy aircraft involved.

Another large operation, CIRCUS 63, was mounted two days later, on Saturday 9 August. This time, the Blenheims' objective was a supply dump in the Bethune area. Once again, Bader's Tangmere Wing formed part of the target support force, but things went wrong right from the start when No. 41 Squadron failed to rendezvous on time. The remainder, unable to wait, carried on across the Channel. For a while, all was peaceful; then, just a few miles short of the target, the 109s hit them hard. For the next few minutes, Bader's pilots were hard put to hold their own, the Wing becoming badly dislocated as the Messerschmitts pressed home determined attacks. Bader misjudged an attack on a 109 and found himself isolated. Six enemy fighters closed in on him and, by superb flying, he destroyed two. The end came soon afterwards, when a third 109 collided with him and severed his Spitfire's fuselage just behind the cockpit. Bader managed to struggle clear of the plunging aircraft, leaving one of his artificial legs still trapped in the cockpit. His parachute opened, and he floated down to a painful landing and captivity.

On 12 August, three days after Bader went down, the medium bombers of the RAF's No. 2 Group made their deepest daylight penetration into enemy territory so far when 54 Blenheims bombed two power stations near Cologne. They were escorted by Westland Whirlwind fighters of No. 263 Squadron, the only fighter aircraft with sufficient range to carry out this task. The Whirlwind was highly manoeuvrable, faster than a Spitfire at low altitude, and its armament of four closely-grouped nose cannon made it a match for any *Luftwaffe* fighter of the day. As it was, the Whirlwind experienced a spate of problems with its twin Rolls-Royce Peregrine engines, and only two squadrons were equipped with the type. Eventually, it was used in the fighter-bomber role with considerable success.

As August gave way to September, some senior Air Staff members began to have serious doubts about the value of CIRCUS operations. Fighter Command losses were climbing steadily, and the results achieved hardly seemed to compensate for them. The only real justification for continuing the sweeps, apparently, was to ensure that Fighter Command remained in a state of combat readiness.

The morale of Fighter Command, however, was soon to suffer a serious blow. On 21 September 1941, Polish pilots of No. 315 Squadron, on their way home after CIRCUS 101, reported being attacked by 'an unknown enemy aircraft with a radial engine'. A few days later, Jim Rosser of No. 72 Squadron was on a sweep over Boulogne, flying No. 2 to Ken Campbell, when he too sighted one of the mysterious radial-engined machines and went down after it, opening fire at extreme range. The enemy aircraft dived into the Boulogne flak barrage and Campbell called Rosser back, but not before the latter had secured some good gun-camera shots.

All sorts of wild rumours circulated in Fighter Command, the favourite among them being that the strange aircraft were ex-French Curtiss Hawk 75As, captured by the Germans and pressed into service. Then RAF Intelligence examined all the data and came up with the answer. The Focke-Wulf 190 had arrived in France.

Focke-Wulf 190s of JG 26 armed with SC 50 bombs. These aircraft undertook many hit-and-run missions against south coast targets.

The first *Luftwaffe* unit to receive Focke-Wulf 190s on the Channel coast was *Jagdgeschwader* 26, closely followed by JG 2, and by October 1941 the RAF was encountering the type in growing numbers. Within weeks, the Fw 190 had established a definite measure of air superiority for the Germans. It completely outclassed the Spitfire VB at all altitudes, and Fighter Command losses rose steadily that autumn. Not until the advent of the Spitfire IX – resulting from the marriage of a Merlin 61 engine to a Mk V airframe – was the balance restored, but the first Mk IXs did not enter service until June 1942, with No. 64 Squadron.

As far as CIRCUS operations were concerned, the crunch came on 8 November 1941, when the Blenheims of No. 2 Group and their escorting fighters suffered unusually heavy losses. The whole 'show' went wrong from the start, with poor visibility making it difficult for the bombers and fighters to rendezvous as planned. Combined with a general lack of co-ordination, this meant that the attacking forces entered enemy territory piecemeal, and the Focke-Wulfs and Messerschmitts were waiting for them. The Intelligence Summary of No. 118 (Spitfire) Squadron gives a typical account.

It was decided in the afternoon to carry out a most ill-conceived scheme, designated RODEO 5, in which the Middle Wallop Wing rendezvoused with the Whirlwinds of 263 Squadron over Warmwell and carried out a sweep of the Channel Islands area. The whole sortie seems to have been one long muddle. The Whirlwinds led the Spits much too far south and then returned right over the flak area. 501 Squadron were sent out to deal with a few Huns that put in an appearance when we were on the way back. 118 went back to help, but 501 were not located. The net result was at least three planes damaged by flak and enemy aircraft, and one shot down, and all we could claim was one enemy aircraft damaged.[53]

It was the end. Winston Churchill himself decreed that there should be no more large-scale sweeps over the continent in 1941; it was now the duty of Fighter Command to gather its strength for the following spring.

While Fighter Command and the medium bombers of No. 2 Group waged an ineffectual war over France and the Low Countries, Bomber Command's heavy bombers had begun to fight a difficult and often costly battle against the German Navy and its port facilities on the French Atlantic coast. In the early months of 1941, one of the biggest threats to the Atlantic convoy routes was the battleship *Bismarck*, which the enemy intended to send into the Atlantic as the central unit of a formidable battle-group that also included the battle-cruisers *Scharnhorst*, *Gneisenau* and *Prinz Eugen*. Of the other major enemy surface units, one, the *Graf Spee*, had been effectively dealt with in December 1939, and another, the *Lützow*, was bottled up in Norwegian waters.

The first major German warships to leave their home ports after the lull in surface ship activity that followed the Norwegian campaign were the battleship *Scheer* and the heavy cruiser *Hipper*. The former sailed at the end of October 1940 and the latter in early December, both reaching the Atlantic by way of the Denmark Strait between Iceland and Greenland. In November the *Scheer* sank five merchantmen in the homebound convoy HX 84, and the toll would undoubtedly have been greater had it not been for the sacrifice

of the armed merchant cruiser *Jervis Bay* (Captain E.S.F. Fegen), which engaged the battleship and gave the convoy time to scatter. Evading strong forces despatched by the Admiralty, the *Scheer* headed for the South Atlantic, and by the end of the year was operating on the latitude of Cape Town.

Meanwhile, on 24 December 1940, the *Hipper* had made contact with the large troop convoy WS 5A far to the west of Cape Finisterre, and attacked at first light on Christmas Day. The convoy, however, was strongly escorted, and the German warship was driven off without having caused any damage. She reached the French Atlantic port of Brest on 27 December, emerging early in 1941 to destroy seven out of nineteen ships of a Sierra Leone convoy before returning to harbour. In March 1941 she was joined at Brest by the *Scharnhorst* and *Gneisenau*, which had broken out into the Atlantic in January and sunk 22 ships in the course of a two-month cruise.

Six days after their arrival, RAF photographic reconnaissance detected the presence of the new arrivals at Brest – the *Hipper* having meanwhile

Halifaxes attacking the *Scharnhorst* and *Gneisenau*. The warships are sheltered by the beginnings of a smokescreen.

departed on another foray into the South Atlantic – and, on Winston Churchill's directive, the two cruisers became a prime target for Bomber Command.

The offensive against the Channel ports and the warships saw the first operational missions by the RAF's new heavy bombers. The first of these was the Short Stirling, which had entered service with No. 7 Squadron at RAF Leeming, in Yorkshire, in August 1940. The rest of the year was spent in crew conversion, and it was not until January 1941 that the squadron moved to Oakington in readiness for its first operational sortie. This was flown on the night of 10/11 February, when three aircraft attacked the oil storage depot at Rotterdam.

The second of the new four-engined heavy bombers, the Handley Page Halifax, went into service with No. 35 Squadron at Leeming in November 1940, and moved to its operational base at Linton-on-Ouse. The first Halifax operation was carried out on 10/11 March, when six aircraft were despatched to attack Le Havre dockyard; four bombed the primary, one bombed Dieppe and one aborted. One of the Halifaxes was shot down by an RAF night-fighter over Surrey while returning to base; the pilot, Squadron Leader Gilchrist, and another crew member survived.

The third new heavy bomber to enter service, the Avro Manchester, was a bitter disappointment for Bomber Command. It was designed to the same specification as the Halifax, but used two Rolls-Royce Vulture engines instead of four Merlins, with unfortunate results. Serious trouble with the Vultures dogged the bomber throughout its operational career, which began on 24/25 February 1941 when six aircraft of No. 207 Squadron, RAF Waddington, attacked warships in Brest harbour. One aircraft crashed on the return flight through engine failure. The Vulture engines were unreliable; often, they would carry the aircraft on long-distance raids without the slightest hint of trouble, only to burst into flames for no apparent reason towards the end of the sortie. To solve the problem, Avro experimented

with a converted Manchester, known as the Mk III, fitted with four Merlins. This aircraft made its first flight on 9 January 1941, and a few weeks later it received a new name: the Lancaster.

Bomber Command's offensive against the *Scharnhorst* and *Gneisenau* began on the night of 30/31 March 1941, when 109 aircraft were despatched to attack Brest harbour without result. On this occasion, all the attacking aircraft returned safely. There was a further abortive attack on 4/5 April by 54 aircraft; their bombs caused considerable damage to the town and one fell in the dry dock alongside the *Gneisenau*, whose captain thought it advisable to move the ship to the outer harbour, where she would be safer while the bomb was defused. She was located there by a photographic reconnaissance Spitfire, and a Coastal Command strike was arranged. The sortie was flown at dawn on 6 April by six Bristol Beauforts of No. 22 Squadron, but only one succeeded in locating the target in bad visibility. Its pilot, Flying Officer Kenneth Campbell, made his torpedo run at mast height through intense flak put up by more than 250 guns around the anchorage, as well as by three flak ships and the *Gneisenau*'s main armament. The Beaufort was shot down with the loss of all its crew, but not before Campbell had released his torpedo at a range of 500 yards. The torpedo exploded on the *Gneisenau*'s stern below the waterline, putting the cruiser out of action for months. For his gallant action, Campbell was posthumously awarded the Victoria Cross. The other members of his crew were Sergeants J.P. Scott, W. Mullis and R.W. Hillman.

The *Gneisenau* was further damaged by Bomber Command on the night of 10/11 April 1941, when she was hit by four bombs; 50 Germans were killed and 90 injured in the attack. Bomb damage to the harbour facilities also delayed the refitting of her companion, the *Scharnhorst*, so the German Naval High Command decided to send out the *Bismarck* from the Baltic port of Gdynia into the North Atlantic accompanied by only one escort, the *Prinz Eugen*. It was a decision that was to have fatal consequences; on 27 May, the battleship was trapped and sunk by units of the British Home Fleet, although not before she had inflicted terrible damage on her pursuers. The *Prinz Eugen*, detached earlier, reached the sanctuary of Brest.

With the arrival of the heavy cruiser conditions at Brest became dangerously overcrowded, and it was decided to redeploy the *Scharnhorst* to La Pallice, a port to the south of her original location, where her refitting was completed. While undergoing sea trials to prove some new equipment she was detected by air reconnaissance, and a major daylight attack was mounted against both Brest and La Pallice. The plan called for Brest to be attacked by 79 unescorted Wellingtons of Nos 1 and 3 Groups, while diversionary sorties were to be flown by eighteen Handley Page Hampdens, escorted by three Squadrons of Spitfires fitted with long-range tanks, and by three Boeing Fortress Is (which had recently entered service with No. 90 Squadron), the latter bombing from 30,000 feet. As a further diversion, Cherbourg docks were to be attacked by 36 Blenheims of No. 2 Group, with a strong Spitfire escort. Meanwhile, the *Scharnhorst* at La Pallice was to be attacked by fifteen Halifaxes of Nos 35 and 76 Squadrons.

The Brest attack was a disaster. The raid was broken up by fierce and prolonged fighter opposition; ten Wellingtons and two Hampdens were shot down by fighters or flak, and the warships in the harbour were undamaged. The Halifaxes attacking La Pallice also met strong fighter opposition and some flak; five were shot down and all the others damaged. However, five hits were registered on the *Scharnhorst*, and although three heavy bombs that penetrated her upper deck failed to explode, the holes they made admitted 3,000 tons of water. Two smaller bombs exploded in the battery deck but caused only negligible damage, and there were no casualties. That night the *Scharnhorst* returned to Brest, making 27 knots despite the volume of water inside her, to take advantage of that port's better repair facilities and stronger flak defences. Although the Halifax crews had lost a third of their number, they had dealt the warship a severe

blow; it would be four more months before she was fully seaworthy again.

This was the last major attack made on the warships until the night of 3/4 September 1941, when 140 bombers were despatched. Most were recalled because of bad weather, but 53 continued to the target and bombed the estimated position of the warships through a smoke-screen, with no result. No aircraft were lost, but three crashed on return to England.

On the night of 7/8 December 1941, Stirlings of Nos 7 and 15 Squadrons made the first of a series of attacks on the warships at Brest using an early type of blind-bombing device known as TRINITY. This was in effect a prototype of OBOE, a radio aid to bombing in which two ground stations transmitted pulses to an aircraft, which then received and re-transmitted them. By measuring the time taken for each pulse to go out and return, the distance of the aircraft from the ground stations could be accurately measured.

Such devices, leading to far greater precision bombing, were to transform Bomber Command's offensive against Germany in the months to come. But they came too late to be of assistance in the attacks on the Atlantic ports; and the best the British could hope for, as 1941 drew to a close, was that the enemy warships would remain bottled up there until they could be eliminated. As events were soon to prove, it was a forlorn hope.

During most of 1941, in parallel with Bomber Command's offensive against the French Atlantic ports, RAF Coastal Command mounted constant attacks on enemy shipping in the North Sea and off the Norwegian coast. As the Command's long-range Lockheed Hudsons were increasingly needed for maritime reconnaissance and anti-submarine warfare, this task devolved mainly on the Handley Page Hampden, which equipped a number of Coastal Command squadrons. Losses were high and results mediocre; in the last quarter of 1941, for example, the Command sank fifteen enemy ships and lost 46 aircraft.

From April 1941, the Admiralty and the RAF launched a combined operation, called

Under the watchful eye of a Catalina flying boat, a convoy heads for the United Kingdom.

The formation of dedicated Strike Wings revolutionized Coastal Command's anti-shipping operations. Here, Beaufighters attack an enemy convoy off the Dutch coast.

CHANNEL STOP, which was intended to close the Straits of Dover to enemy shipping. Because of Coastal Command's shortage of aircraft, much of this task was assigned to the Blenheims of No. 2 Group RAF, which flew regular armed reconnaissance sorties, known as 'beats', off the coasts of Holland, Belgium and northern France. The bombers flew at low level in a rectangular pattern towards, along, and finally away from the enemy coastline; this pattern was designed to surprise any enemy shipping encountered before their defences could react, and was also calculated to be the best tactic to avoid interception by enemy fighter patrols. The steady increase in flak ships assigned to the German convoys, coupled with the inherent risks of low-level operations and the ability of the *Luftwaffe* to mount effective convoy protection patrols, resulted in high losses: around 25 per cent of the Blenheims failed to return. CHANNEL STOP ended early in 1942 and Coastal Command once again became solely responsible for anti-shipping operations, to its cost: in the first four months of 1942 the Command lost 55 aircraft and could claim only six enemy vessels. Costly and unproductive though they were, these anti-shipping operations yielded much valuable experience and led to the formation, at a later date, of specialized anti-shipping strike Wings equipped with rocket-armed Beaufighters and Mosquitoes.

German destroyers carried out four minelaying operations in the Channel area at night during the first three months of 1941, mining areas off the Thames Estuary, Dover and Eastbourne (twice) before lighter nights brought a halt to these activities. The vessels involved, all belonging to the 5th Flotilla, were the *Falke, Greif, Illtis, Jaguar, Kondor, Richard Breitzen, Seeadler* and *Wolf*. On February 1941, a major British minelaying operation was also carried out off Brest by the destroyers *Intrepid, Icarus* and *Impulsive*, operating out of Plymouth with the 20th Flotilla. They were escorted by the 5th British Flotilla destroyers *Javelin, Jersey, Jupiter* and *Kashmir*. The object of the operation was to deny access to Brest by the enemy battlecruisers then at large in the Atlantic; it did not succeed, but the mining of Brest and other enemy-held Channel ports made life extremely difficult and restrictive for the enemy naval forces.

By the winter of 1940-41, attacks on British coastal convoys by enemy *Schnellboote* were presenting a serious threat, and in December 1940, to try to counter it, the 6th Motor Gunboat (MGB) Flotilla was formed. It consisted of three previously converted boats, armed with four Lewis guns and one Oerlikon, and five boats originally built for the French Navy; these were armed with four Lewis guns and four .303

Browning machine-guns in a Boulton Paul power-operated turret. In March 1941 the 6th MGB Flotilla deployed to Felixstowe and was soon in action against the enemy, patrolling lines from the Humber to the Hook of Holland and from Texel to the Thames.[54]

The boats – MTBs as well as MGBs – were established on so-called 'Z Lines' that ran parallel to the convoy routes but up to 20 miles further out to sea. T.C. Parker, one of the crew of an MTB, describes a typical patrol:

> On reaching our Z, which we usually aimed to do just after dark, we would cut engines and put the hydrophone over the side to listen for E-boat screws. These tactics did sometimes work; my boat heard the noise of E-boat screws one night and almost immediately, with one other MTB, encountered six enemy boats. In the ensuing action we scored some hits with our two-pounder Rolls – our main armament, also known as a Pom-Pom – and with the twin 20mm Oerlikon before both were put out of action. We sprayed the E-boats with the only gun we had left, a single .303 Vickers, but it was more of a gesture than anything else. We had three injured, not seriously, but our companion boat, which continued the chase, had four dead and others wounded.
>
> As well as the Z patrols, we used to sweep along the Dutch coast, usually from the Hook of Holland to Den Helder. This type of operation, on which we briefed to attack any enemy ships, was called BANGER. Generally, when we went out on an offensive BANGER patrol our force would consist of seven or eight boats. If, after an action, two or three boats still had ammunition or torpedoes, they would stay on patrol while the others returned to base, which at that time was Lowestoft. One night, my boat and one other stayed out and tacked ourselves on to the tail of about seventeen E-boats which were lining up to enter Ijmuiden harbour. We went down the line firing at as many as possible, and somehow got away with it.[55]

For any sailor or airman unfortunate enough to be immersed in them, the waters of the English Channel in winter could be unforgiving in the extreme. L.E. 'Mick' Aldridge, a crew member on an air-sea rescue craft – the high-speed yacht

'Mick' Aldridge of the ASR craft *Aquamarine*.

Aquamarine, a stepped hydroplane capable of more than 45 knots, attached to the MTB base HMS *Wasp* at Dover – recalls one incident that illustrates the point.

> At the beginning of 1941 the RAF intensified raids on targets in the Pas de Calais area. At dawn early on a January morning we went on immediate standby, and about 10.00 our CO, Lt-Cdr Brown RCNVR, ordered us to take up a position at noon between the Varne and Ridge banks, just over halfway across the straits, until recalled by R/T. Cloud base was about 3,000 feet and visibility four miles, but we managed to find a black conical buoy marking the end of the Varne. Between 13.00 and 14.00 several unseen flights of aircraft passed overhead to the east. The bitter south-easterly wind was increasing, creating an unpleasant sea, and the recall would have been most welcome. Suddenly, we sighted a seaplane with Red Cross markings two miles to the south, and made in that direction. Failing to land, the seaplane flew alongside, its crew pointing, and we discerned an orange lifejacket drifting rapidly towards us. Within a few minutes we hauled an airman aboard,

and from the open door of the seaplane one of the crew gave us a thumbs-up. Only then did we realise that Cap Gris Nez was visible through the gathering gloom, and waited no longer for a recall. Some miles off Dover an MTB contacted us; it was presumed we were in trouble, as we had not acknowledged a recall at 14.30.

The Jerry airman we'd picked up apparently believed the British were ruthless, so when we dressed a minor shoulder wound and wrapped him in blankets his gratitude was profuse. He was only nineteen; the proffered hot cocoa and brandy helped his English. Beyond the aid of his compatriots, and with darkness approaching, he would soon have succumbed to hypothermia. He owed his life to our dodgy R/T, that left us slopping around further from home than we expected.[56]

The *Aquamarine* at sea. A stepped hydroplane, the craft was capable of 50 knots.

Although German minefields continued to be a constant source of anxiety, it was actually the *Luftwaffe* which caused the heaviest British shipping losses during the first half of 1941, and in April, when enemy aircraft sank 116 ships totalling 323,000 tons, they accomplished their highest figure of the whole war. A further 65 merchant ships (146,302 tons) were sunk by air attack in May, and it came as a considerable relief when enemy air activity over the Channel and

North Sea slackened off early in the following month. The efforts of the RAF against enemy shipping in the Home Theatre were far from successful; in the course of some 6,000 direct air attacks made during 1941, only 50 ships were sunk for the loss of 215 aircraft.[57] To balance the picture, however, it must be said that 36 million tons of shipping passed in and out of the Thames in 1941, and the Germans succeeded in sinking only half a per cent of this vast tonnage. In fairness to the RAF's effort, it should also be said the bombers seldom had a large enemy convoy to target; German tactics were to send their merchant vessels out at night, singly or in pairs, under heavy escort.

The reason for the lull in enemy activity across the Channel in mid-1941 became clear when, on 22 June, Germany attacked the Soviet Union, a move that involved a major transfer of bomber and fighter units to the Eastern Front. By the end of the year, the German armies in the east were freezing in the snows of Russia, and although there would be further sweeping offensives in the year to come, they would end in disaster and defeat. Nineteen forty-two would be the decisive year.

Aquamarine in Wellington dock, Dover, for minor repairs.

CHAPTER SIX

1942: The Year of No Retreat

At the end of November 1941, it had seemed that the British people could expect no more than a prolonged and savage struggle against an implacable enemy. It was true that the Soviet Union was now in the war, but the Russian armies had been smashed on virtually every front, and only the onset of winter had brought a halt to the German offensive in the east. Over a year earlier, Winston Churchill had promised nothing but blood, toil, tears and sweat, commodities which the British had in plenty.

Suddenly, the picture changed. On 7 December 1941, Japanese carrier aircraft attacked Pearl Harbor, inflicting crippling damage on the United States Pacific Fleet. Britain now had an immensely powerful ally. Later, Winston Churchill wrote of this momentous event:

> No American will think me wrong if I proclaim that to have the United States at our side was to me the greatest joy . . . I went to bed and slept the sleep of the saved and thankful.[58]

Churchill's attitude was one of immense relief; he was confident, from that moment on, that the Allies would win the war. But there were many, whose menfolk were stationed in the Far East – a safe haven, or so it had seemed up to now, and far from the grey misery of the European war – who heard the news with dread.

On 10 December, three days after Pearl Harbor, the unthinkable happened. The battleship *Prince of Wales*, which had played a prominent part in hunting down the *Bismarck* only a few months earlier, was sunk off Malaya together with the elderly battle cruiser *Repulse*. Of their combined crew, 840 officers and ratings – many of them

natives of the English Channel towns – lost their lives. After that, disaster followed disaster; on Boxing Day 1941 the British garrison at Hong Kong capitulated, and a month later the garrison in the 'impregnable' fortress of Singapore was fighting for its life.

At the beginning of 1942, against this depressing overall backdrop of Allied reverses, Admiral Sir John Tovey, the Commander-in-Chief, Home Fleet, had two main anxieties. The first concerned the German Brest squadron – the *Scharnhorst*, *Gneisenau* and *Prinz Eugen* – which were now believed to be seaworthy again following repairs, and the second arose through the movement of the new and very powerful battleship *Tirpitz* to join the Trondheim Squadron in mid-January, clearly to form the nucleus of a battle group that was well placed to strike at Allied north Atlantic convoys from its Norwegian base.

The battleship *Tirpitz*, seen here in a Norwegian fjord, was seen as a primary threat to Britain's Atlantic convoys.

It seemed likely that the Brest squadron might be making ready for a foray into the Atlantic, and in January 1942 Bomber Command carried out nine attacks on the port. During one of these raids, on the night of 6/7 January, a bomb fell alongside the *Gneisenau*, holing her hull and flooding two compartments, but the damage was quickly repaired.

On 12 January, a week after this attack, Adolf Hitler decided that the warships must leave Brest if they were to avoid further damage, and since it seemed unlikely that they would be able to break out into the Atlantic unscathed, only two options remained open. The first was to return them to Germany by way of a high-speed dash through the English Channel; the second was to de-commission them.

Faced with such a choice, Vice-Admiral Ciliax, commanding the Brest squadron, produced an outline plan for a breakout operation, which was allocated the code-name CERBERUS. (In Greek mythology, Cerberus was the three-headed dog that guarded the gates of hell). The ships would leave Brest at night to avoid detection for as long as possible, as they would pass through the Straits of Dover in daylight, placing them in a better position to fight off torpedo attacks by surface vessels and aircraft. Also, they would have full advantage of the strong air umbrella that could be provided by the *Luftwaffe*.

Throughout January the British maintained their surveillance of Brest. Intelligence reports indicated that repairs to the ships had been almost completed, and on 25 January all three ships were photographed outside their berths and in the harbour. Air reconnaissance also revealed an increasing number of supporting craft at Brest and a concentration of E-Boats at various Channel ports. German naval activity in the Channel increased, and a destroyer bound for Brest was sunk by one of the 1,000 or so mines laid by the fast minelayers *Welshman* and *Manxman* off the French coast between Ushant and Boulogne. (Bomber Command's minelaying aircraft had placed 100 more between Terschelling and the mouth of the river Elbe).

On 2 February, the Admiralty distributed to all authorities a study of the various alternatives open to the Germans, in which it was concluded that their most probable course of action was a dash up the Channel to their home bases. The main onus of countering this move would fall not on the Home Fleet, but on the naval commands at Plymouth, Portsmouth and Dover – especially on the latter, whose forces would be most favourably placed for interception. In addition, RAF Coastal Command, whose No. 19 Group was responsible for reconnaissance in the south-western approaches to the Channel, would be heavily involved. As a preliminary step, the Admiralty ordered certain redeployments of destroyers, submarines, minelayers and motor torpedo boats. To supplement these forces, six Fairey Swordfish torpedo-bombers of No. 825 Squadron, Fleet Air Arm, were deployed to Manston in Kent on 4 February, and every available aircraft of Bomber Command was bombed-up and placed on two hours' readiness. At the same time, Nos 10, 11 and 12 Groups of Fighter Command stood ready to provide air cover, while Coastal Command stepped up its reconnaissance sorties over the Channel area.

After a week, however, the state of readiness was downgraded and squadrons released for other operations, with the proviso that they could immediately be switched to attacks on the warships if need be. Meanwhile, Coastal Command was trying to assemble its available torpedo-carrying aircraft; a far from easy task, for the three squadrons of Beauforts operational in the United Kingdom were scattered all over the country. Number 42 was at Leuchars in Scotland, ready to go into action against the *Tirpitz* if it got the chance; half of No. 217 was at Thorney Island and the other half at St Eval; and also at St Eval was No. 86 Squadron, whose crews had only recently converted to the torpedo-bomber role. Between them they could muster only 35 aircraft, to which were added the six Swordfish of No. 825 Squadron.

On 8 February, British Intelligence received a warning from the French Resistance that the warships were making ready to sail, and subsequent air reconnaissance showed the *Scharnhorst* and *Prinz Eugen* in the harbour and the *Gneisenau* moored just outside. Armed with this knowledge, and with information to the effect that weather conditions would be favourable for a breakout within 48 hours, the Admiralty and Air Ministry concluded that the Germans would make their attempt during the week beginning 10 February. In the meantime, all the British could do was watch and wait, relying on information from the French Underground and on the routine patrols flown by radar-equipped aircraft of Coastal Command from the Brest peninsula to the north-east corner of Britanny and from Le Havre to the Somme estuary.

On 11 February, further air reconnaissance photographs – the first obtained in 48 hours – showed the three principal enemy warships in the main harbour, with six destroyers and a concentration of smaller craft. That night eighteen Wellingtons were sent out to bomb them, with no result other than delaying the start of the breakout by an hour.

The ships eventually formed up in the roads outside Brest at 22.45 hours, and now began an unfortunate chain of circumstances that was to deprive the British of vital intelligence on their movements. A French Resistance worker saw them set sail, but was unable to reach his transmitter because of a strong enemy security cordon around the harbour. A Coastal Command patrol aircraft off Brest had to return early with radar failure, and its replacement – another Lockheed Hudson – detected nothing at all, even though the enemy warships were well within range of its ASV radar. No replacement arrived to cover the gap left by this aircraft, and the fact that this stretch of the enemy coastline was no longer being watched was not reported to the Admiralty or to Dover. In fact, the third patrol Hudson had been recalled because of fog; had it reached its station, patrolling an area off the Sussex coast, it would almost certainly have detected the German ships at first light.

By that time the Brest squadron was steaming at full speed off Barfleur, due south of the Isle of Wight. During the hours of darkness it had been escorted by relays of Messerschmitt 110 night-fighters, flying at very low level to avoid radar detection and keeping station to the left of the ships, between them and any threat that might develop. Now, as dawn broke, the vulnerable Me 110s returned to their bases and were replaced by low-flying Me 109s and Fw 190s. The German fighter commander, *Oberst* Adolf Galland, had at his disposal three fighter *Geschwader*, two based in the Channel area and the other temporarily deployed from Germany – a total of about 280 aircraft. There would never be less than sixteen fighters providing air cover, and the number would rise considerably during the dangerous passage through the Dover Straits.

The Germans had other tricks up their sleeve, too, as Galland explains:

> The German high-frequency experts took a large share in creating the obvious confusion of the British command. Usually we gave little heed to these contraptions, which always remain a mystery to the uninitiated, and indeed to quite a few laymen of the high command of the German *Luftwaffe*, including its C-in-C, who once said to me that his understanding of such things was already overtaxed when operating a radio set. One should all the more value the activities of these experts, who often have to struggle against stupidity, unintelligence and even ill-will! They had created strong interference with the British radar stations by a series of installations and by different methods. They had also directed interference transmissions against the British fighter intercoms, and by special instruments in bombers had simulated radar signals giving false reports of approaching large formations, against which the British actually sent strong fighter forces. The confusion created in this way continued even when the German warships were clearly located and when practical deception was no longer possible.[59]

Surprisingly, the Germans never exploited radar and radio jamming techniques to the full, as did the Allies as soon as such methods became available. This failing was to cost them dearly as the war progressed. They suffered throughout from a lack of appreciation of new technology by those in high command, a point that is highlighted in Galland's comments.

In his account of the operation, Galland states that:

> At eleven o'clock Central European Time an alerting radio message from a British fighter was intercepted by our listening service. It said nothing except that a large naval formation consisting of three capital ships and about twenty warships was steaming at high speed through the Straits of Dover, present position about fifty miles from the mouth of the Somme. The secret was out.[60]

This comment is interesting. By all accounts, the warships were sighted by the pilots of two sections of Spitfires – one from No. 91 Squadron and the other from No. 602 – but they did not report what they had seen until they were on the ground, having previously been warned to keep radio silence. A lot of blame was subsequently attached to these pilots, but if Galland's account is correct – and there is no reason to suppose that it is not – the indications are that R/T silence was indeed broken by one or more of the pilots (the sections were led by Squadron Leader Bobby Oxspring of No. 91 Squadron and by Group Captain Victor Beamish, Station Commander of RAF Kenley) and the alarm raised. The blame for the slowness of the subsequent British reaction, therefore, must lie elsewhere.

For almost thirteen hours the Brest squadron continued its progress up the Channel unmolested. The force best placed to attack it until now – the Beauforts at St Eval in Cornwall – were being rapidly left behind, while those from RAF Leuchars, having been diverted to Coltishall in Norfolk because their original destination, North Coates, was snowbound, would not arrive until 11.30. Three of the seven Beauforts of No. 217 Squadron at Thorney Island were armed with bombs instead of torpedoes, and the weather conditions over the Channel were now so bad that Bomber Command, whose armour-piercing bombs had to be dropped from at least 7,000 feet in order to be effective, would stand little chance

of hitting the warships. The Royal Navy's surface units were also poorly placed for an attack; the destroyers were exercising in the North Sea, and the small force of MTBs at Ramsgate had suffered in an engagement during the night.

At 11.20 the German force reduced speed to ten knots to allow sweepers to clear a path through a minefield laid by British destroyers. The passage took twenty minutes and the ships once again went ahead at full speed; a golden opportunity to attack them during the interval had been lost. At 12.18 the gun batteries at Dover – the first units to try to engage the enemy – opened fire on the warships, which were invisible in the murk, but their shells fell short. At the same time, five MTBs from Dover under Lieutenant-Commander Pumphrey began their attack run, heading for the outer screen of E-boats and the escorting destroyers beyond, the latter laying a smoke-screen. The cruisers were visible beyond the smoke and Pumphrey signalled their position, speed and course, information that was relayed to the MTBs at Ramsgate and the Fleet Air Arm detachment at Manston. Desperately, bereft of any support from fighter-bombers or motor-gunboats, both of which had been promised, Pumphrey's small force tried to slip through the enemy escort screen. Intense fire from the German vessels and from enemy aircraft forced the MTBs to split up and make individual attacks; most of their torpedoes were launched at a range of two miles or more, and no hits were observed.[61]

Meanwhile, alerted by the MTBs' signals, the six Swordfish of No. 825 Squadron had taken off from Manston, led by Lieutenant-Commander Eugene Esmonde, RN, at 12.25. Esmonde had been promised an escort of five Spitfire squadrons, but a combination of bad weather and a timing error resulted in only ten Spitfires turning up three minutes after the Swordfish set course. Within ten minutes, the Spitfires were engaged in a fierce low-level battle with enemy fighters, in the course of which they lost contact with the Swordfish. The latter, flying in two flights of three, pressed on unescorted towards the warships, harassed by fighters all the way.

The pilots of the first three Swordfish selected the *Scharnhorst* as their target as they broke through the outer defensive screen and launched their torpedoes, despite the fact that all three pilots were badly wounded. Esmonde went down into the sea immediately afterwards and the other two Swordfish were forced down within a minute or so, five of their six crew members later being picked up alive by the MTBs. The second flight of Swordfish was seen passing over the E-boat screen, then the three aircraft vanished in the smoke and the geysers of water flung up by the cruisers' heavy armament. All three were shot down and their crews killed. Of the eighteen crew involved in the operation, therefore, only five survived. Lieutenant-Commander Esmonde, who had not expected to return, was posthumously awarded the Victoria Cross.

It was now 13.00, and the warships, still unscathed, were passing Ramsgate, whose MTBs set out to attack. Like their colleagues at Dover, they found the enemy's defensive screen too strong to penetrate and they were soon left behind, returning to harbour in rapidly deteriorating weather and rising seas.

British hopes now rested on the Beauforts of No. 217 Squadron at Thorney Island – or at least, on the four aircraft that were armed with torpedoes. Incredibly, their crews were briefed to attack not battle-cruisers, but 'three large merchantmen', the excuse being one of security. They had also been briefed to rendezvous with a Spitfire escort over Manston at 13.40, but since they did not begin taking off from Thorney Island until 13.25 it was apparent that they would be late. HQ No. 19 Group therefore sent out a radio signal instructing the torpedo-bombers and fighters to make rendezvous in the target area; unfortunately, although the Spitfires received this instruction the Beauforts did not. The four aircraft involved had recently returned from Manston, where they had been engaged in night torpedo attack trials in conjunction with the Royal Navy, and their radios were operating on different fixed frequencies, a fact that Group HQ had apparently overlooked. The upshot was that the Beauforts

arrived over Manston to find that their escort had already departed. After orbiting for some time, two of the Beauforts set course for the target but failed to find the warships, landing back at Manston at 15.35.

The other two, in the meantime, had also landed at Manston, where they were joined by the remaining three, which by this time had exchanged their bombs for torpedoes. These five aircraft now set course for the target.

Unknown to the British, the Brest squadron had encountered trouble. At 14.21, while passing at reduced speed through another dangerous bottleneck – the Ruytingen Narrows – the *Scharnhorst* had struck a mine. Her engines were temporarily stopped and it was half an hour before she could get under way again – half an hour during which not a single British aircraft was sighted. Admiral Ciliax and his staff were transferred to the leading destroyer by cutter, only to be transferred again when the original vessel was damaged by the premature explosion of one of its own shells. The transfer had barely been completed when Bomber Command at last arrived on the scene, the first wave having taken off at 14.20.

In all, Bomber Command launched 242 sorties against the warships before nightfall; most of these were flown by No. 5 Group, the only one retained at four hours' readiness, and involved every type of aircraft except Whitleys, which were based in the north of England. The operation involved 92 Wellingtons, 64 Hampdens, 37 Blenheims, 15 Manchesters, 13 Halifaxes, 11 Stirlings and 10 Douglas Bostons, the latter from No. 2 Group, where the type had just begun to replace the Blenheim. Although most of them reached the target area only one in six managed to bomb the warships. Many crews failed to sight the enemy vessels at all; others located them but were unable to attack, despite repeated attempts, because of the low cloud base. Thirty-nine crews claimed to have aimed their bombs at the warships, but no hits were registered. Fifteen bombers were shot down, bringing to 127 the total number of aircraft lost by

Bomber Command in its offensive against the Brest squadron.

The assault by the first wave of bombers coincided with an attempted attack by six destroyers from Harwich, the *Campbell, Mackay, Vivacious, Worcester, Whitshed* and *Walpole*, led by Captains C.T.M. Pizey and J.P. Wright. The *Walpole* developed mechanical trouble and returned to Harwich, leaving the other five to execute the attack. It was a hazardous operation; not only did the destroyer crews have to contend with enemy fire, but they also had to thread their way through a British minefield – which luckily was clearly marked on their charts – and run the gauntlet of British bombs. The ships reached the outer screen at about 15.30 and initiated individual attacks on the *Gneisenau* and other vessels, but intense fire from the battle-cruisers' heavy armament kept the destroyers at arm's length and they were forced to launch their torpedoes at long range. Only one destroyer, HMS *Worcester*, came within 3,000 yards; she was badly damaged and set on fire, limping back to Harwich with four of her crew dead and nineteen wounded. Once again, the German warships were unharmed.

The five Beauforts of No. 217 Squadron, attacking the *Gneisenau* and *Prinz Eugen* a few minutes later, enjoyed no better fortune. All launched their torpedoes, but none found a target. Although the Beauforts suffered damage, all returned to Manston.

Meanwhile, the Beauforts of No. 42 Squadron had duly arrived at Coltishall from Leuchars, but the mobile torpedo unit transporting their weapons had not. Eventually, enough torpedoes reached the airfield to arm nine aircraft, which took off for Manston at 14.30 to make rendezvous with the fighter escort and some Coastal Command Hudsons, which were to lead the way. Over Manston, after spending several minutes vainly trying to sort out some order from the confusion of Hudsons and Spitfires that were milling around the airfield, the Beaufort leader, Squadron Leader W.H. Cliff, decided to set off independently. He led his formation towards the Dutch coast, intending to sweep back towards the warships; *en route*, one of his pilots mistook the burning destroyer *Worcester* for an enemy vessel and came perilously close to attacking her. By the time he realized his mistake he had lost touch with the rest of the formation and therefore returned to base, still carrying his torpedo.

The remaining Beauforts found the Brest squadron and made their run-in at 60 feet, the crews witnessing an air battle raging overhead. From time to time, sticks of bombs erupted in the sea nearby. The Beauforts split up and made their attacks from different directions against opposition that came mainly from the warships' guns, the enemy fighters being engaged elsewhere. All the Beauforts dropped their torpedoes, without success. Neither did success attend the last Beaufort attack of the day, carried out at 18.00 by twelve Beauforts from St Eval, deployed to Thorney Island for the purpose. Six of the aircraft were manned by crews of No. 86 Squadron, three by crews of No. 217, and three by recalled crews of No. 22, which had been on the point of departing for the Far East.

Three Beauforts failed to return from this last action, bringing the British air losses for the day to 41 aircraft, a total that included seventeen fighters. German losses were one small escort vessel and seventeen fighters.

The Brest squadron slipped away into the darkness. Just before 20.00 the *Gneisenau* struck a mine, but sustained no very serious injuries. Ninety minutes later, however, the *Scharnhorst* was mined a second time and came to a stop, but by this time the British had lost touch with the enemy and were unable to take advantage of this development. On 13 Februrary the *Scharnhorst* limped to safety in Wilhelmshaven while the other two cruisers went on to the Elbe estuary.

The Channel Dash had been a brilliant success for the Germans, and for the British a woeful tale of incompetence, bad planning and humiliation for which not even the courage of the RAF and Royal Navy could compensate. Yet for the enemy, the sequel to the operation was not a happy one. Ten days later, the *Prinz Eugen* was torpedoed and put out of action by a British submarine; the *Gneisenau* was hit by Bomber Command a fortnight later in Kiel harbour and never went to sea again; and the *Scharnhorst*, out of action for six months, was eventually trapped and destroyed off Norway's North Cape by a British naval force in December 1943. And in the final analysis, although the withdrawal of the warships to Germany had been a tactical success, their departure from Brest was a strategic defeat. A fortnight after the CERBERUS débâcle, the British carried out a cross-Channel combined operation which went some way towards saving face. Not only that: it was to have a major significance for the planning of future Allied bombing operations over north-west Europe.

Called Operation BITING, its purpose was to use airborne forces to seize key component parts of a German *Würzburg* installation on the French coast at Bruneval, near Le Havre. Towards the end of 1941, the Air Ministry had received information that the Germans had a new type of radar which was being used to direct flak and also, possibly, searchlights, and which was therefore regarded as a serious menace to RAF aircraft. Radio countermeasures were being investigated, but these were hampered by a lack of information about the enemy apparatus. An object presumed to be one of these installations was identified by photographic reconnaissance at Bruneval.

The station was well protected against assault from the sea, both by military defences and by the nature of the cliffs upon which it stood. A Commando raid against it was likely to prove expensive in casualties and to be too slow to capture any of the equipment before it could be destroyed by the guards. The Commodore, Combined Operations (Commodore Lord Louis Mountbatten) therefore suggested, after consultation with General F.A.H. Browning, the Commander Airborne Forces, that parachute troops should be employed in an attempt to capture the radar apparatus. This suggestion was approved by the Chiefs of Staff Committee on 21 January 1942, and instructions issued for one

operational Whitley squadron of Bomber Command, one company of parachute troops, and sufficient light naval craft to evacuate the force by sea, to be made available.

The airborne unit selected to carry out the attack was C Company of the 2nd Parachute Battalion under Major J.D. Frost. (Two and a half years later, John Frost and the 2nd Battalion would gain everlasting glory in the battle for the Arnhem Bridge). Aircraft and aircrews would be supplied by No. 51 Squadron of Bomber Command under Wing Commander P.C. Pickard,[62] while the evacuation party would comprise assault landing craft under Commander F.N. Cook, RN, supported by MGBs under Lt-Cdr W.G. Everitt, RN. Two specialist personnel to drop with the troops were provided through HQ Combined Operations: Flight Sergeant Cox, RAF, a radar specialist, and Private Nagle of No. 93 Pioneer Company, a German fighting for Britain who was taken to act as interpreter. Both of these men were given a hurried course of parachuting at Ringway. One other specialist took part in the raid: Flight Lieutenant Priest, who was given a temporary commission in the RAF so that he could accompany the expedition. Because of his specialist knowledge, it was too risky to drop him by parachute, but he accompanied the force in one of the ALCs. Finally, the 'seaborne tail' included a section of the 181st (Airborne) Field Ambulance under Captain A.S. Baker.

After some delay caused by bad weather, the operation took place on the night of 27/28 February 1942, the raiding force of 120 men being dropped in groups of 40 by three Whitleys. The first group, dropping at fifteen minutes past midnight, was to attack a garrisoned farmhouse some 400 yards from the site; the second party, which included the technicians, was to make straight for the radar site and begin dismantling it; while the third group, under Lieutenant E.C.B. Charteris, was to secure the beach and the line of retreat to it.

The farmhouse was successfully stormed by Major Frost's party, and the Germans there either killed or captured. All went well too with the technical party, and Cox was soon at work, assisted by a party of sappers under Lieutenant Vernon. They completed their task and then, covered by Frost's party, began the withdrawal towards the beach, only to find that it had not been secured. The third party had, in fact, been dropped in the wrong place; Charteris and his men eventually joined up with the others and rushed the beach, which they captured, and awaited the arrival of the evacuation force.

The 'seaborne tail' was a little late, having sailed during the afternoon of 27 May on the 3,000-ton assault ship MV *Prins Albert*, a former Belgian vessel. The ALCs waited off the French coast for about two hours for a favourable tide, then moved in at about 02.30, escorted by the MGBs. The evacuation was successful, as indeed was the whole operation; at a cost of one killed, seven wounded and seven missing, the RAF was now armed with an invaluable piece of technical intelligence.

A month later, there was a combined operation on a far more grandiose scale. Called Operation CHARIOT, it was born out of desperation. Behind it all lay the presence, in Norway, of the most powerful German naval force so far assembled: the *Scheer*, *Lützow* and four destroyers at Narvik, and the *Tirpitz*, *Hipper* and six destroyers at Trondheim. Of these, the principal threat was the very powerful battleship *Tirpitz*, which, should she make a sortie into the Atlantic, could wreak havoc on Britain's vital merchant convoys.

One way of discouraging such a sortie was to make it impossible for the battleship to dock in western France, and in practice that meant putting out of action the facilities at St Nazaire, which featured the only dry dock capable of handling her. Known as the *Normandie* lock through its association with the famous French passenger liner, or more correctly the *Forme Ecluse*, it was over 1,100 feet in length; and it was towards this haven that the *Bismarck* would have made had she not been sunk in May 1941.

St Nazaire, which had a population of 50,000 in 1942, is 250 miles from the British coast by the most direct route. It is situated on the right, or north bank of the Loire, six miles in from the river mouth which itself is six miles wide and is shaped like the letter L reversed, the town representing the horizontal and the port the vertical, pointing due north.

The port consists of an outer harbour, the Avant Port, formed by two jetties and two docks in a straight line. The outer dock, the Bassin de St Nazaire, is connected with the Avant Port by the South Lock which renders the docks free from tides, and the inner, larger dock, the Bassin de Penhouet, with the Bassin de St Nazaire by a narrow passage spanned by a swing bridge. Ships of up to 10,000 tons can enter the Bassin de Penhouet through the South Lock. There is also an East Lock gate lying about halfway along the Bassin de St Nazaire, reached through a narrow channel – the Old Entrance – which was to play an important part in the operation.

In 1942, directly opposite the Old Entrance on the far side of the Bassin de St Nazaire, were the massive submarine pens, nine completed and five under construction. The great Forme Ecluse lies at the south corner of the Bassin de Penhouet and emerges beside the mouth of the Old Entrance at an angle of about 45 degrees to it. Jutting out into the Loire, about halfway between the jetty of the Avant Port and the lock gate of the Forme Ecluse, is the Old Mole, which then provided the Germans with a perfect site for two anti-aircraft batteries. The narrow strip of land, sandwiched between the waters of the harbour and the Loire, with its power stations, pumping machinery and other lock installations, warehouses and the Old Town of St Nazaire, covered no more than a square mile and was as closely defended as any area along the western seaboard of German-occupied Europe.

The plan for the assault on St Nazaire was more ambitious than any combined operation so far attempted by the British. Its principal objective was the ramming and destruction of the lock gates of the Forme Ecluse by the old ex-American destroyer HMS *Campbeltown*, her bows filled with explosives, while the destruction, first of the smaller South Lock gates and their installation, secondly of other key points such as the pumping machinery for the Bassin, and thirdly of any U-boats and shipping, were to be subsidiary objectives in that order of priority.

The Naval Force comprised the *Campbeltown* (formerly USS *Buchanan*), two escorting Hunt class destroyers, HMS *Atherstone* and HMS *Tynedale*, a motor gunboat, a motor torpedo boat and fifteen motor launches, four of which carried torpedoes and the remainder the Military Force consisting of 44 officers and 224 other ranks of No. 2 Commando and detachments from others. The Naval Force commander was Commander R.E.D. Ryder, RN, in peacetime an Arctic explorer and winner of the Polar Medal, while the Military Force was commanded by Lieutenant-Colonel A.C. Newman of the Essex Regiment.

To achieve the necessary element of surprise a diversionary bombing attack was arranged, 37 Whitleys and 27 Wellingtons being allocated for this purpose. (In the event, because of heavy cloud and icing in the target area, only four aircraft bombed at St Nazaire and six bombed elsewhere; one Whitley was lost.) Aircraft of Fighter and Coastal Commands were also tasked with protecting the force on the outward and return journeys.

The military plan of attack was based on landings at three places, from the bows of the *Campbeltown*, from motor launches on either side of the Old Entrance, and on the north side of the Old Mole. After demolition parties assigned to the three assault groups had done their work, in particular the destruction of bridges that would effectively turn the dock area into an island, the force was to withdraw to the Old Mole for re-embarkation. Two hours was the maximum time allowed for the Military Force to complete its operation, by which time the Naval Force would have to leave in order to get clear before daybreak and rejoin the escorting destroyers.

The expedition sailed from Falmouth at 14.00 on Tuesday 26 March led by HMS *Atherstone*, towing MGB 314. Astern of her came HMS *Campbeltown*, towing MTB 74. Next in line was HMS *Tynedale*, with the MLs forming two columns on either side of the destroyers.

The outward trip was not without incident. At 07.20, on 27 March *Tynedale* sighted a U-boat on the surface at 4,000 yards and opened fire as she closed, forcing the submarine to crash-dive. The U-boat's periscope was sighted soon afterwards and it appeared that she might have been damaged, but *Tynedale*'s captain, Lt-Cdr D. Tweedie, decided against ramming for fear of damaging his own ship and instead dropped a pattern of depth-charges alongside. The U-boat's bow and conning tower emerged from the water and *Tynedale* engaged her with 4-inch and automatic weapons. The submarine assumed a 40-degree list to port and disappeared stern first. No further contact was made with the submarine, but it was by no means certain that it had been destroyed. Later, two French trawlers were encountered and were sunk by gunfire after their crews had been taken off.

Just after 17.00 on the 27th the force received a signal from the C-in-C, Plymouth, saying that five S-boats were believed to be operating in the area, and two hours later another signal informed the Force Commander that two more Hunt class destroyers, HMS *Cleveland* and HMS *Brocklesby*, were being sent at maximum speed as reinforcements. During the afternoon the force had been following a decoy route across the Bay of Biscay towards La Pallice and La Rochelle, but now it turned north-east and headed for St Nazaire at fifteen knots. At 00.45 on 28 March, the force was within sight of the north bank of the Loire; by this time the two Hunt class destroyers had parted company and were patrolling to seaward.

The fact that the expedition arrived at exactly the right place and time was a tribute to the navigational skills of Lieutenant A.R. Green, R.N., the Force Navigation Officer. The vessels now began their final approach, with three Coastal Force craft – MGB 314 and two MLs – ahead of the *Campbeltown* and MTB 74 and two columns of MLs astern. By now a small number of RAF bombers had arrived overhead and the St Nazaire flak defences were putting up a fine barrage.

As the force came abeam Les Morées Tower, three miles from the town, a single searchlight swept the estuary and a challenge came from a German shore station. MGB 314 replied with a false identification, followed by a signal in German that she was 'proceeding up harbour in accordance with previous orders'. The bluff seemed to have worked: then, with two miles to run, the searchlights came on again, fixing on the *Campbeltown*, and the defences opened up.

The force increased speed, returning fire as it forged ahead, and at 01.34 the bows of the *Campbeltown*, with their five tons of explosive, slammed into the lock gates and stuck fast. While the Commandos on board her streamed ashore to carry out their demolition tasks, a party of naval engineers under Chief Engine-Room Artificer H. Howard set about flooding the ship. This part of the operation had been accomplished with fine precision, and it later brought the award of a well-deserved Victoria Cross to *Campbeltown*'s captain, Lieutenant-Commander S.H. Beattie, RN.

The MLs, meanwhile, had been having a difficult time, some having been hit and set on fire as they struggled to land their troops. The port column, heading for the Old Mole, suffered particularly severely as gunfire ripped through their unarmoured hulls. The leading craft, ML 447, got to within ten feet of the jetty before she was set ablaze by machine-gun fire and grenades; her commander, Lt T.D.L. Platt, RNR, persisted in his attempts to land until ML 160 arrived. The latter's skipper, Lt T.W. Boyd, RNVR, placed his craft between the Mole and ML 447 and took off some survivors, including Platt. Both Boyd and Platt were subsequently awarded the DSO. Some time later, ML 160 was joined by ML 443 and ML 446; they were the only three MLs to return to England under their own power and without escort.

Meanwhile, MTB 74 had torpedoed the gates of the submarine pens and MGB 314, with the Force Commanders on board, had been engaging enemy gun positions from a position midstream. Able Seaman W.A. Savage, the layer of the MGB's Pom-Pom, did excellent work amid all the fury and flying metal; he was killed by a shell splinter during the withdrawal, and was awarded a posthumous VC.

Many of the *Campbeltown*'s crew were also rescued by MGB 314, and afterwards Commander Ryder – who also received the VC for his part in the night's work – gave the order to withdraw. It was a severely decimated force that fought its way out of the Loire estuary to make rendezvous with the escorting destroyers; of the 62 Naval officers and 291 ratings who had sailed from England, 34 officers and 151 ratings were killed or missing, and of the total of 44 officers and 224 other ranks of No. 2 Commando, 34 officers and 178 other ranks never returned. In fact, it was not until much later that the true casualty figures were established: 170 men killed or missing out of a total of 621 committed. Given the nature of the operation, it was a remarkably light price to pay for the denial to the enemy of a major and threatening naval facility.

Shortly before noon on 28 March, *Campbeltown*'s demolition charges blew up with devastating effect. The lock gate was blown off its sill and seriously damaged, and the dock itself was put out of commission for the rest of the war.[63]

British special forces mounted several more cross-Channel raids during the weeks that followed. At the beginning of April, 100 members of Nos 1 and 6 Commandos set out in the MVs *Queen Emma* and *Princess Beatrix* to land at the mouth of the River Adour, near Bayonne, and attack enemy shipping there. They attempted a landing on 5 April but found their way blocked by a sand bar, so the mission – Operation MYRMIDION – was called off. The accompanying Hunt class destroyers, *Albrighton*, *Calpe*, *Badsworth*, *Middleston* and *Wheatland*, carried out a diversionary bombardment of St Jean de Luz. A few nights later, on 11/12 April, Captain Montanaro and Trooper Preece of No 101 Commando Troop paddled a canoe into Boulogne harbour and blew up a German tanker, already damaged by MTB 45, with limpet mines.[64]

On 21/22 April, 100 men of No 4 Commando and 50 of the Canadian Carlton and York Regiment, commanded by Major the Lord Lovat, second in command of No 4, carried out Operation ABERCROMBY, a reconnaissance of the beach defences at Hardelot village. For the first time a new landing craft was used, the Landing Craft Support (LCS) which was armed with two machine-guns and a mortar and which was designed to give fire support to the landing parties. The raid was abortive; although the commandos came upon some enemy bunkers, these were unoccupied, and there was no time to attack one of the designated objectives, a searchlight battery. Having experienced some desultory resistance, the raiding force re-embarked without loss.

Meanwhile, the Channel area was once again the scene of much air activity, although with the bulk of the *Luftwaffe*'s medium bomber force assigned to operations in Russia this was confined mainly to fighter and fighter-bomber sorties on the German side. On the British side, after a break of nearly four months, CIRCUS operations were resumed in March 1942, with sweeps by medium bombers and fighters intensified in an effort to prevent the *Luftwaffe* from building up its forces after the losses it had sustained during the winter fighting on the Eastern Front. The mainstay of No. 2 Group's operations on these operations was still the Blenheim, but by the spring of 1942 the American-built Douglas Boston was beginning to enter service in increasing numbers. The first action against a land target by these aircraft was

One that didn't get home: the wreckage of a Focke-Wulf 190 in south-east England.

carried out on 8 March 1942, when Bostons of Nos 88 and 226 Squadrons bombed the Matford works at Poissy while other aircraft of the same squadrons attacked enemy airfields elsewhere.

At sea, skirmishing between British and German coastal forces was also on the increase, with Hunt class destroyers and light craft carrying out offensive hit-and-run attacks on enemy coastal traffic. One notable action took place on the night of 14/15 May, when the German raider *Stier* passed through the Channel *en route* for the Gironde, escorted by the destroyers *Kondor*, *Falke*, *Iltis*, *Seeadler* and sixteen motor minesweepers. The force was heavily shelled by the Dover batteries and attacked by MTBs, the *Iltis* and *Seeadler* both being sunk with heavy loss of life. The rest escaped, despite attempts by British destroyers to intercept them *en route*.

On 16 May, the destroyers *Cleveland* and *Brocklesby* were exercising off Plymouth when four Messerschmitt 109s were sighted, approaching from seaward. The ships engaged them as they attempted to bomb an assembling convoy and shot two of them down.

The principal *Luftwaffe* units involved in attacks on the south coast at this time were *Jagdgeschwader* 2 and 26. Equipped with the Me 109F-4/B fitted with racks for a 550 lb (250 kg) SC 250 bomb, they specialized in low-level intruder operations designed to escape radar detection. Often taking off in poor visibility from their well-defended airfields at Abbeville, Ligescourt, Poix or St Omer, they would hug the ground and head out over the Channel at wave-top height. Favourite targets were the towns of Dover, Brighton, Folkestone, Worthing and Newhaven. JG 2, based in the south around Evreux and Caen, concentrated its attacks on Channel shipping, usually isolated vessels, while JG 26, based further north, attacked Dover and nearby coastal towns. Up to 26 July, 1942, JG 2 claimed the destruction of some 20 ships totalling 63,000 tons, while JG 26 claimed to have destroyed eight railway installations, eight barracks, six ships, five factories, two gasholders and two harbour installations.

This type of attack was hurried and literally hit-or-miss, but it served to keep the RAF's fighter defences in a state of constant readiness. Once the 109s had made their attack, defending Spitfires stood little chance of catching them on the homeward run; it was a matter of pure luck if a patrol intercepted them on the way in. The

The Hawker Typhoon was the answer to the hit-and-run menace, but it was some time before its teething troubles were eliminated.

situation became even worse from June 1942, when the fighter-bomber *Geschwader* on the Channel coast began to equip with the Focke-Wulf Fw 190 A-3, which could carry a 500 kg (1,100 lb) bomb. Enemy attacks, usually carried out by a *Schwarm* of four aircraft, attained a still higher degree of success, and it was fortunate for the British that JG 2 and 26 never had more than about twenty Fw 190s available for operations at any one time. The *Luftwaffe* pilots made full use of the contours of the South Downs, flying what would nowadays be called 'nap of the earth' to pop up and attack coastal targets from the landward side.

Only one RAF fighter, the Hawker Typhoon, was fast enough to catch the elusive intruders, and at low level it was in its element. Three squadrons – Nos 56, 266 and 609 – were operational with the type in the summer of 1942, all based at Duxford. Despite ongoing technical problems, mainly associated with the aircraft's Napier Sabre engine and tail flutter, the Duxford Wing was assigned to air defence duties, although No. 609 Squadron was authorized to carry out a series of operational trials to investigate the Typhoon's usefulness in other roles. These included night interception and – most important of all for the Typhoon's future – ground attack by both day and night, the principal targets being railway rolling stock and shipping. The Typhoon Mk 1A, armed with twelve machine-guns, was now giving way to the Mk 1B, whose four 20mm cannon proved highly effective in the ground attack role.

The Duxford Wing's cannon-armed Mk 1Bs went into action for the first time in August 1942 when, led by Wing Commander Denis Gillam, they flew to West Malling and carried out an uneventful sweep from Dunkirk to Calais. On the following day they took part in Operation JUBILEE, the Anglo-Canadian landing at Dieppe, discussed below.

Soon afterwards the Duxford Wing disbanded. Number 56 Squadron went to Matlask, near Cromer, for air defence duties in East Anglia, while No. 226 Squadron moved to Warmwell in

Dorset and No. 609 to Biggin Hill in Kent. Although the Typhoon continued to have problems well into 1943, when they were at last rectified, and its future still hung in the balance, it was its prowess against the *Luftwaffe*'s low-level intruders that earned its reprieve.

From June 1942, as more Fw 190s were allocated to the fighter-bomber *Geschwader*, Fighter Command began to form special interception squadrons which were based as close as possible to the most severely hit targets and maintained at a high level of readiness. With the shortcomings of the Spitfire *versus* the Fw 190 now apparent, No. 11 Group moved No. 609 Squadron to Manston early in November 1942 to carry out standing patrols over the coastline between Ramsgate and Dungeness, a move spurred by an attack on Canterbury by 30 Focke-Wulfs on 31 October.

On 20 January 1943 the Typhoon at last showed what it could do as an interceptor. On that day, 28 enemy fighter-bombers made a daylight attack on London, while diversionary attacks were made on the Isle of Wight and the Kent coast. The balloon barrage had been grounded before the raid, and so little warning was received of the approaching enemy fighters that the defences were taken almost completely by surprise. Eight bombs were dropped on Lewisham, two on Poplar and twelve at Deptford, Bermondsey and Greenwich, causing heavy damage to a large warehouse in the Surrey docks and inflicting severe civilian casualties.

However, the Typhoons of No. 609 Squadron were scrambled in time to intercept the raiders on the way out, and in the ensuing fight Flying Officer J. Baldwin – who was later to become the top-scoring Typhoon pilot – destroyed three Me 109Gs, while three Fw 190s were shot down by three other 609 Squadron pilots. A fourth Fw 190 was destroyed by Squadron Leader R.H. Harris of No. 91 Squadron, flying a Griffon-engined Spitfire Mk XII.

The other fighter aircraft that made its debut with the RAF in 1942 – and one which was also to play a major part in cross-Channel operations –

was the North American Mustang Mk I. First deliveries were made to No. 26 (Army Co-operation) Squadron in January 1942, and eight more squadrons of Army Co-operation Command were equipped with the type by the end of May. The first Mustang sortie to occupied Europe, a reconnaissance of a sector of the French coast, was carried out by an aircraft of No. 26 Squadron from Gatwick on 5 May 1942. From then on, armed reconnaissance became a regular activity for the Mustang-equipped squadrons, the aircraft operating in pairs and seeking targets of opportunity across the Channel. At Snailwell, near Newmarket, No. 268 Squadron's Mustangs carried out many so-called LAGOON operations from March 1942, the aircraft searching for enemy shipping between Texel and The Hague.

Usually flying at very low altitude, the Mustangs operating on RANGER and RHUBARB sorties across the Channel were not often intercepted by enemy aricraft, and on the occasions when this happened the Mustangs were usually able to get away by using their superior speed. Below 15,000 feet, in fact, the Mustang was superior to the Me 109F, and could hold its own against the Fw 190. It was not until 16 July 1942 that the first operational losses were sustained when two aircraft of No. 26 Squadron failed to return from a tactical reconnaissance in the Abbeville area, having probably fallen victim to the Fw 190s of JG 26. Five days later an aircraft of No. 239 Squadron was shot down by enemy fighters during a TacR mission to Claudebec, and the Squadron lost two more Mustangs during an armed reconnaissance to Bruges on 14 August. No. 268 Squadron also lost a Mustang on 29 July, the aircraft being shot down by flak over the Dutch coast during a shipping reconnaissance.

On 19 August 1942 Operation JUBILEE, the ill-fated expedition to Dieppe, required a maximum effort on the part of British air and naval forces in the Channel area. The plan, termed by Winston Churchill 'a reconnaissance in force to test the enemy defences on a strongly defended sector of coast, and to discover what resistance would

have to be met in the endeavour to seize a part', involved a frontal seaborne assault on the beaches of the small peacetime holiday resort by 4,961 officers and men of the Royal Regiment of Canada, the Essex Scottish Regiment, the Royal Hamilton Light Infantry, the South Saskatchewan Regiment and the Queen's Own Cameron Highlanders, supported by a tank battalion of the 14th Canadian Army, while gun batteries on the headlands east and west of the town were silenced by 1,057 men of Nos 3 and 4 Commandos.

As a prelude to the operation, the assault area was extensively photographed by Mustangs of Army Co-operation Command, and mine-sweepers cleared a way through the German minefield in mid-Channel ahead of the main force, which sailed from Portsmouth, Newhaven and Shoreham on the evening of 18 August. The naval forces supporting the operation totalled 237 craft of all types, including landing craft, the principal units being the destroyers *Calpe* (acting as HQ ship), *Fernie* (reserve HQ ship), *Albrighton*, *Berkeley*, *Bleasdale*, *Brocklesby*, *Garth* and *Slazak*, the latter Polish; the gunboat *Locust* of Dunkirk fame; and the Landing Ships Infantry (LCIs) *Duke of Wellington*, *Glengyle*, *Invicta*, *Prins Albert*, *Princess Astrid*, *Princess Beatrix*, *Prince Charles*, *Prince Leopold* and *Queen Emma*. Thirty-eight craft of the Coastal Force were also committed.

All seemed set to achieve surprise when, just before 04.00 on the 19th, the landing craft on the eastern flank encountered a German convoy. In the brief and confused battle that followed the German escort UJ1404 was sunk and the British steam gunboat SGB5 badly damaged. The engagement delayed the assault on this flank, which crumbled into total disaster under intense enemy fire. Of the 516 troops landed here, 485 were killed, wounded or taken prisoner.

On the western flank the attack achieved better results, but even so the Germans were not dislodged from their batteries and strongpoints commanding the beaches where the main assault was to take place. When this went in at 05.20, therefore, it encountered a murderous and devastating enfilading fire that pinned the troops down on the beaches, while the supporting Churchill tanks failed to penetrate into the town.

Too much has been written about the desperate gallantry of the Canadian infantry in the hours that followed to bear repetition here. Suffice to say that the Canadians lost 215 officers and 3,164 men and the Commandos 24 officers and 223 men. The total military cost was 494 officers and 3,890 men killed, wounded and missing – 68 per cent of the attacking force.

The naval forces offshore did what they could to lend fire support, but since none of the warships mounted guns of more than 4 inch calibre the degree of help from this quarter was limited. Only about 1,000 men were brought away in the assault craft that moved inshore to evacuate them at 11.00, an operation as desperate in its way as the fighting on land. Many craft were lost in the process, including the escorting destroyer HMS *Berkeley*, hit by bombs from a Dornier 217.

RAF air support on the day comprised 70 squadrons, of which 61 were fighters, two were fighter-bombers, and only two (with Douglas Bostons) were actually bombers. Air Vice-Marshal Trafford Leigh-Mallory, the Air Commander, had requested 300 bombers for the operation, but this had been denied by Air Chief Marshal Arthur Harris, the C-in-C Bomber Command, on the grounds that his force was overstretched in its main task – the bombing of Germany – and that he could make no guarantee of bombing accuracy if his aircraft were used in a tactical role. So the attack went in with no fire support other than that provided by the destroyers and two squadrons – Nos 174 and 175 – equipped with Hurricane Mk IIB fighter-bombers and the cannon-armed Hurricane IICs of No. 43 Squadron, operating from Manston, Warmwell and Tangmere respectively. In fact, it was No. 43 Squadron that led the air attack, striking at enemy gun positions, radio stations and key buildings.

The task of the four Mustang squadrons assigned to the operation – Nos 26, 239, 400 RCAF

and 414 RCAF – was to monitor enemy troop movements in the areas to the rear of Dieppe, the aircraft operating in pairs. Their losses were appalling. Of the 106 RAF aircraft of all types which failed to return from operations on 19 August, ten were Mustangs. No. 26 Squadron lost no fewer than five aircraft, No. 239 Squadron three, and the two Canadian squadrons one each. One Fw 190 was shot down by Pilot Officer Hollis H. Hills of No. 414 Squadron – the Mustang's first combat victory.

The RAF claimed the destruction of 43 German bombers and 49 fighters during JUBILEE, with ten bombers and 29 fighters probably destroyed and a further 140 aircraft damaged. The true figures were somewhat different: 25 bombers and 23 fighters destroyed, with 16 bombers and eight fighters damaged. The weight of British air power, nevertheless, kept the *Luftwaffe* away from the beaches, and at 09.56 hours on 19 August, the Military and Naval Force Commanders felt justified in informing AVM Leigh-Mallory that the air co-operation had been faultless.

Without doubt, the most important lesson learned at Dieppe was the absolute need for massive fire support, from both sea and air, in amphibious operations. Another lesson was the need to devise special equipment to overcome defensive obstacles, the realization of which resulted in a formidable array of specially-equipped tanks being available to the forces that went ashore in Normandy two years later. But the overall lesson of Dieppe was how not to do it, and it was better learned in 1942 than in 1944.

Twenty years after the event, Lord Louis Mountbatten unhesitatingly accepted responsibility for the inception of the Dieppe raid in a Canadian Broadcasting Corporation interview, saying:

At Combined Operations Headquarters our job was to create the machine which would eventually make the invasion of the Continent possible, and to devise the new technique for the assault, as well as for the maintenance by sea of the great forces once they had been landed. New landing ships, craft and appliances were to be devised, designed, tested and produced, and hundreds of thousands of soldiers, sailors and airmen were to be trained together to act as a single entity in the assault.

The Chiefs of Staff Committee . . . decided that it would be very necessary to carry out a reconnaissance in force . . . In fact a large-scale raid would have to be made to learn more of the technique required to breach what Hitler called the Atlantic Wall.[65]

The Canadians, to be sure, had paid a terrible price; but as future events were to prove, it had not been for nothing.

CHAPTER SEVEN

1943: The Mounting Offensive

If it was true that 1942 had witnessed its share of Allied disasters, it could at least be said that the year ended on a note of victory, with General Bernard Montgomery's Eighth Army inflicting a decisive defeat on General Erwin Rommel's *Panzerarmee Afrika* at El Alamein and Allied forces going ashore at Algiers and Oran early in November. As the 160 British warships and the many merchant vessels detailed to take part in the North African landings (Operation TORCH) assembled mainly in the Clyde and Loch Ewe, their activities have no part on this narrative, except for the mention that the British coastal convoys were virtually stripped bare of escorts for quite a long period in October and November 1942, when German S-boat activity was again on the increase with the onset of the long, dark nights. On the night of 18/19 November, for example, the German 5th Flotilla, comprising S68, S77, S82, S112, S115 and S116 engaged a convoy off Plymouth and sank the armed trawler *Ullswater* and two coasters with torpedoes.[66]

The success, however, was not all one-sided. On 13/14 October 1942, the German armed merchant cruiser *Komet*, harbour-hopping through the Channel with an escort of four destroyers, was sighted soon after leaving Le Havre by Swordfish aircraft of the Fleet Air Arm. Flares dropped by the Swordfish brought five British destroyers and eight MTBs to the scene, and the fight was on. The *Komet* was hit many times by gunfire from the destroyers and set ablaze, and at 01.16 she exploded. Some of the enemy destroyers were damaged, apparently by the *Komet*'s gunners, firing wildly in the confusion. The destroyer HMS *Brocklesby* was

damaged by a shell from a German coastal battery after the engagement.[67] The damage was not serious and she was at sea again on the last night of October, attacking a small enemy convoy and sinking one of its vessels.

The first major attempt by the enemy to attack a British coastal convoy in 1943 occurred on the night of 24/25 January, not in the Channel but in the North Sea, when sixteen S-boats of the German 2nd, 4th and 6th Flotillas tried to attack a convoy off Lowestoft but were driven off by the destroyers *Mendip* and *Windsor*. On 3/4 February, destroyers made a sortie from Plymouth to attack enemy shipping off Alderney, sinking two coasters, the *Hermann* and *Schleswig-Holstein*, and on the following night the Polish destroyer *Krakowiak*, which had taken part in the Alderney mission, beat off an attempted S-boat attack on a convoy near Start Point.

Since March 1942, enemy shipping and coastal targets had been frequently attacked by the Hurricane IIB fighter-bombers based at Manston with No. 174 Squadron, and No. 175 Squadron at Warmwell. In September 1942 the Westland Whirlwind Mk Is of Nos 137 and 263 Squadrons, newly converted to the fighter-bomber role, also deployed to Manston and Warmwell respectively and were soon engaged in similar operations. Shipping attacks did not meet with much success, but on 10 February the German armed merchant cruiser *Schiff* 14, attempting to break through the Channel under escort by the 8th Motor Minesweeper Flotilla, was bombed by Whirlwinds and forced into Boulogne. She was again attacked there with no result, but the attempt to force the Straits of Dover was

Hurricane Mk IV armed with 60 lb SAP rockets. No. 184 Squadron suffered dreadful losses in attacks on V-1 launching sites.

abandoned and the ship was ordered back to the Baltic. This was the last attempt to send an auxiliary cruiser into the Atlantic.

By this time, RAF Coastal Command was operating its first dedicated Strike Wing. Formed by No. 16 Group at North Coates on the coast of Lincolnshire in November 1942, it consisted of two squadrons equipped with the Bristol Beaufighter Mk VIC; No. 236 Squadron armed with cannon, machine guns and bombs, and No. 254 Squadron armed with cannon and torpedoes. Early in 1943 these two units were joined by No. 143 Squadron, equipped with the Beaufighter Mk XIC for use in the anti-flak role.

The role of the North Coates Strike Wing, and others like it that were formed subsequently, was to assume great importance in 1943, as German

convoy defences grew stronger. In addition to the merchant vessels themselves, which ranged from 1,000 to 10,000 tons (the average being about 3,000 tons) and which were all armed, the Germans used so-called *Vorpostenboote*, armed trawlers crammed with flak guns of all calibres, and *Sperrbrecher* (literally 'barrier breaker' ships

The Beaufighters also ensured long-range fighter protection for maritime aircraft. In this photograph, a Blohm und Voss Bv 138 reconnaissance aircraft goes down in flames.

which were former merchant vessels of up to 8,000 tons). Then there were purpose-built minesweepers, *Minensuchboote* (M-class minesweepers to the British) which swept just ahead of the convoys and which were also heavily armed; *Räumboote* or R-boats, 125-ton close escort vessels armed with 20mm cannon; *Schnellboote*; and sometimes destroyers. Any aircraft attacking the convoy therefore had to contend with a storm of flak ranging in calibre from the heavy weapons – 105mm and 88mm – on the *Sperrbrecher*, down through 40mm, 37mm, 20mm cannon and 7.92mm machine-guns on the smaller escort craft and the transports themselves.

The first attack by the North Coates Wing was made on 20 November 1942, against a convoy near the Hook of Holland. In addition to the naval escorts, it was also protected by Me 109s and Fw 190s. The mission was a disaster. The strike aircraft lost contact with their anti-flak

Beaufighters, a promised escort of Spitfires failed to show up, three Beaufighters were shot down, two more crashed on return and five more were badly damaged. All there was to show on the credit side was one tug sunk and a couple of armed trawlers slightly damaged.

It seemed that the failure of this sortie might have placed the whole future of the Strike Wing concept in jeopardy. But after several weeks of training under the energetic leadership of Wing Commander H.N.G. Wheeler (whose predecessor, Wing Commander Fraser, had been killed in the November attack) the North Coates Wing finally had a chance to prove itself on 18 April 1943, when a strike was laid on against an enemy convoy off the Hook of Holland. Twenty-one Beaufighters, escorted by 22 Spitfires of Nos 118 and 167 Squadrons and eight Mustangs of No. 613 Squadron, hit the convoy hard, sinking the 4,906-ton freighter *Hoegh Carrier*, shattering the

Squadron Leader Jack Rose and Hurricane IID.

minesweeper M-201, which had to be towed into Den Helder, and damaging several other vessels. There was no air opposition, and all the RAF aircraft returned to base.

The real key to success in anti-shipping work, as would later be proved time and again, was the rocket projectile, and in this respect much pioneering work was carried out by the Hurricanes of No. 184 Squadron, formed at Colerne in Wiltshire in December 1942 under the command of Squadron Leader Jack Rose DFC, a highly experienced Hurricane pilot. The Squadron was initially equipped with Hurricane Mk IIDs, armed with two 40mm Vickers 'S' guns – used successfully in the Western Desert by No. 6 Squadron – and two Browning .303 machine guns. Jack Rose describes the Squadron's subsequent activities.

As we collected more aircraft and built up the Squadron, one of our essential activities was the calibration of the 40mm guns, which were remarkably accurate. When the aircraft was set up to fire into practice targets at the butts, the normal standard was all rounds in a pattern of eight inches by five at 540 yards. As the Vickers guns were mounted below the wings, when fired in flight the recoil depressed the nose of the aircraft, so that after each pair of guns was fired the gunsight had to be re-positioned on the target before the next pair was loosed off. After practice, it proved possible to fire off four pairs with high accuracy on the run-up to a ground target, so with 32 rounds – sixteen to each gun – we could achieve a possible average of four attacks.

The Squadron was operational by early March, 1943, and we were expecting a posting to a busier airfield. However, on 4 March we became involved in Exercise SPARTAN, which involved large elements of the Army and many RAF squadrons under simulated battle conditions. We did not know it at the time, but this was the beginning of the preparation for D-Day, some fifteen months away. We lived under field conditions, under canvas – which was no joke in early March – and moved rapidly from one airfield to another. Each squadron which was to work closely with the Army had an ALO – an Army Liaison Officer – permanently attached to it, and apart from a few key personnel all

ground crew became part of a mobile airfield establishment, enabling the squadrons to move rapidly from airfield to airfield and then start up in business immediately on arrival.

Early in 1943 we were equipped with Hurricane IVs, carrying a bank of four rockets under each wing. These had either 25 lb armour-piercing heads or 60 lb semi-armour-piercing high-explosive shells. The damage that these rockets could inflict proved to be very impressive, and I remember being told that if all eight rockets with the larger warheads were fired at once, the result would be approximately that achieved by a broadside from an eight-inch gun cruiser. The most usual technique was to fire the rockets in a ripple, that is one pair at a time during the approach run. As there was no recoil from the rockets, there was no need to re-sight in between each pair of rockets being fired, as in the case of the Vickers 'S' guns. We could, if we wished, use the Vickers guns instead of the rockets and occasionally we did so, but after a time we stuck to the RPs.

The firing range we used was Leysdown on the Isle of Sheppey, where the officer in charge of the range did his best to provide very substantial targets anchored offshore for our benefit; but as none of these targets lasted longer than one or two attacks we cast around for something more substantial. Our Army Liaison Officer, who was with us at the time, arranged for me to meet a brigadier in charge of an infantry tank brigade near Canterbury, and over a drink we discussed our problem. As a result, we

Close-up of the Vickers 'S' gun installation on a Hurricane IID.

were supplied with an unserviceable Churchill tank and later a Sherman too. They were transported to the Leysdown range and were set up on the beach, providing first-class durable targets. All attacks were recorded by the range officers, and my log book shows such scores as 26 and 28 rounds out of 32 fired from the Vickers guns and three or four out of eight using the 25 lb AP rockets.

A Churchill tank used for target practice by No. 184 Squadron's Hurricanes at Leysdown. The 40mm shell holes are clearly visible.

As Jack Rose points out, operations with the Hurricane IVs against heavily defended targets brought their share of problems.

The Hurricane IV's low speed in comparison with contemporary fighter aircraft, and its poor armament after the rockets had been released (one Browning .303 in each wing) meant that operations could only be carried out in selected circumstances: Spitfire fighter cover, when this could be arranged, good low cloud cover or the use of semi-darkness. Spitfire escorts were unpopular with the Spitfire pilots as all our operations were at low level, and to maintain effective contact with us this meant flying lower, slower and longer than they would have liked.

Cloud cover was useless unless we could escape into it quickly, so this ruled out medium and higher cloud. My log book records a number of instances

(usually entered in the log book as Operation TWITCH) when we started out, mostly from Manston, but were recalled before reaching the enemy coast as cloud cover was reported by the Met. people to have lifted. Firing the rockets at low level in the dark was not on, as a regular practice, so we made use of darkness to approach the enemy coast. Timing our arrival for about first light so that, with eyes by then accustomed to the gloom, we could attack and make a quick getaway while there was still half an hour or so to dawn.

In June 1943 a couple of such attacks were made on shipping off the Dutch coast. The first of these, on 17 June, consisted of four aircraft (we normally flew four aircraft on such operations) piloted by myself, Flight Lieutenant Ruffhead, Flying Officer Kilpatrick (Australian) and Flying Officer Gross (Canadian). We each fired our eight 60 lb rockets in ripples at ships anchored close inshore and we all returned with nothing more than a few bullet holes. Soon afterwards we had a visit from someone from Boscombe Down, who was rather put out that a special PR flight had not been laid on to record the damage inflicted by the rockets. This was, I believe, the first use in Western Europe of rockets fired from fighter-type aircraft. Later, of the four of us on that operation, Ruffhead, Kilpatrick and Doug Gross were all killed.

The next such attack, a few days later, was carried out by myself, Warrant Officer Starmer (missing on this sortie), Flight Lieutenant 'Dutch' Holland, and Flight Sergeant Wallace, who was later killed. 'Dutch' Holland later had a miraculous escape when he was shot down in a Typhoon attack on a concentration of enemy armoured vehicles well to the south of the Allied beachhead on D-Day Plus One; he had a series of hair-raising adventures before he managed to link up with friendly troops. 'Humph' Russell of 164 Squadron was shot down during one of the anti-shipping operations and was a PoW for the rest of the war.[68]

While we were at Manston, we thought up, in collaboration with some Swordfish pilots who were stationed there with us, a possible joint action to enable us to make rocket attacks at night. Enemy shipping made maximum use of darkness to slip around the northern coast of France and the Netherlands, spending daylight hours under the protection of the guns of the various ports en route. As the Swordfish had radar and could also drop flares, we thought that it might be possible to synchronise our activities so that a Swordfish, at reasonably safe height, could locate an enemy vessel and drop a flare between it and the land, thus silhouetting the target for a Hurricane IV low-level attack out of the darkness on the seaward side. It was on such an attempt that 'Killy' Kilpatrick, a very capable pilot, disappeared.[69]

Although Jack Rose is correct in his assumption that his squadron pioneered the operational use of rocket projectiles by single-engined fighter-bombers in Western Europe, these weapons had been operational with aircraft of the Fleet Air Arm and RAF Coastal Command since April 1943, although it was not until 23 May that the first success was registered when a Swordfish from the aircraft carrier HMS *Archer* sank the U-752 off the Azores. Five days later, the U-594 was sunk by an RP-equipped RAF Lockheed Hudson north of the Balearic Islands.

By April 1943, rocket rails had also been fitted to the Beaufighters of No. 236 Squadron, and work had begun on those of No. 143 Squadron. Meanwhile, as RP training continued, so did shipping attacks by the North Coates Wing's torpedo and anti-flak Beaufighters, and on 29 April the Wing sank three vessels for the loss of one Beaufighter of No. 143 Squadron.[70]

The Strike Wing suffered a serious reverse on 1 May, when 31 aircraft set out to hunt the cruiser *Nürnberg* and three destroyers off south-west Norway. The mission was beyond fighter escort range and the Beaufighters were badly mauled by Me 109s and Fw 190s, No. 254 Squadron losing three Torbeaus and No. 143 Squadron two anti-flak Beaufighters. The whole Wing was forced to jettison its bombs and torpedoes as the aircraft took evasive action.

The next attack, on 17 May, was accompanied by a strong fighter escort, and the Beaufighters sank the German freighter *Kyphissia* (2,964 tons), the minesweeper M-414 (775 tons) and the flak ship Vp 1110 off the island of Texel.

Meanwhile, a detachment of No. 236 Squadron had been sent to Predannack, in Cornwall, and it was from here that a Beaufighter attacked and

The joint operations room where operations were planned between the Royal Navy and RAF Coastal Command.

sank the U-418 on 1 June, marking the first success for an aircraft of this type using rocket projectiles. The submarine was heading for Brest when it was sighted by Flying Officer Mark Bateman, who was accompanied by a naval specialist, Lieutenant-Commander F.J. Brookes, RN. All four RPs hit the U-418, which went to the bottom with the loss of all hands.

The Strike Wings of Coastal Command now had a viable anti-shipping weapon, and in the months to come they would put it to devastating use. Meanwhile, the spring of 1943 had seen a surge of naval activity in the area of the English Channel. On 27 February, the 5th S-boat Flotilla carried out a particularly audacious sortie, four craft – the S65, S68, S81 and S85 – penetrating into Lyme Bay and attacking a convoy that had assembled there. In a matter of minutes, they torpedoed and sank the freighter *Moldavia* (4,858 tons), the Tank Landing Craft LCT 381 (625 tons) and two escort vessels, the armed trawler *Lord Hailsham* and the whaler *Harstad*. The S-boats retired without loss. On the next night, an attempt to attack a southbound German convoy by four Coastal Force MGBs was broken up by accurate defensive fire from seven escort vessels, MGB 79 being sunk. (The convoy had earlier lost the patrol boat V 1318, which struck a mine off Ijmuiden.)

A mine also accounted for *Schnellboote* S70, lost during a sortie by the 2nd, 4th and 6th S-boat

Flotillas into the area of Lowestoft and Great Yarmouth on the night of 4/5 March 1943. The enemy craft were driven off by the destroyers *Windsor* and *Southdown* and the corvette *Sheldrake*, and the following morning they also lost the S75, attacked and sunk off Ijmuiden by Spitfires and Typhoons. In addition to this sortie, S-boats attempted to attack a convoy off Start Point, but this was frustrated by accurate fire from the Polish destroyer *Krakowiak*. The *Schnellboote* were again active on the night of 7/8 March, attempting to attack shipping near the Sunk Lightship, but the raid was broken up by the destroyer *Mackay* and four MGBs. Two S-boats collided while taking evasive action; one of them, S119, was sunk by MGB20 after her crew had been taken off by S114 the other craft involved in the accident.

The middle of April saw a flurry of intense naval action, beginning on the night of 12/13 when a German convoy was attacked by MGBs 74, 75, 111 and 112, both sides sustaining slight damage. On the next night, the 5th *Schnellboote* Flotilla, led by its redoubtable commander, *Kapitänleutnant* Klug, scored a resounding success off the Lizard Head in an attack on Convoy PW323, comprising six merchant vessels, the Hunt class destroyers *Eskdale* and *Glaisdale*, and five armed trawlers. Four *Schnellboote* (S90, S112, S116 and S121) broke through the defensive screen and S90 hit the *Eskdale* with two torpedoes, bringing her to a standstill. She was later sunk by S65 and S112. Meanwhile, the 1,742-ton freighter *Stanlake* was torpedoed by S121 and finished off by the S90 and S82. All four S-boats returned to their base without loss.

There was a better outcome for the British on the night of 27/28 April, when the destroyers *Albrighton* and *Goathland* attacked a German convoy of two medium-sized merchantmen, escorted by two trawlers and a minesweeper, 60 miles north-north-east of Ushant, off Ile de Bas. Both freighters were hit by torpedoes and heavily damaged, though neither was sunk, but one of the escorting trawlers – UJ 1402 – was destroyed by gunfire. HMS *Albrighton* became involved in a

90-minute close quarter gun battle with some S-boats that arrived on the scene and received damage that put her out of action until the end of May.

With the advent of the light nights of summer, as in the previous year, the excursions of the S-boat into British waters became less frequent, and minelaying by aircraft and destroyers intensified. On the night of 2/3 May, Dornier 217s of KG 2 laid mines in the estuaries of the Humber and Thames and also on the convoy route between Dover and the Thames Estuary, and on 11/12 May 36 aircraft sowed mines on the Humber-Thames convoy route. Six aircraft were lost, mainly to Mosquito night-fighters. On the following night, craft of the 1st, 7th and 9th Minesweeper Flotillas, carrying out Operation STEMMBOGEN – which involved sowing mines in the southern part of the North Sea, west of the Hook of Holland – were attacked by four MTBs, which hit and sank the M8 with two torpedoes. A further major German minelaying operation was undertaken during the last week in May by S-boats of the 2nd, 4th, 5th and 6th Flotillas, which laid mines between Cherbourg and Peter Port, the Isle of Wight and Portland, and in Lyme Bay. The latter objective was mined three times again in June, when mines were also sown off Start Point. In all, the *Schnellboote* laid 321 mines in the course of 77 sorties. The first week in July saw another German 'harbour-hopping' operation, with the *Elbing* class destroyers T24 and T25 moving westwards through the Channel from the North Sea. During the move they were unsuccessfully shelled by the Dover gun batteries, attacked off Dunkirk by three MTBs and attacked in Boulogne by Typhoons. On the night of 9/10 July they joined five minesweepers in escorting a convoy, which was attacked by the destroyers *Melbreak*, *Wensleydale* and *Glaisdale*. The minesweeper M135 was sunk in the ensuing battle, but HMS *Melbreak* was badly damaged.

During this period, the main opportunities for engaging the *Schnellboote* came when the latter were detected moving from port to port. On 24/25 July, for example, S68 and S77, *en route* from

Boulogne to Ostend, were attacked by British MTBs and MGBs, which sank S77 north of Dunkirk, while on 11 August craft of the 4th and 5th S-boat Flotillas, transferring to L'Abervach in readiness for a sortie against Plymouth Sound, were attached by Typhoons. S121 was sunk, S117 badly damaged and four others slightly damaged out of the seven-boat force.

There was a resurgence of German minelaying activities in October 1943, with the return of longer hours of darkness, and an increase in actions against convoys. It was during one such action, on 23 October, that the Royal Navy suffered a further severe loss.

For some time, Allied Intelligence had been aware that a blockade runner, a fast, ultra-modern cargo vessel of 10,000 tons named the *Münsterland*, had been heading back to Germany from Japan with a cargo of rubber and strategic metals, both vital to the German war effort. By a series of incredible circumstances, she had evaded Allied air and naval patrols on the homeward run and had reached Brest, where she was attacked by B-25 Mitchell medium bombers without success. Following the usual harbour-hopping procedure, the *Münsterland* then moved on to Cherbourg, where she was attacked by the Typhoons and Whirlwinds of Nos 183 and 263 Squadrons, both operating from Warmwell.

Meanwhile, the Royal Navy had also tried to intercept her, with unfortunate results, during the passage from Brest to Cherbourg on the night of 22/23 October. The British naval force comprised the light cruiser *Charybdis*, the Fleet destroyers *Grenville* and *Rocket*, and the Hunt class destroyers *Limbourne*, *Talybont*, *Wensleydale* and *Stevenstone*. The *Münsterland* was escorted by six minesweepers of the 2nd Flotilla, two new radar-equipped patrol vessels, V718 and V719, and five Elbing class destroyers providing an outer screen.

Charybdis made radar contact with the enemy force off Ushant at 01.30 on 23 October. Her accompanying destroyers also made contact at about the same time, but no information as to the probable size and composition of the enemy force was exchanged.

By this time the Germans were aware of the British warships approaching to intercept them, and the outer destroyer screen obtained a visual sighting on the *Charybdis*, which was seen turning to port. The leading destroyer, T23, immediately launched a full salvo of six torpedoes at her. At 01.45 the British cruiser opened fire with starshell, and her lookouts at once sighted two torpedo tracks heading towards her port side. One, or possibly both, torpedoes struck home and *Charybdis* came to a halt, listing heavily to port.

By now the other German destroyers had joined in the action, firing several more torpedoes at the British destroyers coming up behind the stricken cruiser. *Charybdis* was hit again, while a torpedo launched by T22 struck HMS *Limbourne*. The cruiser sank very quickly, and despite determined attempts to save her *Limbourne* was also beyond redemption. She was sunk by torpedoes from the *Talybont* and *Rocket*, which returned to Plymouth with the other surviving destroyers.[71]

The action had cost two warships, the lives of 581 officers and ratings, and had achieved nothing. The enemy convoy escaped unharmed, and the next morning air reconnaissance revealed the *Münsterland* at Cherbourg and the five Elbings at St Malo. As mentioned earlier, the freighter was subsequently attacked by Typhoons and Whirlwinds through flak described by one pilot as 'a horizontal rainstorm painted red'. Two Whirlwinds out of twelve were shot down and two more crashed on return to base, and the Typhoons lost three aircraft out of eight, but the *Münsterland* was damaged and her progress delayed. She eventually reached Boulogne, where she was attacked early in January 1994 by rocket-firing Typhoons of No. 198 Squadron and damaged again. This time, although five aircraft were hit, all made it back to base, two crash-landed at Manston. The *Münsterland* story finally came to an end on 20 January, when, after leaving Boulogne, she ran aground in fog west of Cap Blanc Nez and was shelled to pieces by the Dover guns. The Typhoon pilots of Nos 198 and 609 Squadrons, arriving when the fog lifted, relieved

Death of a blockade runner: the *Münsterland* in flames after being pounded by shore batteries on 20 January 1944.

I can remember seeing an intelligence report at about this time in which damage to the NO-BALL sites was given in relation to the weight of bombs dropped by various types of aircraft. The categories were heavy bombers, medium bombers, and rocket-firing aircraft. Although we had loads of only 480 lb (8 x 60 lb), the damage inflicted by our attacks per ton of 'bombs' dropped was, I suppose understandably, very much greater than the damage per ton dropped by the – mostly American – medium and heavy bombers.[72]

their frustration by firing their rockets into what was left of the superstructure.

In the closing weeks of 1943, the tactical air forces were assigned to the first of a lengthy series of attacks on a new threat that had been perceived across the Channel: the launching sites, then under construction in the Pas de Calais, for the V-1 flying bomb. With the heavy bombers of RAF Bomber Command and the USAAF preoccupied with the strategic air offensive against Germany, this new task fell to medium bombers and single-engined fighter-bombers, including the Hurricane IVs of Nos 164 and 184 Squadron, as Jack Rose explains.

In the winter months of 1943-44, just before we re-equipped with Typhoons, we carried out a series of attacks on so-called NO-BALL (V-1) targets in northern France. We were then operating from Woodchurch, one of the airfields scattered over Romney Marsh speedily constructed of wire mesh on grass. My log book records attacks on numbered NO-BALL sites 40, 88, 28, 46, 81 etc and also on named sites at Montorquet, Bois Nigle, La Longueville and so on. We usually flew, again in fours, when the cloud conditions gave the maximum cover if needed. Photographs were always used for the final approach.

Nevertheless, the damage inflicted by the Hurricanes of the two ground-attack squadrons was achieved at considerable cost; on one occasion, during an attack on a NO-BALL site that cost Flight Lieutenant Ruffhead his life, three out of the four Hurricanes he was leading failed to return. Many of the most severe losses were sustained when the enemy defences were fully alerted – as, for example, when a section of Hurricanes made a faulty landfall and consequently had to make a longer approach to their target. Because of the losses, the Hurricanes were given a Spitfire escort whenever possible.[73]

Woodchurch, the rocket-firing Hurricanes' base during their costly anti-NO-BALL sorties, was only one of many similar advanced landing grounds that had sprung up all over southern England, close to the Channel coast, during the year. For in 1943 Britain had been gradually turned into a vast arsenal, and strips such as these would soon enable the Allies to wield the weapons that were now being forged to hurl their armies across the Channel, and to establish a secure foothold in occupied Europe.

Many of the advanced landing grounds (ALGs) that were refurbished in 1943 were originally so-called 'scatter' fields, emergency landing strips created at the time of the Battle of Britain as an insurance against the principal fighter airfields being made unserviceable by enemy bombing, which they sometimes were. With the battle won, hundreds more sites were inspected south of a line from the Thames to the Severn to provide a springboard for the aircraft that would eventually spearhead an assault on the German-held coastline of Europe. The list was eventually shortened to 72, but such was the need for food-producing land that the airfield construction scheme was strongly opposed by the War Agricultural Executive Committee, and in the end only 25 proposals were accepted, of which 23 involved ALGs to be constructed along the Channel coast from Kent to Hampshire. Eleven of the new ALGs were allocated to the United States Army Air Forces, whose advance units had become operational in the United Kingdom in the summer of 1942. The original target date for the completion of the ALGs was March 1943, but construction was set back somewhat by a shortage of materials and, not least, by the English weather.

Hand-in-hand with the ALG construction programme went the formation of a so-called 'Composite Group' of fighter, fighter-bomber, light bomber and reconnaissance squadrons which, operating at first from the new forward airfields near the coast, would support an Allied expedition to France. On 1 June 1943, this formation was re-designated the Tactical Air Force, and with this the old Army Co-Operation Command became defunct. Later, the designation was again changed to Second Tactical Air Force, its role being to support the Anglo-Canadian Group of Armies. The American armies training for the invasion of Europe had their corresponding tactical air support in the form of the IX Tactical Air Command.

In November 1943 a large number of RAF squadrons were transferred from the various other commands to the Second Tactical Air Force, which now comprised four groups. Number 83 and 84 Groups were to provide tactical support for the 1st Canadian and 2nd British Armies, No. 85 Group was to defend the Allied bridgehead across the Channel once it had been established, and the medium bombers Marauders, Mitchells, Mosquitoes and Bostons – of No. 2 Group were to strike at communications and supplies behind the enemy lines. There was also a Reconnaissance Wing and an Air Spotting Pool, and the massive task of furnishing air transport and supply fell to

In 1942-43, No. 2 Group stepped up its attacks on enemy targets in France and the Low Countries. These three photographs show low-level attacks on targets in Holland.

No. 38 Group. All these formations, together with the mighty power of the United States Ninth Air Force, were incorporated into the Allied Expeditionary Air Force, commanded by Air Marshal Sir Trafford Leigh-Mallory.

So, gradually, the machinery that would place a great body of men on the beaches of Normandy in the coming year was being fitted into place. But although the Allied armies were undergoing the type of training that would ensure no repetion of the Dieppe débâcle, and although the Allied air forces were reaching a pinnacle of strength of over five and a half thousand aircraft, enough to ensure complete air supremacy when the landings were achieved, there was still the physical problem of shipping the armies across the English Channel and of safeguarding them in passage, and only the Allied navies could achieve this twin objective.

In December 1943, as preparations for the great leap across the Channel gathered momentum, there was still a long way to go; and there was more than one major obstacle to be overcome *en route*.

CHAPTER EIGHT

NEPTUNE and OVERLORD

The first such obstacle came hard on the heels of the appointment, on 6 December 1943, of General Dwight D. Eisenhower as Supreme Commander for Operation OVERLORD, as the Allied invasion plan was code-named.

The outline plan for OVERLORD had been approved at a conference of Allied representatives held at Quebec in August 1943. It envisaged the landing of three divisions in the assault force, followed up by two more, on a 30-mile stretch of the Normandy coast between the rivers Orne and Vire. The choice of this stretch of coast was dictated by the fact that there were no major harbours there, and so it was likely to be less well defended than beaches elsewhere. The operation was set for May 1944.

The decision to use a relatively slender force of only three divisions in the initial assault wave was dictated, at the time it was taken, by an apparent shortage of landing ships and craft. When General Eisenhower assumed his new posts, however, and had an opportunity to study the plan, he quickly reached the conclusion that a stronger initial punch on a wider front was necessary if the invasion was to have a hope of success, and in this he had the support of General Montgomery, who was to command the military assault forces. Early in 1944, the decision was therefore taken to increase the assault force to five divisions, and to make additional landings at the base of the Contentin peninsula with the object of capturing Cherbourg as quickly as possible. This decision at once created major problems, as the official Royal Navy historian points out.

... To the Admiralty and the Naval Commander this belated change meant that all the plans had to be revised, and that many more warships, merchantmen and combined operations vessels had to be found; and perhaps worst of all – for we were already suffering from an acute shortage of manpower – crews had to be produced and trained to man the additional ships. In the end the Combined Chiefs of Staff agreed to postpone by a month the landing in southern France, which they had originally intended to launch simultaneously with the invasion of Normandy, so releasing more ships and craft for the northern assault; and the Admiralty paid off large numbers of our older warships in order to release their crews for Operation NEPTUNE. But even these emergency measures could not produce enough ships and men, and an appeal for more help was therefore made to the U.S. Navy. This Admiral E.J. King, the Chief of Naval Operations, at first refused – mainly, it appears, because he considered that we were holding back excessive strength in the Home Fleet. When however in April 1944, the manifold responsibilities of that fleet in the Arctic and North Sea were fully explained to him, he agreed to send across three battleships, two cruisers and twenty-one destroyers which was more than we had originally asked for.[74]

The preparations for the naval contribution to OVERLORD, known as Operation NEPTUNE, were quite breathtaking in their extent. As far back as June, 1942, the Admiralty had appointed Vice-Admiral Sir Bertram Ramsay to be 'Naval Commander Expeditionary Force' for the invasion of France and the Low Countries, and a better choice could not have been made. It was Ramsay who, as C-in-C Dover, had masterminded the evacuation from the French Channel ports in 1940, and he had exercised a key role in the invasion of North Africa in November 1942 and in the assault on Sicily in July of the following year.

Now, back in the United Kingdom, Admiral Ramsay was able to devote his considerable energies to the cross-Channel invasion plan, and by 10 April 1944 his final plan for NEPTUNE – a document running to over 700 foolscap pages – was presented to the naval authorities. The primary object of the plan in his own words, was 'to secure a lodgement on the continent from which further offensive operations can be developed,' and to achieve this he assigned the available naval forces to convoy escort, mine-

One of the more spectacular attacks carried out by No. 2 Group in the months before D-Day was the raid on Amiens prison by Mosquitoes on 18 February. These photographs show the attack in progress.

sweeping, fire support for the assault forces, and a multitude of other tasks that were likely to arise.

Two large amphibious task forces were assigned to the assault: an Eastern Task Force under Rear-Admiral Sir Philip Vian, and a Western Task Force under Rear-Admiral A.G. Kirk, USN. The Eastern Task Force was to land three divisions of the British Second Army on three beaches, code-named Sword, Juno and Gold, on a 30-mile front west of the River Orne, while the Western Task Force was to land the US First Army on two beaches, Omaha and Utah, on a 30-mile front to the west of the British assault area. Utah Beach lay at the base of the Cotentin peninsula, and the early capture of Cherbourg depended on how quickly it could be secured and the beachhead exploited. Immediately behind the assault forces were to come two follow-on forces, one British and the other American, which would relieve the assault troops and open the way for a steady flow of reinforcements and supplies that would be necessary to counter and defeat any likely enemy counter-offensive.

To implement NEPTUNE, Admiral Ramsay had a formidable array of 1,213 warships at his disposal, 79 per cent of them British or Canadian, 16½ per cent American and 4½ per cent supplied by other Allied navies. Of these, 107 were battleships, monitors and cruisers, representing the bombardment force; these assembled mainly in the Clyde and at Belfast, while the 286 destroyers, sloops, frigates and corvettes assigned to escort duty assembled at the south coast ports from which the invasion force would sail. The remainder of the force comprised all kinds of naval craft, down to the midget submarines that would approach the beaches well in advance of the assault force and act as pathfinders.

Then there were the combined operations craft, no fewer than 4,126 of them, ranging from big headquarters ships especially fitted out for the role through large merchant vessels converted to Landing Ships Infantry, light assault craft (LCAs) carried by the latter, Landing Ships Tank (LSTs), Landing Craft Tank (LCTs), AA defence craft, rocket-firing craft, smoke-laying craft and obstacle clearance craft, down to repair and maintenance vessels. About three-quarters of the total were of American build.

In addition, hundreds of merchant ships were requisitioned to undertake such duties as channel marking, salvage and cable-laying, for replenishing the warships, for providing harbour facilities and for towing the special constructions that were vital to the success of the invasion. Foremost among these were two artificial harbours, known as MULBERRIES, and five craft shelters called GOOSEBERRIES. The creation of artificial harbours and breakwaters would involve the deliberate scuttling of 55 merchant vessels and some obsolete warships, while 160 tugs would be needed to tow the sections of the Mulberry Harbours across the Channel. About 400 units, totalling one and a half million tons, made up the two MULBERRIES; the huge concrete caissons that formed part of the breakwaters alone weighed 6,000 tons. The MULBERRIES, with their miles of floating piers, were truly remarkable feats of engineering; when assembled, the British one – the larger of the two – would provide a sheltered anchorage for seven deep-laden ships of large tonnage, 20 coasters, 400 tugs and auxiliary vessels, and 1,000 small craft.

In the planning of NEPTUNE, much attention was paid to accurate fire support procedures by the heavy bombardment ships. Each of the five assault forces was allocated a group of fire support warships, their initial targets being the 23 German gun batteries that commanded the assault beaches. An elaborate spotting system was devised that included observation both from the air and from the surface. The lessons of Dieppe, and of subsequent Allied landings in Sicily and Italy, had been well learnt.

The Germans had also learnt from the Dieppe episode, and as a consequence the Atlantic Wall, as they termed their coastal defences on the Channel, was now a formidable obstacle – or rather a series of obstacles, for in places it was incomplete. Since its conception in 1940, after the fall of France, the construction of the Atlantic Wall

had undergone various phases. Initially, its building had been started by the German Navy, with the object of fortifying key port areas. Every port that had fallen into German hands was strengthened by the installation of coastal gun batteries of varying calibres, as well as anti-aircraft defences. After Dieppe, which highlighted the possibility that the Allies might attempt a seaborne invasion at any point on the occupied coastline, a second defensive building phase had begun, with permanent defensive works erected to protect the coasts of Denmark, the Netherlands, Belgium and France. Navy, Army and Air Force were all involved in the building work, and each had an individual task; the Navy's was to improve the existing distribution of naval guns and anti-aircraft batteries, the Army's was to set up its own coastal gun batteries and to defend key positions, and the *Luftwaffe* was responsible for installing coastal radar stations and setting up additional anti-aircraft guns. There was little co-ordination between the three Services, each going virtually its separate way in matters such as the design of coastal gun emplacements. What emerged, in the end, was a series of key points consisting of sealed fortified rings round strategic ports, towns, hills and so on, each garrison being responsible for its own defence. In between were stretches of coast which were relatively weakly defended.[75]

On 15 January 1944, Field Marshal Erwin Rommel was given tactical command of all the troops on the coast confronting England. A few weeks earlier, on the direct orders of Adolf Hitler, he had begun an inspection of the Atlantic Wall defences, working southwards from Denmark, and had been appalled by what he had seen. His concern was to strengthen the weak sectors between the fortified points. Soon after beginning his inspection tour, he had told his senior engineer officer, General Wilhelm Meise:

> When the invasion begins, our own supply lines won't be able to bring forward any aircraft, gasoline, rockets, tanks, guns or shells because of the enemy

attacks. That alone will rule out sweeping land battles. Our only possible defence will be at the beaches – that's where the enemy is always weakest . . . I want anti-personnel mines, anti-tank mines, anti-paratroop mines – I want mines to sink ships and mines to sink landing craft. I want some minefields designed so that our own infantry can cross them, but not the enemy tanks. I want mines that detonate when a wire is tripped; mines that explode when a wire is cut; mines that can be remote controlled, and mines that will blow up when a beam of light is interrupted. Some of them must be encased in non-ferrous metals, so that the enemy's mine-detectors won't register them.

Meise later wrote: 'Quite apart from Rommel's greatness as a soldier, in my view he was the greatest engineer of the Second World War. There was nothing I could teach him. He was my master.'[76]

But the master's appointment had come much too late to turn the forthcoming Allied invasion into a bloody disaster. His plan to create a 'Death Zone' six miles wide along the length of the Atlantic Wall, fell far short of its target; although miles of coastline were fortified with timber stakes festooned with Teller mines, and surrounded by barbed wire, tetrahedra, dragons' teeth and the like, the real machinery for defeating an invasion on the beaches – air power – was never available to him. He was promised 1,000 fighters and fighter-bombers. He never got them.

Besides, the bitter experience of Dieppe had encouraged the British to develop the means of overcoming the obstacles that littered Rommel's 'Death Zone'. Those means were concentrated in Major-General Percy Hobart's 79th Armoured Division, whose task was to clear the way for the assault forces. Its assets included the Churchill Mk III AVRE (Armoured Vehicle Royal Engineers), fitted with a device called a Bobbin; it could lay down a canvas mat, 110 yards long, on a beach surface to support the weight of heavy vehicles. Then there was a Churchill Mk VIII Crocodile, one of the most horrific and spectacular of Hobart's 'Funnies': a flame-

throwing tank which carried 400 gallons of flame-gun fuel in a trailer. Compressed nitrogen forced the fuel from trailer to flame-gun, mounted in the normal machine-gun position beside the tank's main 75mm gun armament, giving a range of about 120 yards.

The first 'Funnies' to reach the shore, however, would be the Sherman M4-A4 DD (Duplex Drive) tanks. The DD was a swimming tank, powered by its own engines and kept afloat by a collapsible canvas screen which was lowered on landing, permitting the tank's guns to be brought to bear immediately. Anti-tank walls and ditches were to be tackled by Churchill Mk III AVREs adapted to carry either huge brushwood fascines, or the SBG – the Small Box Girder bridge, which was dropped over the obstacle by firing a small shearing charge above the turret.

Rommel's minefields would be dealt with by the Sherman 'Crab' Flail, a minesweeping tank fitted with chains that would literally flail a path ten feet wide through which the main landing forces could advance. Bunkers overlooking the beaches would be destroyed by another Churchill AVRE, this one equipped to fire 25 lb Petard heavy mortar bombs.

German Intelligence knew nothing of special weapons such as these, although it must have suspected their existence. In fact, the enemy's intelligence was seriously lacking throughout the build-up phase of OVERLORD, and here again overwhelming Allied air superiority played a key part. In this case it was the activities of the Air Defence of Great Britain, as RAF Fighter Command had been renamed in November 1943 (the title was mercifully short-lived, reverting to Fighter Command in under a year) that denied the Germans the air reconnaissance they so desperately needed if their Intelligence services were to form a true picture of the extent of the massive build-up on the other side of the Channel. The patrols of Spitfires, Typhoons and Mustangs made incursions into UK airspace by daylight prohibitive.

On the Allied side, however, the activities of the Tactical Reconnaissance Wings in the early part of

Everything possible was done to disrupt the enemy's supply system prior to D-Day. Here, a Mosquito attacks a German merchant vessel off Denmark.

The Strike Wings in action again: enemy minesweepers under heavy and accurate attack in the Gironde estuary, June 1944.

1944 were to prove of inestimable value to the eventual success of the invasion. From February onwards, for example, aircraft of No. 35 Recce Wing, acting on Intelligence reports, photographed the sea bed off Normandy, and it was quickly established that the Germans had begun laying anti-invasion obstacles. From then on, regular reconnaissances of the beaches were undertaken to monitor enemy progress, the Mustangs taking some remarkable low-level oblique photographs when high-level photography was not possible because of adverse weather conditions.

On another occasion, an experiment was carried out to see if rocket projectiles would be effective in destroying radar installations, and an enemy radar site in Holland was chosen as the target for rocket-firing Typhoons. Post-strike photographs by Mosquitoes and Spitfires failed to show damage, so the Central Interpretation Unit briefed the Mustang pilots of No. 168 Squadron, No. 39 Wing, to take very close oblique photographs. The sortie, flown on 16 May 1944, showed that the attack had been completely successful, and from then on rocket attacks against enemy coastal radar installations became routine in the weeks prior to D-Day.

A great deal of low-level photo-reconnaissance work was also carried out during the pre-invasion period by the F-6 Mustangs of the USAAF's 67th Photographic Reconnaissance Group, which had been assigned to the Ninth Air Force since October 1943 and whose 12th and 107th Squadrons became operational at Middle Wallop in January 1944. Between 23 February and 20 March they carried out oblique photography of 160 miles of the French coastline, the task being taken over by the 15th and 109th Squadrons in April. These low-level photographs enabled the invasion planners to study the enemy's Atlantic Wall defences – and particularly the new constructions that were appearing under Rommel's direction – in minute detail, to brief assault troops, study local topography and assess activity in marshalling yards and on airfields.

In April 1944, while the RAF's rocket-firing Typhoons attacked enemy radar stations along the occupied coastline and identified V-1 launching sites, other squadrons of the Second Tactical Air Force and IX Tactical Air Command joined the heavy bombers of the strategic air forces in attacking the enemy's transportation

Aircraft of 2 TAF carry out a strafing attack on an enemy coastal installation.

system in France and the Low Countries, the object being to seal off the Normandy invasion area. This period saw the operational debut of a potent new single-engined fighter, the Hawker Tempest Mk V, which became operational with Nos 3 and 486 (New Zealand) Squadrons of No. 150 Wing at RAF Newchurch, seven miles southeast of Ashford, Kent, during April. The Tempests were cleared for offensive action over enemy territory on 8 May 1944; the Second TAF official narrative gives an account of their activities during the remainder of the month, and provides a good insight into the type of operation that was being carried out at this time.

15 May. Between 10.32 and 11.50 hours, eight Tempests carried out offensive patrols over the area of northern France. Four aircraft attacked barges on the Aisne–Marne Canal and one aircraft attacked a railway goods shed at Vitry. The remaining patrols were uneventful.

18 May. Between 11.00 and 17.25 hours, eight Tempests and four Spitfires carried out offensive

sweeps over the area of north-east France and the Brest peninsula. The Tempests sighted a few small vessels in the Boulogne–Le Havre vicinity.

19 May. Between 12.20 and 17.30 hours, seventeen Tempests and fifteen Spitfires carried out offensive sweeps over France, Belgium and Holland. Four Tempests attacked a three-ton lorry on the road to Mons, setting it on fire, and attacked other ground targets in the vicinity of Mons with unobserved results. Three more Tempests attacked 50–60 staff cars, setting 20 cars on fire, five miles south of Louvain and also attacked and set on fire a lorry on the Ninove–Brussels road, setting it on fire.

20 May. Seven Tempests carried out an uneventful sweep over northern France. The same day, between 11.43 and 19.55 hours, ten Tempests and 24 Spitfires carried out offensive sweeps in conjunction with attacks on military targets in northern France and on the airfield at Creil by Bostons and Mitchells.

21 May. Between 04.00 and 14.02 hours, 104 Spitfires, fifteen Tempests and eight Typhoons attacked transport targets in France, Belgium and Holland. Five locomotives were damaged and six were attacked and stopped in the Brussels area.

A Hawker Tempest Mk V at Newchurch, Kent, June 1944.

22 May. Between 10.33 and 20.50 hours, 45 Spitfires and fifteen Tempests carried out offensive sweeps over France and Belgium. The Tempests attacked trains and eight locomotives, damaging and possibly destroying some of them; they were set on fire. Two Spitfires and one Tempest were damaged by flak.

24 May. Between 14.45 and 18.36 hours, sixteen Tempests and four Spitfires swept and patrolled areas of north-east France and Belgium. Twelve Tempests attacked and damaged a barge sixteen miles south-east of Dunkirk, attacked an army lorry with unobserved results, fired at two factories, strikes being seen in the Antwerp-Brussels area, attacked and stopped a car west of Hirson, attacked a locomotive and 20 trucks between Guise and Rivemonde and seven stationary locomotives near Busyny. The Spitfires attacked a goods train and MT vehicles. A tracked vehicle was attacked and forced to stop at Quincon. Four Tempests returned early owing to technical trouble.

Between 10.10 and 20.43 hours a total of 170 Spitfires provided escort and support, uneventfully, to Mitchells and Bostons of 2 TAF, attacking airfields and medium gun batteries in northern France. Four Spitfires returned early with technical trouble. Ten Tempests swept the Cambrai area, uneventfully, in connection with these operations.

25 May. Between 06.05 and 21.05 hours, two Typhoons, six Tempests, and 20 Spitfires carried out weather and shipping reconnaissance patrols over the coast of Belgium and northern France. At Dunkirk, a 1,000-ton ship, with tugs alongside, was seen and one Tempest attacked a motor launch moving at high speed. Strikes were seen and the mast blown away.

26 May. Between 10.00 and 18.05 hours, eight Tempests and four Spitfires carried out weather and shipping reconnaissance patrols over northern France and Belgium. Two Tempests sighted a large barge at Gravelines and a small fishing vessel at

A Junkers Ju 88 burns during a strafing attack by Tempests on an airfield in France.

Dunkirk; otherwise no shipping was sighted. Two Tempests and two Spitfires returned early due to the weather, and two Tempests returned early due to technical trouble.

27 May. Between 13.56 and 19.49 hours, two Mosquitoes, 42 Spitfires and nine Tempests carried out offensive patrols over northern France. Two targets were attacked by 21 Spitfires with good results. Five Tempests attacked a staff car south of Rubemare, which crashed into a wall. They also attacked a lorry and left it in flames near Pas. Between 05.02 and 14.00 hours, fourteen Spitfires and two Tempests also carried out weather and shipping reconnaissance patrols off and over the French and Belgian coasts.

28 May. In conjunction with attacks by Bostons and Mitchells and No 2 Group, between 15.15 and 18.55 hours 62 Spitfires carried out sweeps over northern France, attacking and destroying a lorry and damaging two goods trains, a large streamlined locomotive, a lorry, three large and two small cars and five railway wagons in a siding. At the same time, nine Tempests, patrolled over Cormeille, during which period two Junkers Ju 88s/188s were destroyed and two Ju 88s/188s damaged, all on the ground.[77]

There is an interesting background to this attack on 28 May, more recent accounts of which are slightly at variance with the Second TAF summary, compiled at the time. In the afternoon of 28 May, Spitfire pilots of No. 44 Wing (Wing Commander J.E. Johnson), engaged in a medium-level sweep, reported the sighting of ten Junkers Ju 88s or Ju 188s at Cormeille, near Pontoise. No bombers had been there previously, so it was

fairly clear that these aircraft were a reinforcement, probably intended for a night attack on a British target.

Armed with this information, HQ No. 85 Group contacted Wing Commander Roland Beamont at Newchurch and asked him if No. 150 Wing could lay on a strike. No. 3 Squadron was on readiness at the time, and eight Tempests were detailed to carry out the attack (not nine, as the official account states). Beamont himself took the lead, with Flight Lieutenant Bruce Cole as his No. 2.

The assault on enemy communications began well before D-Day. Here, an important road junction in France shows the scars of air attack.

Over the Channel No. 3 Squadron's CO, Squadron Leader Alan Dredge, was forced to return early with falling oil pressure. He was accompanied back to base by his No. 2, which was standard procedure, so the formation was now down to six aircraft. The formation – callsign 'Harlequin' – continued into enemy territory and reached the target area without opposition. The Ju 188s were sighted in dispersal pens among woods to the south of Cormeille, near a bend in the river Seine. Beamont elected to make a high-speed attack and the Tempests crossed the airfield at 450 mph through heavy flak, having gained speed in a dive from 10,000 feet. They made one firing pass and stayed low until they were five miles from the target area. Climbing back to 10,000 feet, the pilots could see columns of smoke rising from Cormeille. It had been a classic airfield attack of the kind that would become the speciality of Tempest pilots later in the war, against *Luftwaffe* bases in Germany.

The air offensive during the first half of 1944 was not entirely one-sided, although the German effort against targets in Britain was puny in comparison with the Allied strategic bombing campaign. On 21 January 1944 the *Luftwaffe* initiated Operation STEINBOCK, a series of heavy attacks on British targets, with particular reference to London and the south coast ports, by all available bomber aircraft on the Western Front. The night offensive was under the control of the *Angriffsführer* (Attack Leader) England, *General-major* Dietrich Peltz, who had under his command seven *Gruppen* of Junkers Ju 88A-4s, one (I/KG 51 *Edelweiss*) with Messerschmitt Me 410s, and two *Staffeln* of Heinkel He 177s.[78]

The first attack, on the night of 21/22 January, involved 447 aircaft; of the 500 tons of bombs dropped, only 30 tons fell in the London area. The raid was led by 'pathfinder' Dornier Do 217s of I/KG 66 using DUPPEL, the German equivalent of the British WINDOW radar countermeasures equipment.[79]

In the first attack, nine bombers were shot down by Mosquito night-fighters. The so-called 'Little Blitz' of 1944 cost the *Luftwaffe* dearly; 57 bombers were claimed by fighters and AA in the two raids that took place in January, 72 in February, 75 in March, 75 in April and 50 in May. Mosquitoes equipped with Mk VIII Airborne Interception radar accounted for 129 of this total.

It was during April that Peltz turned his attention to the bombing of British ports in the hope of disrupting the build-up of invasion shipping. On 23/24 April, 100 sorties were flown against Portsmouth, and two nights later 130 aircraft bombed the Poole/Swanage areas. Bombing accuracy was very poor, a reflection of the low quality of the crews that were now reaching the *Luftwaffe*'s operational units; in one attempted raid on Bristol no bombs at all hit the city, the majority falling on Weston-super-Mare, twenty miles away.

Sporadic enemy activity continued during May, tailing off towards the end of the month. On 15 May the enemy flew 106 sorties, 60 of which were directed against the Portsmouth area. Squadron Leader Gill of No. 125 Squadron chased a Ju 88 and shot it down near Cherbourg, and an Me 410 was damaged north of Portland Bill. A Ju 88 of 9/KG 54, shot down by a Mosquito of No. 456 Squadron after being coned by searchlights, fell at Medstead, near Alton, and a Ju 188 was shot down by No. 604 Squadron. A week later No. 125 Squadron destroyed a Ju 88 and a Ju 188 in the

The Germans used Dornier Do 217 pathfinder aircraft during the 'Little Blitz' of 1944.

Southampton area, while two more Ju 88s were shot down by No. 456 Squadron. The 'Little Blitz' ended on 29 May 1944, the last attacks being made by fast aircraft – Me 410s and Fw 190s – on the south coast harbours which, by now, were crammed with shipping.[80]

The early months of 1944 also saw an increase in German naval activity in the Channel area, the S-boat flotillas having been reinforced. On the night of 5/6 January, seven S-boats of the 5th Flotilla attacked the convoy WP.457 off the south-west coast of England. The boats fired a total of 23 torpedoes, swamping the escort, which was led by the destroyer HMS *Mackay* and sank the freighters *Polperro* (403 tons), *Underwood* (1990 tons) and *Solstad* (1,408 tons), together with the trawler *Wallasea*. The escorts had better luck on 16/17 February, successfully driving off seven S-boats of the 5th Flotilla that tried to intercept a convoy off Lizard Head; the enemy fired eleven torpedoes, but all missed. On the last day of January, however, six boats of the 5th Flotilla attacked convoy CW.243 off Beachy Head and

sank the freighters *Caleb Sprague* (1,813 tons) and *Emerald* (806 tons) as well as the trawler *Pine*.

A few days later, on 5 February, there was a sharp engagement between the British destroyers *Brissenden*, *Talybont*, *Tanatside* and *Wensleydale* and the German minesweepers M156 and M206, escorted by the destroyer T29, off the coast of northern Brittany. The M156 was badly damaged and limped into L'Abervach, where she was destroyed later by air attack.

In fact, the most intense actions during February 1944 took place in the North Sea, where S-boats were carrying out minelaying operations off Grimsby and Great Yarmouth. In the Channel itself, a combination of radar and rapid reaction by the escort forces were gradually getting the better of the periodic S-boat forays towards the south coast.

There were, nevertheless, some frenetic actions in the Straits during March, beginning on the night of the 14th/15th, when British MTBs attacked two groups of the German 36th Minesweeping Flotilla off Gravelines and sank

A U-boat returns to its French harbour after a successful Atlantic sortie. By 1944, the heyday of the U-boats was over.

the enemy leader, M3630, with a torpedo. Return fire was heavy and the British lost one boat, MTB 417. On the following night, ten S-boats of the 5th and 9th Flotillas attempted to attack convoy WP.492 off Land's End, escorted by the corvettes *Azalea* and *Primrose*. The German force was detected by air reconnaissance and other British warships in the area – the cruiser *Bellona*, the Tribal class destroyers *Ashanti* and *Tartar*, the Hunt class destroyers *Brissenden* and *Melbreak*, two minesweepers and some MTBs – diverted to intercept. Faced with this formidable weight of firepower the Germans had little choice but to disengage, but not before S143 had been damaged.

The value of the British coastal radar defences in combating the S-boat threat was again demonstrated on two nights in March, when the 5th and 9th Flotillas set out to attack shipping off the Lizard and Weymouth on the 16th/17th and 20th/21st. The crafts' radar detection equipment alerted the crews that they were being tracked, and the sorties were abandoned.[81]

The British coastal forces were also in action on the night of 20/21 March, when five MTBs attacked the German convoy HECHT, comprising the tanker *Rekum* escorted by the 18th *Vorpostenboote* Flotilla. The MTBs were beaten off, but the tanker was sunk by the Dover guns.

The real breakthrough in this phase of the Channel naval war came in April, when the British adopted new tactics. These involved the use of the cruisers *Bellona* and *Black Prince* in the role of command ships, using their radar to direct destroyers of the newly-formed 10th Flotilla on to enemy targets and then maintaining a constant plot of the action, using their long-range guns to engage the enemy force while illuminating it constantly with starshells while the destroyers closed in. The tactics worked well, and on 26 April they resulted in the sinking of the Elbing-class destroyer T28, two more destroyers – T24 and T27 – being badly damaged and forced to seek shelter in Morlaix. They broke out on the night of 28/29 April and were intercepted off St Brieux by the Tribal class destroyers *Haida* and

Athabaskan. The Germans fired twelve torpedoes at their pursuers and *Athabaskan* was hit, sinking at 0442, but T27 was further damaged by shells from the *Haida* and ran aground, to be finished off later by MTBs.

On the previous night – 27/28 April – the S-boats achieved their greatest victory since 1940, and it happened more or less by accident. On that night, nine boats of the 5th and 9th Flotillas sailed from Cherbourg to attack a convoy that was reported to be off Selsey Bill. Instead, they encountered a convoy of landing craft – eight US LSTs, escorted by the corvette *Azalea*, heading from Brixham and Plymouth for Slapton Sands in South Devon where they were to take part in Exercise TIGER, a dress rehearsal for the American landing on Utah Beach. The convoy should also have been escorted by the destroyer HMS *Saladin*, but she had been damaged in a collision with a landing craft in Plymouth harbour and no replacement had been assigned.

Nine S-boats fell upon the convoy as it entered Lyme Bay, and in the torpedo attack that followed LST507 and LST531 were sunk and another, LST289, was damaged. The loss of life was severe: 441 soldiers and 197 seamen. The attackers were pursued by the destroyers *Onslow*, *Obedient*, *Ursa*, *Piorun* and *Blyskawica*, but got clean away. The incident was hushed up for a long time after the war, and even today there is still controversy over the actual loss of life, some sources putting it as a high as 749.[82]

Long before the British, Commonwealth and American forces landed in Normandy, the Allied air forces had succeeded in establishing total air superiority over the invasion areas. The month between 5 May and 5 June 1944 saw the heaviest period of bombing of the war as the Allied air forces maintained a non-stop onslaught on the enemy's communications in France and the Low Countries. As D-Day approached, a large proportion of the Allied striking force was earmarked to carry out heavy attacks on enemy coastal batteries and radar installations. Since Allied air supremacy had virtually eliminated *Luftwaffe* reconnaissance flights over the Channel area, the Germans depended almost entirely on their coastal radar to give warning of the approach of an invasion fleet, and the destruction of their coastal stations became of the utmost importance.

By the first week of June 1944 air attack had knocked out some 80 per cent of the enemy's coastal radar capability, and to confuse the remaining stations about 250 warships that were to accompany the invasion fleet were equipped with radar-jamming devices. Jamming was also to be undertaken by radar countermeasures aircraft, notably Stirlings and Fortresses of No. 100 Group RAF forming a so-called MANDREL screen over the Channel.

These measures in themselves, however, were not enough. To ensure complete surprise, and to maintain deception, it was necessary to mount a decoy operation that would lead the enemy to believe that the main weight of the invasion would fall on a different point of the French coast from that actually intended. As the Allied surface forces would be stretched to their limits in support of the actual invasion, it was obviously out of the question to employ a large fleet of 'ghost' vessels to simulate the invasion force. The only real solution was to use aircraft, dropping bundles of WINDOW at precise intervals.

In the early hours of 6 June, 1944, as the massive Allied invasion fleet turned in towards the Normandy coast, eight Lancasters of No. 617 Squadron RAF set out over the Channel towards a point north of Le Havre. The aircraft formed up in two lines, each consisting of four aircraft abreast with four miles between each and with a distance of eight miles between lines. The Lancasters flew a series of 30 orbits, each describing an oblong eight miles by two, and each orbit was a mile ahead of the previous one to simulate a surface force moving across the Channel at a speed of about seven knots. On each of the eight-mile legs the Lancasters dropped twelve bundles of WINDOW per minute. To ensure the exceptionally high standard of navigational accuracy required, each aircraft carried two GEE sets.[83]

To produce larger echoes on the enemy's radar with the passage of time – fostering the illusion that a fleet was heading towards the coast – the size of the WINDOW bundles was gradually increased, and the Lancasters maintained an altitude of 3,000 feet to prevent the bundles from dispersing before they hit the water. As an added precaution, in case the ruse was detected and analysed for what it was by enemy airborne radar, a small force of harbour defence boats and air-sea rescue launches kept station beneath the orbiting Lancasters, The vessels carried a device known as MOONSHINE, which picked up enemy radar pulses, amplified them and re-transmitted them, giving a 'solid' radar impression of a large concentration of ships forging slowly ahead. The boats also towed FILBERTS, 29-foot-long barrage balloons with nine-foot-diameter radar reflectors built inside their envelopes. Each FILBERT produced an echo similar to that of a 10,000-ton ship.

The Lancasters' mission – code-named Operation TAXABLE – ended at a point exactly ten miles from Cap d'Antifer, within range of the German coastal batteries. As 617 Squadron returned to base their accompanying boats moored their FILBERT floats and laid a smokescreen, as the same time broadcasting recorded sounds of large vessels dropping anchor over powerful loudspeakers.

As the boats turned for home a second force of aircraft – this time six Stirlings of No. 218 Squadron, accompanied by six launches – was carrying out Operation GLIMMER, a similar mission over the Straits of Dover off Boulogne. Both these missions were so successful that, as the respective forces headed back towards the English coast, the German coastal batteries opened up a furious barrage on a large expanse of empty sea, and when the first Allied troops hit the Normandy beaches the Germans at first believed that the landings were a feint, and that the main assault was about to take place further north.

Other acts of deception also played a part in the overall plan. On the night of 2/3 June, 271 aircraft of Bomber Command attacked four coastal gun batteries in the Pas de Calais area, and there were more attacks in this sector on the next two nights. Then, on the night of 5/6 June, 1,012 bombers attacked ten coastal batteries in the Normandy invasion area while Nos 617 and 218 Squadrons were carrying out their 'spoof' operations elsewhere. In addition, 36 Halifaxes and Stirlings dropped dummy parachutists and explosive devices to simulate airborne landings away from the invasion area.

Throughout the buildup to the invasion, Allied fighter aircraft maintained their tight web of patrols by day and night over the Channel and North Sea. The RAF's Mosquitoes were now fitted with the latest Mk VIII AI equipment, but as yet were not allowed to venture over the continent with it; bomber support was left to Mosquitoes still fitted with the earlier Mk IV. It could sometimes be a frustrating business for the night-fighters, as Flight Lieutenant Stuart Watts, a navigator with No. 157 Squadron, explains.

> I can't tell you the number of times we got so close to something fast – a 190, for example, which the Mosquito had the legs on in a dive. You'd go through the 'gate', catch him up and then you'd hear a faint voice in the background saying 'Atora 12, return to base. I say again, return to base.' It was highly upsetting because we could have shot the bugger down; but we were not allowed to cross the coast, not allowed to cross into enemy territory. It was just about as much as your commission was worth to press on.[84]

D-Day itself, meanwhile, had been subjected to several delays and uncertainties, having been postponed from the original May date. Now, at last, the uncertainty was a thing of the past. The British landings were scheduled to begin at 07.25 on Tuesday, 6 June 1944, one hour after the United States assault units hit UTAH and OMAHA beaches on the western flank; the difference in the tide accounted for the time-lag. The troops had already been embarked on their LSIs (Landing Ships Infantry) for the best part of a week, suffering agonies of seasickness while the great armada assembled in the Solent and off Spithead. Their miseries had increased on Sunday, 4 June,

when heavy storms had lashed the Channel, resulting in one last 24-hour postponement.

The 50th (Northumbrian) Division had come a long way since the dark days of May 1940, when it had battled its way across Flanders in the British Expeditionary Force's epic fighting retreat to Dunkirk. Those three weeks in Flanders had turned the Division's young territorial soldiers – boys from the area of Durham and Northumberland, and North Yorkshire – into hardened veterans, and ever since then they had been in the forefront of battle: Dunkirk, Gazala, Mersa Matruh, Alamein, the Mareth Line, Wado Akarit, Catania, names that recorded the British Army's slow uphill struggle to victory.

Now, four years almost to the day after Dunkirk, 'Fifty Div' was going back to France, selected by General Sir Bernard Montgomery to be one of the spearhead divisions in the greatest Allied undertaking of the war. The Division's objective was GOLD Beach, the strip of coastline between Le Hamel and La Rivière. This lay at the centre of the invasion front and formed a vital link between the assault forces of the American First Army on the right flank and the remainder of the British Second Army on the left. The 50th Division's initial task was to penetrate the beach defences between Le Hamel and La Rivière, and to secure a position inland stretching from Bayeux on to the west to the neighbourhood of St Leger, on the Bayeux–Caen road to the east.

The Divison was no longer exclusively a Tyne–Tees formation; four years of war had changed that. The units earmarked for the initial assault were the 231st Brigade, comprising the 1st Battalion the Hampshire Regiment, the 1st Battalion the Dorsetshire Regiment and the 2nd Battalion the Devonshire Regiment; and the 69th Brigade, consisting of the 5th Battalion the East Yorkshire Regiment and the 6th and 7th Battalions the Green Howards. After capturing the beaches and the ground overlooking them, the assault brigades were to push on and expand their bridgeheads. If these operations were successful, two reserve brigades would be sent in: the 56th Brigade to follow up the 231st, and the 151st Brigade to follow the 69th. These two reserve brigades would be mainly responsible for capturing the Bayeaux–St Leger position in the last phase of the assault. A further task assigned to 50th Division was the capture of Arromanches, on the right of GOLD Beach area; this was the site designated for the first of the MULBERRY Harbours,

On 50th Division's left, between la Rivière and St Aubin, was JUNO Beach. This was the target of the Canadian 3rd Division, whose 7th and 8th Brigades – comprising the Royal Winnipeg Rifles, the 1st Canadian Scottish, the Regina Rifles, the Regiment de la Chaudière, the Queen's Own Rifles and the North Shore Regiment – were to carry out the initial assault. The reserve brigade in this sector was the 9th.

On the left of the Canadians, SWORD Beach formed the eastern flank of the invasion. This was assigned to the British 3rd Division, which Montgomery had commanded during the retreat to Dunkirk four years earlier, and which had held the line on the Channel coast during the Battle of Britain. The 3rd Division's spearhead was 8th Brigade, consisting of the 1st Battalion the South Lancashire Regiment and the Second Battalion the East Yorkshire Regiment. Backing up the assault force was the 1st Special Services Brigade (Nos 3, 4, 6, 41 and 45 Commandos) followed by the 185th and elements of the 9th Brigade.

On the morning of 5 June, all units were feeling the strain, their nerves keyed up to breaking point by the endless waiting. On board the LSI *Empire Lance*, men of the 6th Green Howards – who were to lead 50th Division's assault together with the 5th East Yorkshires – wept through sheer relief when, at 17.00 hours, the Senior Naval Transport Officer announced over the tannoy: 'At 17.45 hours this ship will weigh anchor and, in passage with the remainder of the armada, sail for the coast of France.' Others showed their emotions in different ways; in introspective silence, in enforced jocularity. But the underlying emotion was one of

Tank Landing Ships (LSTs) were very large vessels, as this photograph shows. They were the original 'roll on, roll off' ships. (*Fred Winter*)

The wartime caption to this photograph states that it shows a high-speed launch bringing aboard airmen who have crashed in the sea. In fact, it was taken a few yards from Ramsgate jetty! Nevertheless, ASR launches performed valiant work throughout the war in the Channel area. (*Richard Derwent*)

pride, of a deep sense of dedication and purpose. Once again, a British army was about to wage a war of liberation on the continent of Europe, joined by powerful allies from across the sea.

Now that the invasion was on the move, the troops were in remarkably good spirits, despite their seasickness. Many, conscious of the stern task that lay ahead, tried to snatch a few hours' sleep that night, but it proved almost impossible; apart from the physical discomfort of the cramped vessels, the hours of darkness reverberated with noise as wave after wave of aircraft – some on bombing missions, others towing gliders and carrying paratroops of the British 6th and US 82nd and 101st Airborne Divisions, on their way to seize key objectives inland – roared through the night unseen.

By 05.00 the LSIs had reached their lowering positions, some seven or eight miles off the French coast, and the assault battalions embarked in their landing craft – no mean feat in itself, for a heavy swell was running and the craft were tossed up and down like corks. Nevertheless, the operation was accomplished with remarkably few mishaps. In 50th Division's sector, the rough sea presented an additional problem, for it prevented the launching of the DD amphibious tanks which were to have supported the initial assault waves on the beaches. It was now decided that these were to be landed directly on to the beach from their LSTs, which meant that they would arrive after the infantry. Armoured support in the early stages would be provided by the armoured fighting vehicles of the Westminster Dragoons and the 81st and 82nd Assault Squadrons, Royal Engineers. These units, forming part of the 79th Armoured Division, were equipped with a variety of Hobart's

'Funnies'. The 79th Division was to perform valiant service that day, blasting a path for the infantry all along the beaches.

Visibility was poor as the assault craft and their supporting tank landing craft began their run-in towards the beaches, with the coastline obscured by haze and smoke. A terrible blanket of noise lay over everything, as warships of Vian's Eastern Naval Task Force hurled their broadsides at the enemy's positions. Opposite the British beaches, the bombardment was opened at 05.25 by the battleship HMS *Warspite*, engaging the shore battery at Berneville; she was followed by another veteran battleship, HMS *Ramillies*, the monitor *Roberts*, and the cruisers *Mauritius*, *Arethusa*, *Frobisher*, *Danae* and *Dragon*, the latter Polish-manned.

The warships' gunfire was generally much more accurate than the tactical bombing had been, being directed by aircraft of No. 34 Reconnaissance Wing – also known as the Air Spotting Pool – based at Lee-on-Solent. This unique formation comprised Nos 808, 885, 886, and 897 Squadrons of No. 3 Wing, Fleet Air Arm, equipped with Seafire L. IIIs and Spitfire Vbs, Nos 26 and 63 Squadrons RAF, also equipped with Spitfire Vbs, and the Typhoons of No. 1320 flight – about 110 aircraft in all. The Pool included seventeen American pilots of Observation Squadron VOS-7, made up from aviation units on battleships and cruisers assigned to bombardment duty. They flew Spitfires from D-Day to D plus 4. The usual technique was for the aircraft to operate in pairs, one acting as spotter while the other provided cover. The first spotting mission was flown at 04.40 on D-Day, and by nightfall the Pool had lost three Seafires and three Spitfires, some of them to friendly fire.

The leading units of 50th Division could see no sign of enemy opposition behind the drifting smoke clouds as they forged through the breakers towards GOLD Beach. Major R.J.L. Jackson, one of the Beachmasters – whose task it was to co-ordinate the first phase of the assault – recalled later:

> The beach was completely deserted as we approached and I remember being puzzled by the comparative silence. Of course, the Allied bombardment was landing far ahead and we could see some of the big shells passing over us, but the absence of any fire directed at us was strange. As Beachmaster, my job was like that of a traffic controller except that my traffic was on foot. I had to see that everyone was directed to their correct positions as soon as they arrived. Our biggest fear concerned the first few seconds when the landing craft doors were opened and we presented a tight, congested target for any machine-gunners. Because of this we lost a sergeant, who jumped too soon into the sea when we hit a false bottom. The water there was some eight feet deep, but he thought we had struck the beach. He was carrying so much equipment that he sank straight away and drowned.
>
> Ironically his fears were without foundation. When we landed the doors opened, we jumped out, but there were no bullets. The beach was still apparently deserted. The water was only about a foot deep and I quickly advanced up the beach flanked by a radio operator and a regimental policeman carrying a Sten gun. At every step we expected to be fired at, but were not. Lack of opposition became eerie.
>
> Then, after about 200 yards, we must have reached a German fixed line. Suddenly they threw everything at us. The mortars took us first and I was hit badly in the leg. My radio operator and policeman were both killed outright by the same explosion.[85]

Everywhere along GOLD Beach it was a similar story. There was a false illusion of calm as the spearhead companies jumped from their LCAs at about 07.25 and waded through the shallows, then all hell broke loose as the Germans opened up with mortars, machine-guns and artillery on the infantry advancing across the exposed beach. On the extreme right of 231st Brigade's assault, the 1st Hampshires became pinned down by accurate fire among minefields, and it was 90 minutes before two companies managed to get off the beach and attack the pillboxes and machine-gun nests manned by the troops of the German 352nd Infantry Division. Even then, they might not have got off the beach at all had it not been for the support of the Churchill 'Petard' tanks, which knocked out several pillboxes. The 1st Hampshires suffered heavy casualties in the day's fighting, but succeeded in capturing Le Hamel and Arromanches before nightfall. The 'Petards' and 'Flails' of the Sherwood Rangers also gave invaluable support to the 1st Dorsets and 2nd Devons, the other two battalions of 231st Brigade, who battled their way off the beach to take the high ground beyond and push on towards Bayeaux.

On the left of GOLD Beach, meanwhile, the leading units of 69th Brigade had gone ashore near La Rivière. The 5th East Yorkshires were in the forefront, closely followed by the 6th Green Howards on their right. Heavy machine-gun and mortar fire greeted the East Yorkshires as they crossed the beach, and one company – nearest La Rivière – was pinned down. It, too, was extricated by a couple of Petard tanks, which knocked out the troublesome pillboxes. The East Yorkshires fought their way off the beach and pushed inland, threading their way through minefields towards the German coastal battery at Mont Fleury.

On their right, the 6th Green Howards also had to contend with heavy mortar fire and machine-gun fire from pillboxes. Adding to their problems, the Germans had an 88mm gun in a reinforced concrete bunker, protected from infantry attack by machine-guns, and this opened up an accurate fire on the LCAs and LCTs as they closed the beach. The 88 hit two Petard tanks as they came ashore and they blew up with terrific explosions, showering debris on the heads of the advancing troops, and without their support the forward sections of 'A' Company, 6th Green Howards were pinned down behind the sea-wall. Help arrived in the shape of a solitary DD tank of the 4th/7th Dragoons, which engaged the enemy machine-gun posts. Under cover of its fire, two platoons leaped across the sea-wall and systematically began to wipe out one enemy position after another.

On the left of 'A' Company, 'D' Company suffered heavy casualties when it encountered deep water, mines and heavy mortar fire during its landing. Nevertheless, the company commander managed to assemble the remainder of his men and led them across the enemy

minefields towards the Mont Fleury battery, which the East Yorkshires had not yet reached. The company's progress was so rapid that the enemy troops defending the battery were taken completely by surprise, and were either killed or captured.

Shortly afterwards, Major Lofthouse, 'D' Company commander, noticed that two enemy pillboxes had been by-passed in the advance and went back with Company Sergeant-Major Stan Hollis to make sure that they were clear. This decision was to lead to the award of the only Victoria Cross to be won on D-Day. The citation tells the story.[86]

> In Normandy, on June 6th, 1944, during the assault on the beaches and the Mont Fleury Battery, CSM Hollis's Company Commander noticed that two of the pillboxes had been by-passed, and went with CSM Hollis to see that they were clear. When they were twenty yards from the pillbox a machine gun opened fire from the slit, and CSM Hollis instantly rushed straight at the pillbox, recharged his magazine, threw a grenade in through the door, and fired his Sten gun into it, killing two Germans and taking the remainder prisoner. He then cleared several Germans from a neighbouring trench. By this action he undoubtedly saved his Company from being fired on heavily from the rear, and enabled them to open the main beach exit.
>
> Later the same day, in the village of Crepon, the Company encountered a field gun and crew, armed with Spandaus, at a hundred yards range. CSM Hollis was put in command of a party to cover an attack on the gun, but the movement was held up. Seeing this, CSM Hollis pushed right forward to engage the gun with a PIAT[87] from a house at fifty yards range. He was observed by a sniper who fired and grazed his right cheek, and at the same time the gun swung round and fired at point blank range into the house. To avoid the falling masonry CSM Hollis moved his party to an alternative position. Two of the enemy gun crew had by this time been killed, and the gun was destroyed shortly afterwards. He later found that two of his men had stayed behind in the house, and immediately volunteered to get them out. In full view of the enemy, who were continually firing at him, he went forward alone using a Bren gun to distract their

attention from the other men. Under cover of his diversion, the two men were able to get back . . . It was largely through his heroism and resource that the Company's objectives were gained and casualties were not heavier, and by his own bravery he saved the lives of many of his men.

While the Green Howards – joined now by the 7th Battalion, which had landed and entered the battle – and the East Yorkshires pushed on to take their early objectives, supported by the DD tanks of the 4th/7th Dragoon Guards and the 79th Division's 'Funnies', the units of the 231st Brigade over on their right continued to make steady, albeit laborious, progress. In the afternoon the 1st Hampshires took Les Roquettes, which had originally been the objective of the 1st Dorsets, then swung round to the right through Asnelles-sur-Mer to attack the strongly defended sanatorium at Le Hamel. Several infantry assaults failed, but the sanatorium eventually fell in the afternoon after a series of devastating attacks by Petards. Meanwhile, the 1st Dorsets had succeeded in gaining the high ground to the south of Arromanches.

By 11.00 the Flail tanks had cleared seven lanes through the minefields on GOLD beach and the DD tanks were pushing inland, supporting the troops of the newly-landed 56th and 151st brigades in the centre. An hour later the bridgehead had reached a depth of three miles; 56th Brigade was astride the La Rivière–Bayeaux road and 151st, on its left, was capturing the high ground before working its way into the Seulles Valley. Further left still, 69th Brigade pressed on towards Creuilly, while 231st Brigade continued mopping up around Le Hamel and Ryes before driving on to reach the outskirts of Bayeux at nightfall. Completing the picture on GOLD Beach was No. 47 (Royal Marine) Commando, which had gone ashore some two hours after the initial landings with the task of capturing Port en Bessin, a key point at the junction of the British and American beaches.

The Commandos encountered severe difficulties right from the start. Three of their landing craft were sunk during the approach to the beach,

An LST with bow doors open. (*Fred Winter*)

and when the remainder landed at Le Hamel they found the 1st Hampshires who should have cleared this sector by this time, still involved in heavy fighting. After a stiff fight with a company of Germans, during which they suffered 40 casualties and took 60 prisoners, the 400 Commandos set off on the ten-mile march through enemy territory to strike at Port en Bessin from the rear. They reached their objective at nightfall and attacked at dawn. The town was strongly defended by about 500 enemy troops of the 352nd Division, plus some Naval personnel, who were entrenched in pillboxes and strong-points, and the battle raged all day. By the time Port en Bessin fell, No. 47 Commando's effective strength had been reduced to 200 men.

Meanwhile, in the centre of the British Second Army's front, the Canadian 3rd Division had been having a hard time on JUNO Beach, between La Rivière and St Aubin. Supported by the 2nd Canadian Armoured Brigade, the 3rd Division had to negotiate a strongly-defended open expanse of beach and clear the towns of Courseulles and Bernières before pushing inland to capture the airfield at Carpiquet, on the outskirts of Caen. Allied Intelligence had known for some time that Caen was the key to the whole German defensive system in Normandy, and General Montgomery had consequently assigned high priority to its capture. Everything hinged on the Canadians' speedy exploitation inland during the first day, before the defenders of Caen – the 716th Infantry Division and 21st *Panzer* Division – had time to get over their initial surprise.

The Canadian assault, however, got off to a poor start. Bad weather delayed it for an hour, and by the time the leading assault craft closed the beaches at about 08.30 the rising tide had covered many dangerous obstacles. At one point, underwater explosives and accurate artillery fire from the shore destroyed 20 out of 24 craft, leaving the surviving troops to struggle to the beach as best they could.

The assault on the right flank was spearheaded by the Canadian 7th Brigade, with the Royal Winnipeg Regiment and the Regina Rifles leading the attack west of the Seulles River. They were supported by a handful of DD tanks of the Canadian 1st Hussars, which had been launched 800 yards out and wallowed ashore with extreme difficulty. It was fortunate that they succeeded, for the Allied naval and air bombardment had left many enemy strongpoints untouched in the Canadian sector, and if it had not been for the tanks the infantry might not have got off the beaches at all. To add to their problems, the incoming tide had reduced the width of the beach to a maximum of 100 yards, and the masses of troops and equipment that piled up on this narrow strip provided excellent targets for the enemy artillery, mortars and machine-guns. Despite the difficulties, however, the DD tanks managed to blast enough holes in the enemy defences to enable the infantry to break out, and

by the time the Engineer assault armour of the 22nd Dragoons and the 26th Assault Squadron, Royal Engineers, arrived to support the 7th Brigade, the DDs and infantry were already pushing inland. By mid-afternoon the advance had reached a depth of seven miles, and the Canadian armour had cut the Caen–Bayeux road.

On the left, the Queen's Own Regiment of Canada and the North Shore Regiment had to land without the benefit of armoured support, and enemy machine-guns cut great gaps in their ranks as they raced for the shelter of the sea wall at the rear of the beach. The position eased with the arrival of some DD tanks and Engineer assault armour, which crawled up the beach to blast holes in the twelve-foot-high wall. Flail tanks came up to clear paths through the minefields, and with their assistance the infantry began to make better progress, and when the 8th Brigade's reserve, the French-Canadian Regiment de la Chaudière, came ashore 30 minutes later the worst of the enemy resistance had been overcome.

Further inland, however, the enemy rallied and counter-attacked the 8th Brigade at Bernières, and although this danger was overcome by the Regiment de la Chaudière it had the effect of slowing up the Canadian advance. Caen did not fall that day, nor the next. In fact, it was to be 10 July before British and Canandian troops penetrated the town, and by that time air attacks had reduced it to a sea of rubble. Nevertheless, the Canadians advanced further inland than any other troops on D-Day, joining up with 50th Division and carving out a beachhead fifteen miles long and seven deep on Second Army's front.

JUNO Beach and SWORD Beach, on the extreme left flank of the Second Army's assault, were separated by a five-mile stretch of rocky coastline dotted with a number of hamlets, all heavily defended. To clear these, two Royal Marine Commandos were detailed to go in some two hours after the main assault, No. 48 Commando landing at St Aubin on the left of the Canadians and No. 41 Commando at Lion-sur-

Mer, on the right of the British 3rd Division. The two Commandos were to push inland, swinging left and right and clearing all obstacles in their path before joining up with one another and forming the vital link between the British and Canadian beachheads.

In practice, however, it was not so easy. Heavy fighting was still going on around St Aubin when No. 48 Commando closed the beach, and several of their landing craft were knocked out by 88mm gunfire. By the time the Commando assembled it had already suffered some 40 per cent casualties, but despite this it managed to take its initial objectives. Number 41 Commando also encountered difficulties; it, too, suffered casualties during the landing, and then it ran into armoured and infantry elements of the 21st *Panzer* Division outside Lion-sur-Mer. It was a long time before any progress was made, and days before the two Commandos succeeded in joining up as planned.

Meanwhile, SWORD Beach – lying just to the west of Ouistreham, at the outlet of the Caen Canal – had also been the scene of bitter fighting as the leading units of the British 3rd Division struggled to get ashore. Despite rough seas and obstacles, the leading DD tanks of the 13th/18th Hussars had crawled ashore almost exactly on schedule, engaging the enemy strongpoints practically at point-blank range while the Engineer assault groups made their landings in turn. Under cover of the armoured duel the spearhead infantry of the 8th Brigade – the 1st Battalion the South Lancashire Regiment and the 2nd Battalion the East Yorkshire Regiment, closely followed by the 1st Suffolks – fought their way through intense machine-gun and mortar fire to gain footholds on the beach.

The Petards and Flails of the 5th Assault Regiment, Royal Engineers, supported by the 22nd Dragoons and the Westminster Dragoons did their work well, and by 09.30 the armour had beaten seven lanes through the German forward defences. The South Lancashires pushed on towards Hermanville, a mile and a half inland; beyond it was the vital high ground of Périers

Ridge, strongly defended by anti-tank units of General Feuchtinger's 21st *Panzer* Division and infantry of the 716th Division. By this time, the spearhead troops of the 8th Brigade were practically exhausted, and so they dug in while the three battalions of the reserve 185th Brigade moved up to attack the ridge. The plan called for the tanks of the Staffordshire Yeomanry to break through and then push on rapidly to Caen with the men of the Shropshire Light Infantry, but the battle situation had become so confused that the tanks could not be disengaged from the general mêlée.

When the enemy guns on Périers Ridge were finally silenced after a hard struggle, the Shropshires were forced to advance without armoured support, trudging along the road out of Hermanville with their flanks unprotected. There was to have been a parallel advance by the East Yorkshires, but they had lost 70 officers and men killed and 150 wounded and were in no fit state to engage in more fighting for the time being. Despite the lack of support, the Shropshires fought their way through and reached Biéville, less than four miles from Caen, at about 16.00, when they were joined at last by the tanks and self-propelled guns of the Staffordshire Yeomanry.

The reinforcements arrived just in time, for soon afterwards the Shropshires' advance ran into a battle group of the 21st *Panzer* Division, trying desperately to carve a gap between the British and Canadian beachheads. Five Tiger tanks were knocked out by the British self-propelled guns and the rest withdrew. The British infantry tried to press on, but were soon pinned down by heavy fire from Lebisey Ridge, commanding the road to Caen. Here, as in the Canadian sector, it was fast becoming clear that Montgomery's gamble of taking Caen was doomed to failure.

Meanwhile, the American assaults on UTAH and OMAHA Beaches had seen mixed fortunes. On the extreme western flank of the invasion, the landing at UTAH Beach was supported by a bombardment force comprising the US battleship

Nevada, the British monitor *Erebus*, the US cruisers *Tuscaloosa* and *Quincy*, the British cruisers *Hawkins*, *Black Prince* and *Enterprise*, eight US destroyers and a Dutch gunboat, the *Soemba*.

The Field Order governing the operations in this sector was concise: 'VIII Corps assaults UTAH Beach on D-Day at H-Hour and captures Cherbourg with minimum delay.' It was an important mission, for as soon as Cherbourg and the Brittany ports were opened they could be supplied directly from the United States, whereas the British would rely, ultimately, on resupply through the northern Channel ports and Antwerp. In the meantime, all would rely on the two *Mulberries* and the five *Gooseberries*.

The beach-head at UTAH was to be established by the 4th Infantry Division, the 8th Infantry Regiment leading with the 1st Battalion on the right, heading for GREEN Beach, and the 2nd Battalion on the left, its objective RED Beach.

Forty minutes before the assault, the beach area was bombed by 276 aircraft of the US Ninth Air Force. Then, under cover of the naval bombardment, 600 men closed the beach in twenty landing craft, supported by 28 DD tanks of the 70th Tank Battalion. The 2nd Battalion were the first ashore – the first troops, apart from the airborne forces fighting to the rear, to land in Normandy. They encountered only desultory fire as they advanced up the beach, and in a sense they were lucky, for they had landed about a mile south of their target, at a spot where the enemy defences were lighter.

The leading troops were off the beach in about two hours, enemy strongpoints being mopped up with relative ease. Long before noon, the 1st Battalion had overrun a key fortified position at La Madeleine, opening up the causeway to the Audoville-la-Hubert road, while the 2nd and 3rd Battalions, the latter in the centre, crossed the causeways to Pouppeville and Houdienville, flanked by their DD tanks.

By 10.00 six battalions of infantry had begun to move off the beach, the spearhead force having now been joined by follow-on troops of the 12th and 22nd Infantry Regiments. Shortly after noon,

the three battalions of the 22nd Infantry Regiment moved off to open the northernmost exit, the 3rd Battalion pushing along the coast road to anchor a flank on Hamel-de-Cruttes, while the 1st and 2nd Battalions had a miserable advance to St Germain de Varreville, wading waist-deep – and sometimes neck-deep – through flooded terrain. The 12th Infantry Regiment found the going even worse; tired of waiting for the 8th Regiment's 1st Battalion to clear its exit from the beach, the men struck out diagonally, wading through chest-deep water across the line of march until they reached dry land. But the discomfort mattered little; what did matter was that, at the end of the day, the two regiments leading the assault at UTAH Beach – the 8th and 22nd – had lost twelve men killed between them.

OMAHA Beach was different. OMAHA Beach was a nightmare and a tragedy, and the assault on it was to account for nearly half the D-Day casualties. It was defended by the best German coastal infantry division on the Normandy coast, the 352nd; British Intelligence knew that it had been assigned to the sector and had duly informed the US First Army, which treated the information with suspicion and appears to have taken little action on it. At any rate, the assault forces were never briefed on the calibre of the defending troops they were likely to encounter.

The nature of the defences themselves, however, were well known, thanks to air reconnaissance and night-time infiltration by members of the special forces during the build-up period. OMAHA Beach was a shallow arc of sand, enclosed in the west by the outcropping rocks of the Pointe de la Percée and in the east by Port-en-Bessin. Inland, bluffs rose gently to a plateau 150 feet above the beach, giving way to small fields enclosed by hedges, deep lanes and scattered hamlets. Behind the beach were three coastal villages, Vierville, St Laurent and Colleville, a mile and a half apart and linked by a narrow lane. There was a stretch of paved promenade along the front, bordered by a low sea-wall. Narrow gullies running up from the beach gave access to this promenade and the area beyond. Between the beach and the bluffs there was also a shingle bank, ten feet high in places. The area was readily defensible, the rocky outcrops providing concealment for gun positions to enfilade the beach and its approaches. Behind the shingle bank and the sea-wall there were trenches, pill-boxes and gun emplacements, all sited to bring a devastating crossfire to bear on the beach, which itself was mined.

The assault on OMAHA Beach was to be made by the 16th and 116th Regimental Combat Teams of V Corps, supported by armour and artillery. While these made a frontal attack on the strongest points, engineer teams would clear lanes through the obstacles and minefields for the follow-on forces, and would then blow gaps through the shingle bank and sea-wall. The follow-on force would then drive on through the three villages nearest the coast to the Isigny–Bayeux road, its right flank on the flooded areas bonding UTAH Beach and its left on the boundary between the US First and British Second Armies. At H-Hour, a powerful enemy battery on the sheer cliffs of the Pointe de Hoe, west of OMAHA Beach, would be attacked and eliminated by US Rangers, who would then advance on Isigny with the 1st Battalion of the 116th Regiment on their left.

Such was the plan, and it went wrong from the moment when, at about 03.00, the assault craft were lowered into the water twelve miles offshore. Many foundered in the heavy seas, leaving men struggling for their lives.

Whereas at UTAH Beach the supporting DD tanks were launched from a point 3,000 yards out, at OMAHA the 32 tanks due to land at H minus five minutes were launched into steep seas 6,000 yards off shore; 27 were swamped within minutes and sank. Two more were jammed in the ramp of the LCT, and only two reached the beach. Other LCT commanders had the sense to get closer inshore, but even so the 96 tanks that should have been available to provide close support for the 1,450 men in the assault wave were reduced in number by almost a third because of this rash action.

The DUKW amphibious vehicles that were to bring in the supporting artillery also met with disaster. The 111th Field Artillery Battalion lost all its 105mm howitzers except one, and other artillery units fared little better. Nevertheless, it was still a formidable array of men and material that forged its way towards OMAHA Beach when the supporting bombardment force opened fire, 40 minutes before landfall. The naval bombardment, in this case, was provided by the US battleships *Texas* and *Arkansas*, the British cruiser *Glasgow*, the French cruisers *Montcalm* and *Georges Leygues* with eight American and two British destroyers. At the same time, 329 B-24 Liberators of the US Ninth Air Force bombed thirteen targets in the OMAHA area.

The friendly barrage lifted when the assault craft were less than half a mile from the beach and was instantly replaced by an enemy one. Here, the German gunners were wide awake and the assault troops floundered ashore through murderous fire, many of their craft being sunk before they hit the beach. In the next half-hour about a thousand assault troops and engineers managed to get ashore, but of the sixteen engineer teams, each assigned to a particular objective, only five came near to completing their tasks. On the beach there was chaos, a maelstrom of smoke and flame and corpses, the living struggling forward to the shelter of the sea-wall and the shingle bank. Yet incredibly, as the morning wore on, order began to emerge out of the chaos. As one account put it:

> The day belonged to the few, to the lieutenant and a wounded engineer sergeant who walked erect, cut wire, and blew mines, taunting those who lay at the water's edge more by their examples than with words, until at last the scattered remnants on 'Easy Red' staggered forward; to an engineer lieutenant crawling through mud and sand, probing for mines with a hunting knife; to the infantry lieutenant who assaulted a strong-point single-handed with grenades, and handed over his map and compass to a sergeant as he died, riddled with bullets. They were there, such men, in ones and twos, all along the line of smoke and mines, chaos, exhaustion and death, gathering their small groups, taunting, cursing, urging, moving forward off the beach, usually blind, but the daylight would come.

Presently the fog of war would clear, and these men would combine to new tasks.

But on 'Dog-Green' and 'Fox-Green', where the leading companies had been blown to pieces, literally at the cannon's mouth, as their craft had come in against the powerful defences of the Vierville and Colleville gullies, the pattern had a different form. On the left at 'Fox-Green' sections of the 16th and 116th came in late, scrambled together, and with their supporting DD tanks at the bottom of the sea. Deprived of almost their entire officer and NCO leadership, battered threequarters to death, these remnants were beyond rallying. In taking the first shock these men had played such parts as they were to play that day, and the wreckage of their dead, the sodden corpses floundering in the rising tide, in all the ugly maze of lost equipment, bore witness.

The struggle belonged to those following in their wakes.[88]

Meanwhile, the 2nd Ranger Battalion had assaulted the gun battery on the Pointe de Hoe, swarming up and over the clifftop with the aid of grappling irons, only to find the position abandoned. This group then moved off inland. The remainder of the battalion, landing opposite the Vierville gulley in the wake of the 116th Infantry, suffered heavy casualties; only 62 men out of 130 reached the dubious sanctuary of the sea-wall. The 5th Ranger Battalion, on the left, met very little opposition; 450 strong, it lost only a handful of men before reaching the sea-wall, where it joined up with a company of the battered 116th Infantry.

Gradually, with many individual and collective acts of gallantry, the Americans fought their way off the bullet-swept beach and secured the heights beyond, clearing the way for the follow-up force. Supported by the guns of warships that came close inshore, they penetrated inland to a depth of 1,500 yards. It was not much, but they were ashore, and they were there to stay.

As 6 June drew to a close, the Allies were off the beaches everywhere. The only attempt at a counter-attack, by 90 tanks of Feuchtinger's 21st *Panzer*, had lost its momentum and petered out; the infantry divisions were falling back everywhere, and the only other formation that might have intervened in strength – 12th *Panzer* Division, coming up from Lisieux under air attack all the way – had arrived at Caen only to find its vital fuel dump in flames.

That evening, General Montgomery reported to his superiors: 'As a result of the D-Day operations a foothold has been gained on the Continent of Europe.' It had been gained at a cost of some 2,500 Allied dead, the lion's share on OMAHA Beach.

CHAPTER NINE

The Channel Secured

To meet any possible seaborne threat to the invasion, the Allies had deployed a formidable range of warships, supported by the reinforced No. 19 Group, RAF Coastal Command. Ten support groups of destroyers, sloops and frigates, supported by a host of Coastal Force MTBs and MGBs, formed a screen at either end of the Channel; six of these groups covered the Western Approaches and the Bay of Biscay,

Admiral Karl Dönitz, the architect of the U-boat war, lost two sons in the German submarine service.

supported by the escort carriers *Activity*, *Tracker* and *Vindex*.

When the assault convoys crossed the Channel, the special anti-invasion groups of U-boats which had been held in the Biscay ports and Norway were all still in harbour, but as soon as the Germans realized that the invasion had really started the Biscay U-boats, and also three destroyers which had been lying in the Gironde estuary, were ordered to proceed to the scene of the landings. The destroyers, constantly harassed from the air, were soon forced to put into the shelter of Brest, but on 6 June seventeen U-boats put to sea from that harbour, fourteen from St Nazaire, four from La Pallice and one from Lorient.

They were soon in trouble. On 7 June, aircraft of No. 19 Group sank the U-955 and U-970 in the Bay of Biscay, and four of the Brest boats, U-963, U-989, U-256 and U-415 were all damaged and forced to return to base. On the following day, a Liberator of No. 224 Squadron sank the U-629 and U-373 in quick succession, and on 9 June U-740 was also destroyed.

It was clear that the Germans had little hope of penetrating the invasion area using submarines which were not equipped with SCHNORCHEL apparatus. Nine boats of the Biscay group were fitted with this device, which enabled them to recharge their batteries and air while remaining submerged and also greatly reduced their chances of detection by ASV-equipped aircraft, and eight of these attempted to infiltrate the Channel area from 7 June. Between that date and 11 June three made abortive torpedo attacks, and U-821 was destroyed by an aircraft.

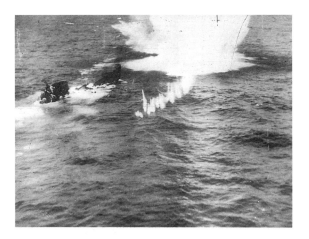

Seek and sink. The U-boats had little chance of penetrating the invasion area without being detected. These photographs show a submarine under air attack, its end marked finally by an oil slick on the surface.

It was not until 15 June that they enjoyed some success, the U-621 sinking the tank landing ship LST280, the U-767 the frigate *Mourne*, and the U-764 the escort destroyer *Blackwood*; the latter was taken in tow, but was a total loss. On 18 June, U-767 was sunk by destroyers of the 14th Support Group, and the U-441 by a Wellington of No. 304 (Polish) Squadron.

A second group of SCHNORCHEL-equipped boats penetrated the invasion area during the second half of June, and these suffered an early loss when U-971 was sunk in the western part of the Channel by the destroyers *Haida* and *Eskimo* on the nght of 22/23 June. Two nights later, the destroyers *Affleck* and *Balfour* sank the U-1191, while the U-269 was destroyed by the *Bickerton*; the destroyer *Goodson* was torpedoed and damaged by the U-984. On 27/29 June, U-988 torpedoed the corvette *Pink*, which was a total loss, and sank two ships of 9,444 tons before she was sent to the bottom by the 3rd Support Group. The biggest German success came that same day, 29 June, when the U-984 attacked convoy EMC.17 and torpedoed four ships of 28,790 tons, three of which were sunk and the fourth beached. This attack showed what a SCHNORCHEL boat could achieve under favourable circumstances, and it must be said that the U-boats had suffered their share of bad luck during operations in June; often, their torpedoes had detonated prematurely, or their motors had failed to work properly.[89] On one occasion, on 18 June, torpedoes from the U-621 had narrowly missed the American battleships *Texas* and *Arkansas*.

After these excursions, the surviving U-boats never again presented a serious threat to the invasion. Neither did the *Luftwaffe*, although on the few occasions when enemy aircraft eluded the Allied fighter screen they were still capable on inflicting damage. In the early morning of 13 June, for example, a lone Junkers Ju 88 avoided detection by tagging on to an Allied bomber force, then broke away and torpedoed the destroyer HMS *Boadicea*, which sank with the loss of 175 officers and men. The loss of this ship was particularly sad; one of the old 'B' class destroyers that had formed part of the original Dover flotilla in 1939, she had survived five years of war in waters ranging from the South Atlantic to the Arctic Circle. Another surprise air attack of this type also sank the American destroyer USS *Meredith II*. Six Allied destroyers were also sunk by mines – the US *Corry*, *Glennon* and *Rich* and the British *Fury*, *Swift* and *Wrestler* – while the French destroyer *Mistral* was sunk by coastal gunfire.

The S-boat flotillas were much in evidence during the first two weeks of June, making frequent sorties and scoring several successes against Allied landing ships and landing craft. Such was the expenditure of torpedoes and ammunition, especially by the Cherbourg-based flotilla, that the Germans attempted a risky re-supply mission by the destroyers based at Brest on the night of 8/9 June. The four destroyers involved – ZH1, Z24, Z32 and T24 – were intercepted off the Ile de Bas by the 10th Flotilla, comprising the *Tartar*, *Ashanti*, *Haida* and *Huron*. In the ensuing battle ZH1 was sunk, Z32 beached and blown up, and the other two damaged, Z24 later being sunk by air attack off Bordeaux. On the British side, HMS *Tartar* was severely damaged.

In the evening of 14 June, the German light naval forces in the Channel area received a severe

blow when 221 Lancasters of Bomber Command attacked Le Havre. Twenty-two Lancasters of No. 617 Squadron dropped 12,000 lb *Tallboy* bombs on the S-boat pens, while the remainder carpeted the harbour with 1,320 tons of high explosive. The attack destroyed the destroyers *Falke*, *Jaguar* and *Möwe*, fourteen S-boats and seventeen patrol boats and escort vessels, as well as many smaller craft, and effectively removed the S-boat threat to the invasion area from this port. On the following day, 297 Lancasters, Halifaxes and Mosquitoes attacked Boulogne, sinking fourteen minesweepers and patrol craft.

A 12,000 lb TALLBOY bomb exploding on the U-boat pens at Le Havre. These weapons were used to good effect in the latter stages of the war.

On 26 June, after a heavy bombardment by Allied naval forces, Cherbourg fell to the Americans, and another vital port was lost to the Germans. The S-boats continued to make gallant sorties against the cross-Channel supply routes during July, but the back of their offensive had been broken; the majority of their missions were disrupted by British Coastal Force craft – joined now by American PT boats – and destroyers.

On the night of 5/6 July the Germans brought a new weapon into action: the NEGER one-man torpedo, 26 of which were deployed against the assault area from Villers-sur-Mer. On this occasion they sank the minesweepers *Cato* and *Magic*, and later in the month they sank the

A U-boat, desperately trying to dive, is attacked by a Mosquito of RAF Coastal Command.

destroyer *Isis*, the minesweeper *Pylades* and disabled the Polish cruiser *Dragon* so badly that she had to be scuttled as part of a Gooseberry Harbour breakwater. NEGER operations ceased in mid-August, their operating unit having suffered horrendous losses. Some success was achieved during this period by Small Battle Unit Flotilla 211, which used LINSEN explosive boats to sink the destroyer *Quorn* and the anti-submarine trawler *Gairsay* on 2/3 August.

Tragically, one of the worst losses suffered by the Royal Navy during the invasion period was caused by friendly fire. It happened on 27 August 1944, when fifteen Typhoons of Nos 263 and 266 Squadrons, led by Wing Commander J.R. Baldwin, located six ships heading south-west off Cap d'Antifer. Suspecting that they were Allied, Baldwin quered their identity with Operations, but was told that no Allied shipping was in the area. Despite querying the instruction to attack three more times and describing the coloured recognition signals fired by the ships, the attack

order remained in force. The Typhoons went in and opened fire with rockets and cannon.

Their target were the ships of the 1st Minesweeping Flotilla. Within minutes, HMS *Hussar* and HMS *Britomart* had been sunk and HMS *Salamander* damaged beyond repair. Of the Royal Navy crews, 78 were killed and 149 wounded. The incident, apparently, was caused by a failure to communicate a change of course by the minesweeping flotilla to Naval HQ, who therefore did not expect any friendly shipping to be in the area and authorized the attack. Two accompanying trawlers, the *Colsay* and *Lord Ashfield*, were also attacked and damaged. No blame for the error was laid at the RAF's door.

In mid-August another group of U-boats made an attempt to penetrate the Channel, but four were quickly sunk by surface forces and the rest were recalled to Norway. To all intents and purposes, it was the end; the Channel was secure.

For at least part of the bombardment force that had covered the Normandy landings,

Escort carriers like the one pictured here (HMS *Ameer*) covered the approaches to the Channel during the D-Day operations.

though, there was still work to be done. In the first week of November, 1944, a bombardment force led by HMS *Warspite* and the monitors *Roberts* and *Erebus* shelled the island of Walcheren, in the Scheldt estuary, in support of a hard-fought and costly landing there by Canadian forces and the Royal Marine Special Service Brigade. On 8 November, the German commander and his 29,000-strong garrison surrendered.

Elsewhere in Holland, the Germans clung on tenaciously, and it was from this foothold that the surviving S-boats made their last forays into the North Sea and the English Channel. On 22 March 1945 – for the last time – boats of the 2nd and 5th Flotillas set out from Ijmuiden and Den Helder to attack shipping between the Thames Estuary and the Scheldt. The mission was intercepted by the destroyer HMS *Mackay*.

And so it was almost over. The end came at last on 8 May 1945, when the destroyers *Beagle* and *Bulldog* sailed to St Peter Port in Guernsey to receive the surrender of the German garrison in the Channel Islands. It was from these islands, on 8/9 March, that the German Navy had carried out its last raid of the Channel war, when four minesweepers of the 24th Flotilla under *Kapitänleutnant* Mohr, supported by several smaller craft, had landed a raiding force in the harbour of Granville, on the French coast. The assault troops blew up four freighters, disabled a PT boat, captured a small collier and set free 67 German prisoners.

Now, littered with the debris of war, the Channel was silent. Over five years, the war had spread out over the oceans of the world; but it was here, in and over the Narrow Seas, that the decisive acts had been played.

Notes and References

1. The battleships were the *Resolution* and *Revenge*; the other aircraft carrier was the *Hermes*; and the light cruisers were the *Cairo*, *Caradoc* and *Ceres*.

2. The Portland-based destroyers were the *Veteran*, *Whitshed*, *Wild Swan*, *Windsor* and *Wren* (18th Destroyer Flotilla) and the *Echo*, *Eclipse*, *Electra*, *Encounter*, *Escapade* and *Escort* (12th Destroyer Flotilla). The Portsmouth-based boats were the *Malcolm*, *Venomous* and *Wivern* (16th Destroyer Flotilla), while the 19th Destroyer Flotilla at Dover comprised the B-class destroyers *Basilisk*, *Beagle*, *Blanche*, *Boadicea*, *Boreas*, *Brazen* and *Brilliant*. Making up the two flotillas at Plymouth were the *Mackay*, *Vanoc*, *Vanquisher*, *Versatile*, *Vimy*, *Walker*, *Warwick*, *Whirlwind* and *Winchelsea* of the 11th Destroyer Flotilla, and the *Keppel*, *Vanessa*, *Viscount*, *Vivacious*, *Vortigern*, *Wakeful* and *Wessex* and the 17th Destroyer Flotilla.

3. The U-Boats destroyed in the minefields, which were laid between the Goodwin Sands and the Dyck Shoal, were the U-12 (8 October), U-40 (13 October) and U-16 (24 October).

4. The minimum sweeping height for these operations was 35 feet.

5. Captain S.W. Roskill: *The Navy at War, 1939–1945*, pp 47–48.

6. Captain D.J.R. Simson and Lt-Cdr C.G.W. Donald were respectively captains of the *Keith* and *Vimy*.

7. Peter Verney: *The Micks – Story of the Irish Guards*, London 1970.

8. This signal appears to have been sent entirely on Dewing's own initiative.

9. Winston Churchill, *The Second World War*, II, *Their Finest Hour*, p. 72. London, 1949.

10. At this time, vessels organized by Admiral Ramsay were already standing by to evacuate the Calais garrison.

11. Churchill, *Their Finest Hour*, p. 73.

12. Personal letters of Commander Thomas Kerr, RN (Imperial War Museum archives).

13. The first operational MTB base in the 1939–45 War was Felixstowe, the 1st Flotilla becoming operational there in January 1940. In March the 4th and 10th Flotillas also assembled at Felixstowe. The three flotillas used British Power Boat Company 60-footers, Vosper and Thorneycroft boats respectively. When the Germans invaded Holland on 10 May 1940, the 4th Flotilla deployed to Ijmuiden with the task of preventing enemy seaplanes from landing on the Zuider Zee. One He 115 was destroyed by MTB 24 (Sub-Lieut R. Parkinson, RN); this was the first enemy aircraft to be shot down by the Coastal Force.

14. Bryan Cooper, *The Battle of the Torpedo Boats* (London, 1970).

15. The British referred to the fast enemy craft as E-boats, the 'E' denoting enemy, but I have used the more correct S-boat throughout – except where the term E-boat appears in a British combat report.

16. Personal account of Mr F.G. Hutchinson (Author's archives).

17. Personal account of W.T. Elmslie (Author's archives).

18. Personal account of Lt-Cdr Archie Buchanan (Author's archives).

19. Personal account of W.T. Elmslie (Author's archives).
20. Personal account of Lt-Cdr Archie Buchanan (Author's archives).
21. Personal account of Major A.E.G. Steede (Author's archives).
22. Quoted in Major L.F. Ellis, *The War in France and Flanders 1939–40* (London 1954).
23. Report of Captain A.P. Fisher, RN Sick Quarters, Dover (Imperial War Museum archives).
24. Personal account of Mr T. Collins (Author's archives).
25. Personal letters of Commander Thomas Kerr, RN (Imperial War Museum archives).
26. Personal account of Mr W.E. Williamson (Author's archives).
27. Quoted in Michael Glover, *Invasion Scare 1940*, p. 52.
28. Ibid, p. 75.
29. Churchill, *Their Finest Hour*, p. 233.
30. A very full account of the deployments of all British warships in the Channel area at this time may be found in Peter C. Smith's book *Hold the Narrow Sea* (Moorland Publishing Co. Ltd, 1984).
31. On the night of 1/2 July, a Hampden of No. 83 Squadron attempted to drop the first 2,000 lb bomb of the war on the battle cruiser *Scharnhorst* at Kiel. The bomb overshot the target and exploded in the town, killing ten people – the biggest loss of German civilian lives to date in one raid. The Hampden was flown by Fg Off. G.P. Gibson, later of Dams Raid fame.
32. Churchill, *Their Finest Hour*, p. 566.
33. The term 'Air-Sea Rescue Launch' was not yet in common use.
34. The Americans supplied 55,000 Thompson guns and 800,000 P-14 rifles.
35. Hajo Herrmann, *Eagle's Wings*, Airlife, Shrewsbury 1992.
36. The Dutch schuit *Bill S.*
37. Shipping casualties on 11 July were the patrol vessel *Warrior II*, sunk off St Abb's Head; the steamer *Eleanor Brook* sunk and the merchant vessels *City of Melbourne* and *Peru* damaged in Portland harbour; and the small tanker *Kylemount* sunk off Dartmouth. On 14 July, *Stukas* sank the coaster *Island Queen* and damaged the destroyer HMS *Vanessa* and the coasters *Mons* and *Dlader*, the latter a Norwegian vessel.
38. During the attack on this convoy, CW7, dive-bombers sank the destroyer HMS *Brazen* and the coaster *Pulborough*, and also damaged the destroyer HMS *Beagle*, the anti-submarine trawler *Lady Philomena* and the coaster *Westown*. On the following day they hit and sank the steamers *Terlings* and *Kollskeg* west of St Catherine's Point.
39. In the attack on this convoy, CW8, the bombers sank the merchant vessels *Corhaven*, *Leo*, *Polegrange*, *Henry Moon* and *Portslade*, as well as damaging the *Hodder*, *Gronland*, *Newminster*, *Summity* and *Tamworth*. The destroyer HMS *Boreas* was also damaged by air attack later in the day, and her sister ship HMS *Brilliant* was hit by two bombs that passed completely through her before exploding.
40. The vessels sunk or damaged in the attacks on this convoy, CW9, were the *Fife Coast*, *Holme Force* and *Ouse*, sunk by S-Boats of the 1st Flotilla (the *Ouse* as the result of a collision while taking evasive action), the *Coquetdale*, *Empire Crusader* and *Tres* sunk by air attack, and the *Polly M*, *Balmaha*, *John M. Scheldt*, *Veenenburgh*, *Omlandia* and *Surte* damaged.
41. This marked the end of the convoy attack phase, during which the *Luftwaffe*, surface craft and mines had sunk about 30,000 tons of the five million tons of shipping that had passed along Britain's coastline.
42. There were four main long-range German gun batteries between Cap Gris Nez and Calais: the *Batterie* Lindemann (three 16-in guns), *Batterie* Todt (four 15-in guns), *Batterie* Grosse Kurfurst (four 11-in guns) and a mobile railway battery with four 11-in guns. The construction of the fixed sites had been delayed by air attack, mostly by Blackburn Skua dive-bombers of the Fleet Air Arm.

43. *The Battle Re-Thought: A Symposium on the Battle of Britain.* Royal Air Force Historical Society/Royal Air Force Staff College, Bracknell, 25 June 1990, paper by Dr Horst Boog, Senior Air Historian, Military Research Office, Freiburg.

44. Ibid.

45. Petroleum weapons – possibly an early version of napalm – appear to have been used in this action, although details are sparse. The survivors were landed at Antwerp docks, and the burns casualties treated in Antwerp and Tielt before transfer to Berlin via Brussels. The American war correspondent and historian William L. Shirer referred to the incident in his Berlin Diary (18 September 1940).

46. Churchill, *Their Finest Hour*, p. 405.

47. *The London Gazette*, 1 October 1940.

48. Roskill, *The Navy at War, 1939–1945*, p. 88.

49. Olive Walker: *Sailor Malan*, Cassell 1953.

50. Correspondence: W.J. Rosser and author.

51. Ibid.

52. Ibid.

53. War Diary, No. 118 Squadron.

54. Peter Scott, *Battle of the Narrow Seas*, p. 33.

55. Correspondence, T.C. Parker and author.

56. Correspondence, L.E. Aldridge and author.

57. During the entire war, RAF Coastal Command operations in the Home Theatre sank 366 ships totalling about half a million tons by direct attacks, and damaged 134 more, for the loss of 856 aircraft. Mines laid by the RAF, on the other hand, accounted for 762 ships (738,000 tons) and seventeen U-boats, aircraft losses on minelaying sorties totalling 533.

58. Churchill, *The Second World War* Vol. III, *The Grand Alliance*, p. 539.

59. Adolf Galland, *The First and the Last*, Methuen, London 1955.

60. Ibid.

61. For a very good eye-witness account of this action, seen Peter Scott's *Battle of the Narrow Seas*, pp. 30–32.

62. Wing Commander Pickard, veteran of many special operations, was to lose his life in February 1944, leading the celebrated Mosquito attack on the walls of Amiens Prison.

63. It has not been possible to give more than a precis here of this remarkable operation, but several excellent accounts have been written. See, for example, *Combined Operations 1940–42* (HMSO), published a year or so after the raid.

64. See Charles Messenger, *The Commandos, 1940–46*, p. 134.

65. Record of a statement made to the Canadian Broadcasting Corporation by Admiral of the Fleet Earl Mountbatten of Burma, 12 July 1962. Quoted in the *Right of the Line* by John Terraine, p. 560.

66. The coasters were the *Birgitte* (1,595 tons) and *Yewforest* (815 tons).

67. For a fuller account of this action see Peter C. Smith, *Hold the Narrow Seas*, pp 170–172. The British destroyers involved were the *Cottesmore*, *Albrighton*, *Eskdale*, *Glaisdale* and *Quorn*. The *Brocklesby* was part of a second group comprising the *Fernie*, *Tynedale* and the Polish *Krakowiak*, which were not directly involved in the action. The two groups sortied from Dartmouth and Plymouth respectively.

68. No. 164 Squadron, also with Hurricane IVs, moved to Manston from Warmwell on 5 August 1943 and remained there until 22 September, when it went to Fairlop in Essex to begin training as a close support squadron.

69. Account written for the author by Wing Commander Jack Rose, CMG, MBE, DFC.

70. The ships were the Dutch *Aludra* of 4,930 tons, the Swedish *Narvik* of 4,251 tons and the 385-ton flak ship Vp 807.

71. For a very comprehensive account of this action, see Peter C. Smith, *Hold the Narrow Seas*, pp 184–200.

72. Correspondence, Wing Commander Jack Rose and author.

73. For an interesting, if somewhat lurid, account of one of these operations, see Pierre Clostermann, *The Big Show* (Chatto and Windus, London, 1952) pp 76–84.

74. Roskill, *The Navy at War 1939–1945*, p. 369.

75. For a very good description of the Atlantic Wall fortifications, and others in wartime Europe, see *Fortress Europe* by Rudi Rolf and Peter Saal (Airlife, Shrewsbury, 1988).

76. See David Irving, *The Trail of the Fox: the Life of Field-Marshal Erwin Rommel* (Weidenfeld & Nicolson, London, 1977).

77. Operations Summary, May 1944, No. 85 Group, Second TAF: narrative held in the Air Historial Branch, MoD (RAF).

78. On the night of 28/29 August 1942, a He 177A-1 of I/KG 40, carrying out operational trials from Bordeaux-Merignac, had dropped a single 550 lb (250 kg) bomb on the Broad Weir district of Bristol, killing 45 people and injuring 66 – the worst single bomb incident suffered by the city during the war.

79. WINDOW: strips of tinfoil, cut to the wavelength of enemy warning radar and dropped in bundles from attacking aircraft to confuse the enemy's defences. It was first used during Operation GOMORRAH, the heavy RAF attacks on Hamburg of July 1943.

80. For a very good account of RAF Mosquito night-fighter operations during this period, see C. Martin Sharp and Michael J.F. Bowyer, *Mosquito* (Faber and Faber, London, 1967).

81. By early 1944, S-boats were equipped with a derivative of the METOX radar warning receiver, originally fitted to U-boats to detect the signals as ASV equipment used by maritime patrol aircraft.

82. The S-boats involved in this action were S136, S138, S140, S142, S100, S143, S150, S130 and S145. There are two very good and detailed accounts of the incident: *The Invasion Before Normandy – the Secret Battle of Slapton Sands* (Edwin P. Hoyt, Robert Hale, London 1987) and *Channel Firing – the Tragedy of Exercise Tiger* (Nigel Lewis, Viking, London 1989).

83. Gee: Fixing system relaying electronic pulses from three ground stations to receiver equipment in the aircraft. The latter measures difference in time of receipt of signals from ground stations and converts the resulting information into terms of distance. Two sets of readings are plotted on a special chart known as a Gee Lattice Chart; the point of intersection is the aircraft's position.

84. Taped interview, author and the late Flight Lieutenant S.J. Watts, DFC.

85. Regimental History of the Green Howards.

86. Ibid.

87. PIAT: Projector, Infantry, Anti-Tank.

88. *D-Day: Spearhead of Invasion*. R.W. Thompson, Macdonald, London, 1968.

89. These malfunctions may have been caused by sabotage; more probably, they resulted from over-hurried and dispersed production caused by the Allied strategic bombing offensive.

Index